D1571919

WEYERHAEUSER ENVIRONMENTAL BOOKS

Paul S. Sutter, Editor

WEYERHAEUSER ENVIRONMENTAL BOOKS explore human relationships with natural environments in all their variety and complexity. They seek to cast new light on the ways that natural systems affect human communities, the ways that people affect the environments of which they are a part, and the ways that different cultural conceptions of nature profoundly shape our sense of the world around us. A complete list of the books in the series appears at the end of this book.

BRINGING WHALES ASHORE

*Oceans and the Environment
of Early Modern Japan*

JAKOBINA K. ARCH

UNIVERSITY OF WASHINGTON PRESS
Seattle

Bringing Whales Ashore is published with the assistance of a grant from the Weyerhaeuser Environmental Books Endowment, established by the Weyerhaeuser Company Foundation, members of the Weyerhaeuser family, and Janet and Jack Creighton.

Design by Thomas Eykemans
Composed in OFL Sorts Mill Goudy TT, typeface designed by Barry Schwartz
22 21 20 19 18   5 4 3 2 1

All maps by the author, made with Natural Earth
Jacket illustration: Hiroshige Utagawa, *Hizen gotō kujiraryō no zu* (Whale hunting at the island of Goto in Hizen), 1859, Library of Congress

University of Washington Press
www.washington.edu/uwpress

Library of Congress Cataloging-in-Publication Data on file
ISBN (hardcover): 978-0-295-74329-5
ISBN (ebook): 978-0-295-74330-1

To my parents, with gratitude for all the experiences,
on the water and off, that led to this book

CONTENTS

FOREWORD

The Aquamarine Archipelago

PAUL S. SUTTER

Three decades ago, Conrad Totman, the distinguished historian of early modern Japan, began his masterwork of Japanese environmental history, *The Green Archipelago: Forestry in Preindustrial Japan* (1989), with a riddle: "Japan today should be an impoverished, slum-ridden, peasant society subsisting on a barren, eroded moonscape characterized by bald mountains and debris-strewn lowlands," he wrote, but instead it was a densely populated archipelago with an advanced industrial economy and high levels of consumption that had somehow also retained its verdant forests. How had the Japanese managed this? Totman's answer was that a remarkable series of developments during the Tokugawa period (1603–1868)—a sustained era of peace when the Tokugawa shogunate consolidated power in Japan and tightly controlled contacts with the larger world—resulted in a sophisticated system, or systems, of sustainable forest management. As the seventeenth century dawned in Japan, the environmental indicators had not been good. Population growth accelerated, placing heavy resource demands on the archipelago's forests; elites engaged in a spree of monumental construction, with ruinous environmental impacts; and Japanese cities, built primarily of wood and fueled by wood and charcoal, boomed and then often burned and had to be rebuilt. All of this led to what Totman evocatively called "the early modern predation," a period of increasingly widespread deforestation, and subsequent soil erosion, that seemed to portend disaster. But disaster never came. Instead, by the early nineteenth century, well before the Meiji Restoration opened Japan to the world, the archipelago's leaders and citizens alike had not only pre-served key remnants of their once forested realm, but they had devel-oped silvicultural methods that had regenerated Japan's once-extensive forests.

Conrad Totman's interpretation of these sanguine developments, though it was more complex than my quick summary can capture, nonetheless helped to launch Tokugawa Japan on its career as a hopeful environmental parable. Islands have long been popular subjects for cautionary tales about environmental collapse, of growing populations stripping a limited land base of its resources and then paying the price. But here was an island chain that had done the opposite. Here was a place that had turned inward, a place whose leaders had disciplined its citizenry to control their wants and live within their means, a place that had developed its own sophisticated approaches to regenerative forest management entirely outside the influence of European forestry. Here, it seems, was an historical example of wise human adaptation to envi-ronmental limits through the creation of a sustainable closed system. Except that it wasn't.

Toward the end of *The Green Archipelago*, Conrad Totman fleetingly turned his gaze to the sea. While noting that the Japanese had eased pressure on the archipelago's forests by reducing wood consumption and increasing the efficiency of forest exploitation, he also noted that the nation had achieved this easing by "extending its exploitation farther out into the ocean." Intriguingly, he observed that "expanded exploita-tion of marine products, as protein for humans and fertilizer for agricul-ture, meant that the human population could meet more of its needs without increasing the burden on forests." To a degree, at least, the pres-ervation of the terrestrial environment had come at the expense of the accelerating exploitation of the marine environment. But Totman did not elaborate, perhaps because this topic was beyond the scope of his study. Nonetheless, his strong focus on forests reflected, and perhaps perpetuated, a persistent terrestrial bias in Japanese historiography.

Jakobina Arch's innovative and multifaceted study of Japanese whaling during the Tokugawa period, *Bringing Whales Ashore*, is, on one level, the elaboration that Totman never provided. Arch gives us an aquamarine archipelago to attach to the green one that has so fascinated historians' environmental imaginations. While whaling was only part of a larger story of Japan's turn to the ocean during the early modern era, Arch makes a compelling case that it was the most important and reveal-ing part of the story. Her rich history flows from several foundational observations. First, she shows that "organized whaling"—an activity in which large numbers of Japanese, organized in coastal villages, actively hunted near-shore whales for profit—dates from the Tokugawa period and no earlier. While there is a deeper history to the Japanese oppor-tunistically availing themselves of the resources that whales might offer up, before the late sixteenth century the Japanese did not actively hunt whales in any systematic manner. Like regenerative forestry, then, organized whaling was a resource strategy distinctive to the Tokugawa period, one that highlighted the importance of the near-shore marine environment to the environmental history of the era.

Arch's second foundational point is that while organized whaling occurred at the periphery of Japanese society, in isolated villages along rocky coastlines, whales and the whaling economy were nonetheless central to early modern Japanese economy, society, culture, and even religion. Here the full force of the metaphor in the title comes into play, for *Bringing Whales Ashore* is a remarkable tour through all of the myr-iad ways in which whales mattered to even the most land-locked of Japanese lives. Whale meat, which today sits at the heart of Japanese claims for whaling's deep cultural importance, was the least of it. Arch shows that whale meat, either fresh or salted, simply did not travel well and was thus of minor dietary importance during the early modern period. But whale oil served as a vital illuminant, other whale products helped the Japanese fertilize and work their fields, and, in one of this study's most surprising insights, we learn how whale oil was also widely used as a pesticide that allowed the Japanese to intensify rice culture. If whale products were ubiquitous during the Tokugawa period, whale meanings were even more so. As Arch demonstrates in great detail, and in ways that reveal the depth of her research, early modern Japanese not only consumed whales, but they put them on display, they made them the subjects of anatomical drawings, they memorialized whale deaths, they wrote comic stories about whales, and they even dreamed about whales. By materially and culturally "bringing whales ashore," Arch has not only given us a sophisticated environmental account of whaling in the Tokugawa period, but she has also provided us with a vivid history of Tokugawa society and culture viewed through the lens of whaling.

Arch's final foundational point sets her study apart from Totman's *The Green Archipelago* in another important respect: early modern Japanese whaling, she suggests, was not sustainable. Declining yields largely told that story. It is true that, unlike European and American enterprises, which had industrialized and turned to pelagic or open ocean whaling with accelerating voraciousness during the nineteenth century, Japanese whaling remained a shore-based activity and thus had a limited reach into surrounding waters. Whale decline was thus a fairly localized phenomenon around Japan as the Tokugawa period progressed. Still, as a growing number of environmental historians have demonstrated for other early modern places and resources, organized whaling in early modern Japan had degraded ecological baselines even before modern industrialized whaling spread throughout the Pacific during the middle of the nineteenth century. This is not a story of a deep historical sustainability followed by modern industrial collapse. And because whales are highly migratory, even near-shore whaling had far-reaching marine environmental implications. It is certainly true that by the time of Admiral Perry's arrival in Edo Bay in 1853—an event that marked the beginning of the end of Tokugawa isolation and was itself driven by the spread of American whaling throughout the Pacific—industrial pelagic whaling had also diminished Japan's near-shore whale populations. But Arch convincingly shows us that these outside impositions did not undo a traditional and sustainable Japanese whaling culture. Rather, they intersected with the tail end of an economically sophisticated and culturally rich form of marine resource exploitation, both new to and central to the Tokugawa Period, that was taking its toll.

Why does this deep dive into organized whaling, the commerce in whale products, and the circulation of whale meaning during Japan's Tokugawa period matter to us today? One answer is that it challenges a powerfully consequential environmental narrative in Japanese society: the story about traditional whaling that justifies Japan's continuing exploitation of whales in defiance of the international community. In 1986, the International Whaling Commission put in place a moratorium on commercial whaling and allowed for exceptions only for scientific research or indigenous subsistence. The Japanese have objected to the moratorium under the logic that whaling in Japan is a cultural tradition that dates back nine millennia and thus deserves to continue. Theirs is an argument that invokes a variation on indigenous subsistence, though they use the mechanism of scientific permits to allow commercial whaling to continue. *Bringing Whales Ashore* suggests that organized whaling in Japan is a much more recent development, that it has always been a commercial rather than a subsistence practice, and that it was never sustainable. With this history in hand, the grounds for seeing whaling in Japan as a deep cultural tradition are shaky indeed. Beyond that, though, Arch shows that whaling today has almost no resemblance to the rich practices that constituted organized whaling and its cultural milieu during the Tokugawa period, a quarter millennium when, despite what the historiography has maintained, the Japanese people were deeply connected to the sea and its resources, with whales and whaling as the consummate example. Contemporary Japanese whaling is more the product of discontinuity than deep tradition. It is symptomatic of a cultural alienation from the ocean that has allowed the Japanese to forget their history of marine connection during the early modern period—a period that the marine environmental historian Jeffrey Bolster has aptly called the "Age of the Ocean." By restoring that history for us, Jakobina Arch has not merely replaced Totman's green archipelago with an aquamarine version. Rather, she demonstrates that early modern Japan was "an archipelago both isolated from and tied to the Pacific," and that the lines separating the terrestrial from the aquatic in Japanese history have kept us from seeing the ocean for the trees.

ACKNOWLEDGMENTS

This book has grown immensely from its original seed, and I owe a great debt to all the people who helped me nurture it along the way. Shigehisa Kuriyama started me off with what seemed to be a simple question about a whale anatomy illustration. He continued to provide invaluable support as the question became ever more complicated and gradually evolved into this book. I also owe many thanks to Ian Jared Miller, Andrew Gordon, and David Howell, as well as to Harriet Ritvo for her help in the field of animal history. I also want to thank Hal Whitehead for his earlier support while I was studying whale behavior, even though neither of us had any idea at the time that I was going to end up writing a history of whales instead of becoming a biologist.

All of the members of the Japan at Nature's Edge conference in 2008 gave me an early indication of how much interest there would be in work on the history of whales in Japan before the modern era, and helped me to start thinking about the project as an environmental history. In particular, I want to thank the organizers and editors of the conference volume *Japan at Nature's Edge*, Ian Miller, Julia Thomas, and Brett Walker, as well as my fellow marine scholars William Tsutsui and Micah Muscolino, for the encouragement that this was a fruitful direction for my research.

Presentations (both my own and others') and conversations at conferences for the American Historical Association, Association for Asian Studies, American Society for Environmental History, Association for East Asian Environmental History, and the International Society for the Study of Religion, Nature, and Culture have also been essential for this project.

My early work on this project was greatly improved with the support of my colleagues at Harvard and elsewhere, especially but not limited to Victor Seow, Jeremy Yellen, Jürgen Meltzer, Di Yin Lu, Shi Lin Lo, Ian Matthew Miller, Kuang-chi Hung, Sakura Christmas, Bian He, Sean O'Reilly, Kjell Erikson, Melinda Landeck, Rebecca Woods, and Michaela Thompson.

A year of research in Japan was supported by a generous grant from the Japan Foundation, during which time I am indebted in particular to the assistance given me by Setoguchi Akihisa, Tsukada Takashi, Fukunaga Mayumi, Yasuda Akito, Hayato Sakurai, Taiji Akira, Nakazono Shigeo, and Kuronaga Ryohei. I also greatly appreciate the conversations and assistance offered by all of the members of the early modern history *kenkyūkai* at Osaka City University, the Dōbutsukan *kenkyūkai*, the Kyoto Asian Studies Group, and the Osaka Medicine, Society and the Environment *kenkyūkai*.

Other funding that has supported this research includes a Reischauer Institute grant, Whitman College's generous sabbatical plan that helped me pull the book together, and an NEH Summer Institute fellowship at the Mystic Seaport's Munson Institute in 2016.

I also wish to thank my fellow participants at the Munson Institute as well as the coordinators and guest speakers for the fantastic conversations about maritime history. Without that experience, my sabbatical would not have been nearly as productive, and this book likely would not yet be finished. In particular I want to thank Sharika Crawford for her generous comments on some of the draft chapters. The members of the 2016 Cascadia Environmental History retreat and participants in the University of California at Irvine's Of Soils, Roots, and Streams: A Symposium on Ecology and Japan also provided helpful feedback and commentary on chapters in progress.

All of my colleagues in the history department at Whitman have been incredibly supportive: Julie Charlip, John Cotts, Sarah Davies, Brian Dott, Nina Lerman, David Schmitz, Elyse Semerdjian, Lynn Sharp, and Jacqueline Woodfork. This book would be far less coherent without my discussions with them and with all of my other colleagues at Whitman. I also want to thank my editors Regan Huff, Catherine Cocks, and Paul Sutter, as well as the two reviewers, Phil Brown and Brett Walker, who so generously helped me improve this book.

For all the people who showed such enthusiasm when I discussed what I was working on, whether or not your name is included here, thank you for the encouragement that this was a story that needed to be told.

NOTE ON THE TEXT

Names. All Japanese names are given in the text with the family name first. For authors who have published in English with their name in Western order, names appear in the bibliography with the same format as Western names: Family name, Given name. Other Japanese authors appear in the bibliography as Family name Given name (without the comma), so that they are more easily findable in alphabetical order by family name. In premodern Japanese history, individuals are commonly referred to by their given name rather than family name. For example, when discussing the work of Takizawa Bakin, I refer to him as Bakin. However, in the citation of his work in the notes, I use his family name Takizawa to match the bibliographic listing.

Measurements. The value of different monetary units varied widely over the course of the Tokugawa period. However, the shogunate set the following official exchange rates in 1700:

1 ryō or koban (gold) = 50 monme (silver) = 4,000 mon (copper)

1 koku = 5 bushels, the amount of rice that should feed 1 adult for 1 year, supposedly worth 1 ryō (in reality, rice prices were affected by supply and demand)

1 ri = 2.4 miles

1 hiro = 1 fathom (6 feet)

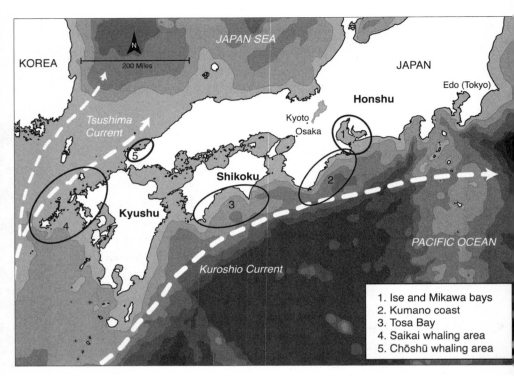

MAP 1. Regions with organized whaling groups in Japan (ca. 1570–1900), baleen whale migration routes (dotted arrows, following typical routes of the Kuroshiō and Tsushima currents), and corresponding organized whaling areas (circled). The whaling practiced on the Bōsō Peninsula southeast of Edo focused on entirely different species of non-baleen beaked whales and thus is not included.

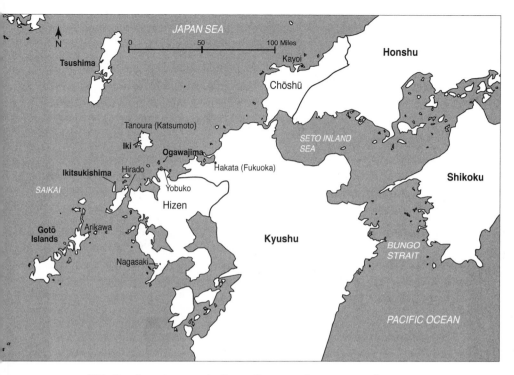

MAP 2. Whaling locations on the Japan Sea coast (ca. 1590–1900), in two major whaling areas: the Saikai area and the area surrounding Kayoi. The relevant domains of Chōshū, Hizen, and Iki are also indicated.

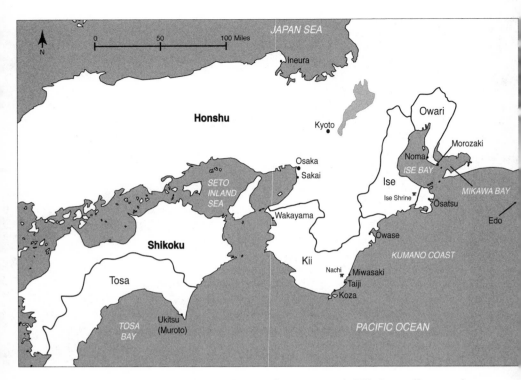

MAP 3. Whaling areas on the Pacific coast (ca. 1570–1900). Whaling villages and other landmarks in the whaling areas of Ise and Mikawa bays, the Kumano area on the Kii Peninsula, and Tosa Bay. The relevant domains of Owari, Ise, Kii, and Tosa are indicated. Note the location of the net whaling village of Ineura to the north.

BRINGING WHALES ASHORE

INTRODUCTION

CENTURIES AGO, TENS OF THOUSANDS OF RIGHT, GRAY, AND HUMP-
back whales swam through huge swathes of the Pacific Ocean. Today,
only a few traces of their vast migrations remain. For someone standing
on the rocky coast of Japan's Wakayama Prefecture, the bushy whale
spouts and glimpses of the slick backs of migrating whales that would
have been commonly visible on a winter's day in the early 1600s have
given way to clear, open water as far as the eye can see. The large numbers of whales that used to swim through the scattered islands on the
northeastern coast of Kyushu, headed back and forth from the Sea of
Okhotsk through the Japan Sea, have diminished today to the point
where the sighting of a single whale can make the news.[1]

Despite this decimation of whale populations, the nation of Japan
continues to catch whales today. The controversy over this practice is
particularly heated because most other nations ceased whaling under
the moratorium on commercial whaling that the International Whaling
Commission (IWC) proposed in 1982 and enacted in 1986. Only two
exemptions to the moratorium were allowed for IWC members. First,
the IWC agreed that aboriginal whalers who hunted only for subsistence, such as the various peoples in the Arctic whose entire way of life
and culture depended on a small harvest of whales every year, should
not be treated the same as the nations who had instigated massive commercial depredations of whale populations. Japanese whalers tried to
argue that their whaling culture was just as threatened by the moratorium as aboriginal whaling cultures, but they were not allowed an
exemption under this rule. Instead, they made use of the second exemption, which allowed member governments to issue permits for small
catches for scientific study. Because almost all biological information
about whales to that point had been obtained by scientists on board

3

whaling ships, and nonlethal sampling methods were not yet prevalent in the 1980s, the IWC had included this permit option to make sure that biological information about whale populations could still be collected.

Although the Japanese government issued so-called scientific permits for yearly harvests in Antarctica and the North Pacific, opponents of Japanese whaling have long argued that they are merely a front for attempts at continued commercial whaling. The International Court of Justice agreed in 2014 that whaling under such permits was not actually for the purposes of scientific research, but the Japanese government–subsidized Institute of Cetacean Research (ICR) continues to send out whaling ships.[2] Taking advantage of the requirement that sampled whales not be wasted, the ICR passes along the meat harvested after data collection to an associated corporation that sells it within Japan. Their studies are mostly intended to find the sustainable level of harvest that would allow the moratorium to be lifted.[3] For instance, the director-general of the Institute of Cetacean Research said at the Traditional Whaling Summit in 2002 that "Japan is proud of the tradition of whaling which she has built up over nine thousand years and firmly believes in the sustainable use of whales as a food resource, which is why we can never give up the issue and remain strong advocates of whaling."[4] Other members of the summit also prioritized the idea of whaling culture and traditions, with the argument that the practice of eating whale meat and its associated "rituals and performing arts that has [sic] been developed over years" were in danger of vanishing if commercial whaling could not continue in the twenty-first century.[5] Thus, despite operating under the scientific exemption, Japanese whaling supporters rely heavily on arguments similar to those used to create the aboriginal exemption: they say that their whaling tradition and practice are so integral to their culture that Japan should be exempted from the IWC's commercial ban.

One problem with these arguments is that they deliberately create an exaggerated sense of cultural continuity by focusing on broad trends and generalizations rather than specific historical details. In other words, the case for "traditional" whaling rests more heavily on an invented tradition than on a comparison between the historical reality and the current reality of whaling.[6] Untangling the threads that have led to a modern misconception of the historical role of whaling, whales, and marine resources more generally requires examining early modern Japan from different perspectives. Without a thorough understanding of the era's natural history, development of whaling techniques, development of different whale products and their economic role, new forms of knowledge and storytelling, and even spiritual understandings of animals like whales, it is easy to miss the dramatic changes in the ways that Japanese people have interacted with whales between the Tokugawa period (1603–1868) and today. There is plenty of information about historical interactions between whales and Japanese society, but much of it is scattered throughout a wide variety of historical records, including whaling business records, illustrated scrolls, scientific and natural history writing, literature, monuments, religious texts, and whale-based artifacts. Japanese scholars who study the histories of specific whaling groups have collected some of this material, and local historians have collected other pieces, but very little of this information has been made available in English. Thus, the wider international audience for Japanese prowhaling arguments has only a few texts to help them understand what the call for the importance of traditional whaling culture actually means.[7]

Since the moratorium, interest in and discussion of the earlier history of whaling in Japan has increased, but usually as a short commentary within works focused on the issue of modern Japanese whaling.[8] Whaling supporters tend to produce works inextricably tied to the prowhaling agenda, particularly the many books by former Ministry of Agriculture, Forestry, and Fisheries official Komatsu Masayuki. He was one of the people who helped plan the current scientific whaling program in Japan, and in his many books argues to a popular audience for the importance of whaling in Japanese culture as part of his agenda to keep modern whaling alive.[9] With such a strong bias toward highlighting the importance of whaling in Japan today, his books can exaggerate continuities with the past instead of demonstrating changes within whaling practices, attitudes toward whaling, or uses of whales.[10] Such ahistorical arguments do a disservice to the reality of the particular ecocultural context of Tokugawa Japan as an archipelago dependent on the contents of local waters containing organisms that moved throughout the Pacific Basin.

There is evidence that people may have sometimes hunted or at least opportunistically killed stranded whales in prehistoric times, but there is no reason to believe in an unbroken whaling tradition lasting for nine thousand years, through the transition from hunter-gatherer society to settled agriculturalists and across the many different political and social configurations in the Japanese archipelago's whole recorded history. And in fact, most prowhaling arguments do not rest too heavily on the prehistoric uses of whales, because the Jōmon culture of hunter-gatherers is not the best model for the earliest form of a recognizably Japanese civilization centered around settled rice-growing agriculturalists. The first point at which we have any useful records for a recognizable whaling tradition is with the rise of organized, harpoon-wielding whaling groups in the 1570s in Ise and Mikawa bays, a large combined bay on the Pacific coast between Tokyo and Osaka.[11] These groups were successful enough that the practice spread all along the southern coast of Japan after 1600. Any traditions that surround the consumption of whale meat for Japan as a whole, rather than a few elites at court offered pieces of rare stranded whales for feasts, belong at the earliest to this era of organized, shore-based whaling (approximately 1570–1900), roughly contemporaneous with the Tokugawa period. The overlap is even closer if the early modern era is defined to include the political consolidation from 1590 onward, which formed the basis of the Tokugawa peace, and the first decades of the Meiji era (1868–1912) before the largest transformations of the modern era took hold. But even if the Japanese whaling tradition is limited to the last 450 years, the final century and a half of that span includes a dramatic industrialization and modernization that transformed Japan so thoroughly that comparisons between modern practices and early modern ones are far more likely to find differences than continuities. When there are similarities, they are not always the things that prowhaling arguments focus on today, such as the fact that early modern whaling was also a big business focused on profit more than subsistence. It is true that people hunted whales in Japan in both the early modern and modern eras, but the techniques, equipment, location, and people involved have all changed so much that referring to both practices as Japan's whaling tradition is misleading.

In early modern Japan, the structure and techniques of organized whaling were quite different from modern whaling. Whalers belonged to a specific whaling group based out of a coastal village that had space on the beach for processing whales. Groups were managed by an individual who was usually a member of the local elite—someone whose rank was high for their local area but who owed allegiance to the government at relatively low levels, rather than being directly under the lord of a domain (daimyo) or other major political figure. Whaling groups each required a minimum of three hundred people to operate, the largest having around three thousand.[12] They targeted whales in the waters within sight of the coast, then hauled the carcasses back to the beach for processing. Whaling groups then sold the meat, oil, and other parts like baleen or bonemeal to both local and regional buyers. Although the total number of groups operating at any given point is difficult to determine, by the middle of the seventeenth century, there were whaling groups operating out of villages from Ise Bay (about halfway between Tokyo and Osaka) to southern Shikoku's Tosa Bay and throughout the islands on the northwest coast of Kyushu. As long as whales were still abundant in coastal waters, shore-based whaling easily made use of the kinds of shipbuilding and coastal maritime expertise available throughout fishing communities in Japan. Just like European and American whalers, who only moved to pelagic whaling once whales were no longer available nearer land, Japanese whaling focused on the closest available whale populations. The major difference between Japanese and Western whaling history is that the coastal migration routes and configuration of the continental shelf near Japan allowed Japanese whalers to continue shore-based whaling much longer than other commercial whalers had.

Modern factory ship whaling, in Japan and elsewhere, was a commercial business where multiple corporations ran factory ships to process whales in the open ocean—mostly in Antarctic waters. As Pacific whale populations collapsed under American whalers' hunting pressure beginning in the 1840s, Japanese whalers gradually realized they needed to adopt the new technologies being developed by the global whaling industry to hunt the faster open-ocean whales that no one had yet overexploited. By the time the factory ship was invented in the

1920s, Japanese whaling corporations were ready to give up on shore-based whaling, which they had already restructured into a more modern form using larger pelagic whaling ships to haul whales back to processing plants on shore, because inshore whale populations had become too small to support commercial whaling efforts. Factory ship whalers from all nations hunted from sixty- to two-hundred-foot-long engine-driven catcher boats that were much faster than the open rowboats used in coastal whaling. A whale caught with the bow-mounted harpoon gun on one of these boats was towed to a larger factory ship, which processed all the whales brought in by its catcher-boat fleet. The few hundred people employed by each whaling company fleet were the only ones who interacted with the whales as anything other than processed oil or, in the case of Japan and Norway, meat. The new technologies of catcher boat and factory ship made twentieth-century whalers far more efficient at killing whales than ever before. In 1938, whaling observer and United States Coast Guard lieutenant Quentin Walsh noted: "One modern factory ship can take more whales in one season than the entire American whaling fleet of 1846 which number [sic] over 700 vessels."[13]

By uncritically linking earlier whaling practices with modern factory-ship whaling, as if current practices reflect a natural progression of technology but with similar cultural meanings as the earlier form of whaling, the reality of early modern whaling is reduced to a few images and talking points divorced from context and centered on the commonality of killing whales. Even in Japan, people cannot read historical texts written before the twentieth century without special language training, so most of the information easily available to the general public about Tokugawa whaling and attitudes toward whales is from secondary sources published about the history of whaling, many of which are explicitly intended to promote the continuation of whaling today.[14] The problem of information access is even worse for people who cannot read this Japanese-language scholarship and must rely on the scant descriptions of earlier Japanese whaling that have been published so far in English.

When writers acknowledge the differences between modern and early modern whaling, they tend to assume the earlier version was somehow a more sustainable fishery than the twentieth-century whaling

industry that visibly and rapidly decimated Antarctic whale populations. Even Morikawa Jun, whose work explicitly deconstructs the
culture- and tradition-based arguments for the continuation of Japanese whaling today, says that Tokugawa period whaling was sustainable.[15] Those like him who assume "traditional" whaling was sustainable
frame the early modern form of whaling as small-scale, local, and with
limited impact on the rest of Japan's economy and society. For example,
Nishiwaki Masahiro's unsupported statement that there were only
sixty whales caught per year in all of Japan during the seventeenth century (in contrast with the catch of tens of thousands per year that was
driving environmentalist concerns in the Save the Whales movement
when he was writing) is clearly an underestimate.[16] While a total catch
for the whole of Japan cannot be compiled due to the loss of some whaling group records, two different whaling groups alone each caught over
eighty whales in a single year in the seventeenth century.[17] By the early
nineteenth century, when there had been whaling groups operating in
Japan for at least 150 years, ninety groups or more were whaling simultaneously. If the catch over the whole period was only twenty whales
per year per group (averaging bad years and highly successful ones), and
the average number of whaling groups operating at any given time was
closer to fifty, to reflect expansion of the industry from around 1600 to
1800, whalers would still have harvested over two hundred thousand
whales in the two centuries before any influence of Western whalers in
the Pacific appeared.

The assumption of limited impact, while it sometimes comes from
a lack of detailed information about historical whaling practices, also
arises in part from the massive difference in whale populations between
the two eras, for which the responsibility rests solely on humans. Even
today, we lack important information about the migrations and life
cycles of the whales that used to be found in abundance along the coasts
of Japan. However, in combination with historical sources like whaling records and scrolls depicting whales, one can begin to re-create
the place of whales in the marine environment near Japanese shores.
The specific impact of early Japanese whaling is partially concealed by
the much more dramatic loss of around thirty thousand right whales
(*Eubalaena japonica*) from the Pacific in the 1840s alone at the hands of
American whalers (in comparison, the current population of Pacific

right whales is estimated to be around five hundred individuals).[18] By the twentieth century, having tapped out most of the readily available whales in the rest of the world's oceans, modern industrial whaling (including Japanese offshore whaling) further diminished the whales of the Antarctic to the point where people became seriously concerned about their impending extinction. It is hard to imagine what the seas must have been like before these two massive depredations, but an abundance of migratory whales was an important element of the environment of coastal Japan before the mid-nineteenth century not at all visible today.

These two points of population collapse were just the most recent in a global history of whaling-caused collapses leading to changes in target species and searches for new whaling grounds.[19] With the possible exception of the subsistence whaling practiced by native populations in the Arctic and surrounding northern oceans, how long a particular form of localized whaling lasted depended most strongly not on the culture of whaling but on its scale. Early Japanese whaling was no different, particularly because their organized whaling was just as much about making money as it was about producing food. Even though they did not expand offshore until the late nineteenth century, Japanese whaling groups were still forced to shift focus from right whales to gray and humpback whales, after whaling pressure caused a decline in right whale availability. Then in the nineteenth century, after American whalers began to hit Japanese migratory whales before they reached the coast, near-shore Japanese whalers either shifted to smaller targets like dolphins or pilot whales, or gave up entirely.[20] In most cases, whaling groups simply went out of business, and former members found some other livelihood as Meiji modernization projects offered new opportunities in factories or cities away from the village. Offshore whaling corporations employed some formerly coastal whalers, but they also established bases in entirely new places like Ayukawa which had no ties to the earlier traditions of whaling.[21]

Adaptation to changing whale populations thus led to changes in the process and the role of whaling throughout its history in Japan, but some of these changes were more dramatic than others. Even though current whaling supporters emphasize the continuous and ongoing tradition of whaling in Japan, the leap to modern industrial whaling was a major shift concurrent with rapid changes in all areas of Japanese life during the Meiji industrialization and modernization push. As whalers were drawn further out into the Pacific and eventually the Antarctic, whaling became far less attached to the daily lives of most of the population of Japan. Thus, while there was certainly some connection between older coastal whalers and modern Japanese whalers, the interconnections between whales and people discussed in this book were generally quite specific to the society of early modern Japan.

Far more people had a chance for direct or close second-hand experience with fisheries and shipboard work in early modern Japan than in the twenty-first century. Paradoxically, modern Japan is a society more embedded in global trade and international fisheries than its early modern counterpart. However, as with everywhere else in the modern industrial world, it is one where the personal connection between the ocean and its products is reserved for a smaller portion of the population. Mechanization dramatically decreased the proportion of the global population who work in ports, ships, and fishing boats. Even before the Great East Japan Earthquake destroyed major fishing communities all along the Tōhoku coast of northeast Japan in 2011, such communities and others throughout the country had been declining. The Statistics Bureau of Japan counted only 173,000 people working in all fisheries nationwide in 2015, or only 0.14 percent of the population, down from 0.91 percent of the population in 1953.[22] A census from 1891, in contrast, showed 3.3 million people (8.3 percent of the population) involved in fisheries. While we do not have such detailed numbers for the preceding two and a half centuries, it can reasonably be assumed that the proportion was not less than in 1891, given the Tokugawa era rise of fisheries for whales, bonito, herring, sardines, and other marine organisms.[23]

The tens of thousands of people who were directly involved in hunting and processing whales in the Tokugawa period have diminished now to only a few hundred crew and researchers operating supposedly noncommercial hunts under the direction of the Institute of Cetacean Research.[24] What this dramatic shift in personal experience on the water means is that even those practices that do have continuity with the coastal whaling groups of Tokugawa Japan exist in a very different setting than they did in the past. There are far fewer whales visible in coastal waters, there are far fewer people who have any contact with whales even outside of those waters, and the whales that are brought ashore by Japanese whalers have generally already been cut up into their component parts.[25] The striking change in the numbers and presence of Pacific whales from the mid-nineteenth through twentieth centuries reflects a similarly striking change in the way that people in the Japanese archipelago interact with their local marine environment.

THE PACIFIC OCEAN AND EARLY MODERN JAPAN

As important as a more complete view of Japan's historical whaling practices is to understanding the whaling problem today, research on whales in early modern Japan also has the power to illuminate broader issues in Japanese history. Organized whaling groups in early modern Japan integrated the marine environment into Japanese society through the various whale-derived products that they made available throughout the country. The sheer variety of interactions between people and whales (whether physical whales or imagined versions of them) shows how embedded the Japanese archipelago was in the maritime space around it. This space included not just the coastal waters connecting the islands of Japan, but also the broader Pacific through which the whales moved. Previous histories that have relegated fishing villages and coastal trade networks to the unimportant margins have diminished our ability to see the whole archipelago, land and sea, but following whales brings the maritime component back into the picture.

It is puzzling, given the extensive coastline of Japan, with its four main islands and thousands of lesser islands, that so little attention has been paid to the influence of the sea in Japanese history. The problem is not a lack of sources dealing with maritime topics, as is demonstrated by the rich set of sources focused on whales and whaling used in this book. With much of the interior filled with uninhabitably steep mountains, it could be argued that there are no truly nonmaritime communities in the archipelago. However, apart from Amino Yoshihiko's work on medieval Japan and the scholars who follow his lead, most histories of Japan tend to draw a line at the shore, marginalizing or completely ignoring fishing villages and coastal peoples.[26] While the study of Japan in fields like archaeology, folklore studies, and cultural anthropology has begun to turn to the world of the ocean, it has been much more difficult to get historians of Japan to consider topics beyond rice-centered agricultural society. The dependence of prehistoric hunter-gatherer populations on coastal products is readily acknowledged (especially with the clear archaeological traces left by reliance on shellfish), but after the arrival of rice cultivation, consideration of fisheries' importance in later Japanese history is sparse.[27] Within Japan, a historical viewpoint cutting out any nonfarming peoples has deep roots in the Japanese school system, where the most widely published high school history textbooks characterize agriculture as the center of feudal society.[28] Fisheries, including whaling, simply do not enter the general picture of Tokugawa society taught to students today, leaving the information accessible only to people specifically searching for local histories or specialized books about historical fisheries, rather than those learning a basic history of the period.

The minimal role of the ocean and coastal waters in Japanese culture today also helps to create assumptions about maritime space that shape what kinds of things seem worth researching, and what kinds of impressions of the past carry the most weight. When the total number of people on the working waterfront declined with the modern rise of labor-saving fishing technologies and cargo transfer facilities, Japanese recreational uses did not fill in that newly emptied space in the same way that they did in the Western world. In the United States, for example, yacht clubs flourished and recreational boating spread beyond the upper class over the course of the late nineteenth and twentieth centuries.[29] There is a striking contrast between American marinas and harbors packed with recreational boats, and the few lonely docks with less than a dozen boats found in good Japanese harbors like Hakodate, a city of just under three hundred thousand people. When I visited in 2002, most of the few sailboats appeared to be from New Zealand or Australia rather than local yachts, and the harbor was far less crowded with recreational vessels than even a much smaller American port. The romance of sailboats or, later, motorboats clearly did not drive a move to the waterfront in modern Japan on the same scale as the transformation of the waterfront in the United States. The beach also is less of a recreational draw in modern Japan than in the ancient cultures of the Mediterranean or in modern America.[30] While vacationers do go to the beach in the summer in Japan, you will rarely if ever find any Japanese visitors to beaches after September 1, when the season is considered over, no matter how hot the weather remains.[31] The beach as a place for play is more constrained, perhaps as a reflection of the more constrained role for the ocean in general in modern Japanese life.

Japan's apparent lack of interest in ocean recreation compared to America or Europe could be explained by geographical differences between the steep land falling quickly into the ocean in Japan and the more gradual run to the sea and more sheltered estuaries and harbors found along the Mediterranean or on the East Coast of the United States. But if geography determines the liveliness of a nation's coast, then it would be easy to assume that the present relative disinterest in the ocean would stretch backward through all eras of Japanese history. In other words, since beaches, harbors, and other maritime spaces in and around Japan today are minimally populated and do not have a central cultural role, it makes sense that the marine environment is not at the forefront of scholarship about either contemporary or historical Japan. Without research that is aware of the seascape as well as the landscape of the archipelago of Japan, the centrality of maritime space to historical Japan is too easily forgotten.

With very little work touching on the marine environment's role in Japanese history, it becomes even easier for scholars who do not specialize in Japan to leave the country out of histories centered on the Pacific Ocean, especially for the supposedly isolated and inward-focused Tokugawa period. The idea of Tokugawa Japan's unimportance and isolation from the rest of the Pacific world comes from shogunal government restrictions on foreign trade and movement of Japanese people beyond coastal waters, a policy known as "closed country" or sakoku. Scholars of Japanese history have long since countered the myth of complete isolation arising from the sakoku policy, recognizing that there was interaction with foreigners even during this period of tightly controlled trade. But for people who do not know much about Japan, the notion of the closed country still lingers, making it easy to assume Tokugawa Japan was simply not a part of or influenced by the Pacific World.[32] However, in this era of controlled maritime movement, the ocean was still important, as this was a period when the Japanese people deepened their reliance on their coastal waters. Even when inhibited from making far-flung connections across the ocean, they needed near-shore waters to flourish. New specialized fisheries like whaling increased investment in local waters. Coastal shipping, especially from Kyushu through the Inland Sea to Osaka, also boomed during the Tokugawa peace. It was essential for getting rice taxes from distant domains to the mercantile and political centers of the country. Although foreign trade was limited, Japanese coastal shipping was most likely the largest in the world at the time.[33] The supposed limitation during sakoku to strictly coastal waters was possible because humans were the only ones being constrained: there is no clear boundary between those waters and the open Pacific for the migratory whales or fish that gave rise to the Tokugawa period's flourishing specialized fisheries. Thus, whatever ignorance the Japanese people might have had about other peoples in the Pacific, they were still heavily reliant on the Pacific Ocean's bounty and thus part of an early modern Pacific World, even if only on the margins.

To understand what it meant for early modern Japan to be an archipelago both isolated from and tied to the Pacific, we need to consider a combination of different environments, from the mountains to the plains, from the shore to the coastal currents, from local waters to connections across the entire Pacific. Whales bridge a surprising number of those environments, in part because they are so large and so impressive that they cannot help but draw attention. They also offer a new way to consider the history of the Pacific, as whales and currents have some of the most sweeping circulations throughout the ocean basin.[34] They were not the only marine organism embedded in many aspects of life in Tokugawa society, but they can be found in so many aspects simultaneously that they highlight a number of different changes made possible by limited expansion out into the coastal waters of the archipelago. This small first step into seeing the Japanese archipelago as both the land of its islands and the seas surrounding them is crucial for understanding the success of the empire that followed. Upon these early foundations of maritime resource expansion, the modern nation of Japan stretched its borders into a far-flung Pacific empire in the twentieth century, chasing whales even beyond those wide territorial boundaries to the Antarctic.[35]

The ways that people wove whales into their terrestrial lives in the Tokugawa period show that maritime endeavors like whaling, fishing, and transportation were not just isolated work on the water, but rather integral to the society as a whole. Given the new specialized fisheries and massive growth of coastal transport during the Tokugawa period, this is actually a period when Japan's archipelagic nature was critical. Because of the volcanic and geologically new nature of Japan's mountainous interior, there is a relatively abrupt transition between the human-usable lowlands and the approximately 80 percent of land area too steep to cultivate.[36] As the Tokugawa peace promoted a dramatic population increase in the seventeenth century unmatched in earlier Japanese history, availability of arable land quickly reached its limits. High growth continued through improved agricultural production, urbanization, and resource intensification. The population settled into overall equilibrium in the latter half of the Tokugawa period (with some regions declining in population while others continued to grow).[37] Without increased use of maritime resources available along the extensive coastline of the many islands making up the archipelago, this intense population growth might have just as quickly collapsed rather than finding relative equilibrium; the major famine crises of the late Tokugawa reflect a population without a large cushion to see them through sustained or particularly severe bad weather affecting harvests, even with these new resources.[38] Environmental historian Conrad Totman argues that the development of new and specialized fisheries, promoted by the conjunction of peace and restricted foreign travel for mariners as well as geographically restricted terrestrial agricultural expansion, was an integral part of the maintenance of Japan's large population after its initial explosion just after the institution of peace in the early seventeenth century.[39] However, even he only gives a few pages to the maritime environment in his history of early modern Japan.

A far more common view of preindustrial Japan is not as an archipelago depending on both land and sea, but as an island (i.e., small) nation that somehow operated as a closed system. This is particularly so for scholars of global environmental history, who have found a sustainability object lesson in Tokugawa Japan. In his discussion of global civilizational inequality and collapses, Jared Diamond notes that Japan relied on and caused depletion of non-Japanese resources like those traded for with the northern Ainu in Ezo, but he carefully denotes this as separate from Japan itself (despite the fact that this area became part of the country in the late nineteenth century), diminishing the force of his argument for domestic sustainability. Also, he does not talk about how the use of marine resources to supplement agriculture tapped into a larger maritime space than just the waters next to shore territories. His recognition of Japanese use of coastal waters undermines his argument for contained resource use, as the organisms in those waters were not necessarily constrained to territory near Japan.[40] Similarly, John Richards depicts early modern Japan as an inward-focused conservationist society, one that "could satisfy virtually all its requirements from its own resources."[41] He concludes that "Japan under the Tokugawa was a bounded world with finite resources defined by islands in an archipelago," without considering what the fluid spaces between those islands might contribute from outside those bounds.[42] This is despite the fact that five years before Richards' book, Brett Walker had already begun to challenge this basic assumption of resource scarcity by dating Japanese colonialism to the pre-Meiji period and demonstrating that Japanese people were exploiting resources from foreign (particularly marine) environments as far as the Amur Estuary and the Kuril Islands in the early modern period.[43]

While the boundaries of one single island can indeed enclose and limit a terrestrial system, Japan's island nature needs to be seen as a collection of islands, whose boundaries are thus not closed at all because they must be drawn somewhere in the waters that connect those islands to each other and to the Pacific Ocean as a whole. A closed system could not be dependent on whales, sardines, bonito, and other migratory marine populations that cross far vaster distances than the length of Japan's coast. Fishermen were not bounded to sessile populations of prey within some arbitrary boundary of Japan's premodern ecosystem. They were in fact dependent on the regular movement of new specimens from far out in the Pacific along the Kuroshio and Tsushima currents, on the arrivals and departures of whales and fish in coastal waters to mark predictable harvest seasons.

If one looks at Japan as an archipelago rather than a collection of small landmasses, oceanic characteristics like movement, dynamism, and fluidity are more visible than the stasis or equilibrium that is assumed for a sustainable closed system. This is true not just for the appearance and disappearance of whales in particular coastal areas, but also for the movement of whalers, their products, and knowledge about whales between coastal villages and interior cities. In particular, the perception of whales as living spiritually within the same space as humans forces us to reconsider the idea of a sharp boundary for early modern society at the shoreline of Japan's islands. Such interconnections between the ocean and the land, the reliance on marine products and curiosity about and knowledge of marine organisms outside of direct experience with coastal living show us that the people of early modern Japan were truly living in an archipelagic space that included both terrestrial and marine areas.

A marine environmental history focusing on an archipelago rather than the open ocean benefits from the fact that liminal spaces have two sides: both the ocean and the land sides of the boundary were crossed by whales and whale products. Early modern whaling groups in Japan were not just tied to particular species now rarely appearing off Japan's coasts; they were also tied to the land-shore boundary by their use of beaches for processing space. This tie to the local environment has been severed by modern industrial whaling centered on factory ships out in the open ocean. Reliance on a shore base meant that whalers worked in a liminal space blending land and sea even before the whale carcass was hauled up on the beach. Mountain lookouts coordinating the movement of whaleboats were an essential component of the whaling group, which not only kept the boats within sight of the shore but also meant that there was not a solid boundary between land and sea for whalers—they depended on aspects of both environments for success.

This interdependence of shore and marine positions helps explain another striking dimension of the place of whales in Japanese society during the Tokugawa period: the sense that whales, too, inhabited human spaces, and at least in spirit form easily crossed back and forth between the waters in which they swam and the terrestrial spaces they visited in human dreams. In contrast, ship-based whalers were constrained to a very small human outpost moving through a space that was otherwise threatening to human existence, one in which cetaceans easily survived. In such a setting, a strong division between humans and cetaceans as simple animal resources to be exploited as thoroughly as possible would develop more easily than the more fluid perception of the place of whales and people in early modern Japan. Thus, it is important to consider not just the fact that whales were hunted, but also where and how they were hunted to understand people's investment in this aspect of the marine environment.

Because of the massive habitat range of whale species, a history of the ways that people interacted with whales along a small slice of their migration routes that happens to intersect with one country (Japan) still perforce speaks to histories of the Pacific as a whole. There is increasing interest in looking at the history of the Pacific in a new light, particularly during the period when European explorers began stitching together an image of the Pacific Ocean as a whole rather than as a series of widely divergent regions.[44] Tokugawa Japan under sakoku may seem to fit poorly into this narrative of a Pacific World. Matt Matsuda's history of the Pacific, for example, talks about Japan's part in the sixteenth century, and then skips ahead to consider the impact of empires expanding into Japanese territory around the turn of the nineteenth century, leaving much of the Tokugawa period as something apparently outside of this overarching Pacific narrative.[45] However, by looking at the ways that whales, with territories unlimited by human political boundaries, were integral to the lives of even those Japanese people living away from the coast, we can see that this archipelago did not and could not entirely withdraw from the greater Pacific Basin in the seventeenth and eighteenth centuries. The intersection between whales and humans in early modern Japan is another of the "direct engagements . . . tied to histories dependent on the ocean"[46] foundational to Matsuda's concept of Pacific history—one that reaches outside purely human communities to bring part of the living Pacific into the story.

We also need to have histories of the ocean that include not just those people directly working in maritime spaces, but also all the other people who interact with it indirectly, even without having been there.[47] Our interactions with the ocean are not limited to the people who physically touch it, float upon it, and pull organisms out of it. To fully understand the impact of the Pacific on human history, we must consider the cultural particularity of those interactions with imagined as well as physical oceans. As an archipelago with a large proportion of oceanic space within its borders, Japan even in the relatively isolated Tokugawa period is a prime example of the kind of place where interactions with the oceans were both integral to their culture and also particular to a specific aspect of the Pacific Ocean as a whole. If we discount the Japanese experience from Pacific history, our understanding will remain incomplete.

Finally, we cannot solve current problems with overfishing and destruction of the oceanic environment if we mischaracterize past smaller-scale impacts that still lead to collapse (merely over a longer span of time) as sustainable use. Whale populations collapsed most dramatically under the focused attention of factory ships in the Antarctic in the twentieth century, but just because that harvest was clearly excessive does not mean it was unique. Tokugawa whalers were part of a history of dubiously sustainable fisheries even before they met whalers from other nations or felt their impacts on the populations they shared as targets in the nineteenth century. Their contribution is not just another tally in the list of pressures diminishing historic whale populations, however, since the sources they left behind also contribute to the sparse information we have about baseline whale populations in the era before major collapses. A richer understanding of premodern whale populations and the ways humans lived with them is crucial if we are to judge whether and how whales will recover under the protections afforded by endangered species regulations and commercial whaling moratoriums instituted in the late twentieth century.

ORGANIZATION

Each chapter of this book looks at interactions between whales and humans on sea and shore from a different perspective. Chapter 1 introduces, as much as possible with the minimal information humans have collected, the whales themselves and how the space we know as Japan might have been part of their lives in the premodern era. The rest of the book then moves on to focus on various relationships between humans and whales, beginning with the closest contact with whales and moving further away with each chapter. Chapter 2 begins with the whaling groups along the coasts of Japan whose harpooners leapt onto the backs of whales to deal the killing blow, and whose work centered on hundreds of people gathering together on the beach to finish the messy deconstruction of a whale into component parts before it began to rot—a necessarily rapid hands-on process, given the fact that the insulating properties of blubber cause whale corpses to begin decomposing almost immediately after death. The following chapter turns to the products made from those whale parts, and the wider group of people who interacted with those smaller portions of a whale throughout Japan in the growing mercantile economy and consumer culture of the period. The final two chapters move away from direct physical contact to consider different ways that people thought about whales. Chapter 4 focuses on types of knowledge, from natural history and anatomy to illustrations and stories that featured whales for entertainment. The final chapter focuses on religious thought, and how people dealt with dead whales' spirits, where the human-whale relationship involved close contact only in the metaphysical realm.

Although interest in the history of whaling in Japan often begins with the modern whaling problem, this is not a book about how modern whaling developed from earlier traditions. Instead, it focuses on the importance of this first form of Japanese organized whaling within the culture of the Tokugawa period, before the dramatic changes brought by modernization and industrialization. While the conclusion does consider what happened to whales and whaling after the end of the Tokugawa, the main focus of the central chapters is on the premodern role of whaling in Japan. In part this is because, in comparison to the scant resources focused on Tokugawa whaling, much more information is already available in English about twentieth- and twenty-first-century Japanese whaling. But more importantly, the rich interactions between people and whales in Tokugawa Japan are interesting in and of themselves, rather than just as precursors to modern practices. Just as they are now, whales in the Tokugawa were treated as natural resources serving human purposes. The difference lies in each period's interpretation of what that meant for the people making use of whales.

Human life in the Tokugawa period was heavily reliant on the vast marine ecosystem of the Pacific Ocean, and our interpretations of the history of this era must take these wider resource boundaries into account. Organized whaling developed into an influential and dynamic business in the context of changing species availability and particular geographies of the coast. Changes in the techniques for catching whales and the areas in which they were caught show that whaling developed into a relatively large-scale endeavor—at least enough to have impacts on the whale populations in coastal Japanese waters (chapter 2). Both the scale of whaling efforts and the scale of whale bodies then further shaped the lives of nonwhalers as their products and ideas about these creatures spread throughout Japan. Whales are a particularly good model for understanding the diversity of natural resources used in this period because so many different products came from a single whale, representing a cross section of the possibilities provided by marine resources (chapter 3). Encounters with whales or their parts also pushed people to articulate an understanding of nature particular to this new, heavier reliance on a marine resource base (chapter 4). By describing and telling stories about whales and their spirits, people were also working out how to think and feel about the maritime influence on their world (chapters 4 and 5).

The history of Tokugawa Japan must include its maritime spaces, because parts of that space were so integral to its terrestrial spaces that drawing a line between them is nonsensical. The examples explored in the following chapters show the many ways that, if one ignores the specialized fisheries of the period like whaling, Tokugawa history is incomplete. Far from being just a marginal coastal business only relevant to people on the fringes of mainstream society, whaling influenced such basic aspects of early modern Japanese life as their understanding of anatomy and natural history, and even the consumption of meat and rice.[48] This book follows whales ashore and into the terrestrial and metaphysical spaces of the early modern Japanese archipelago, tracing the ways in which there was no clear dividing line between the ocean's inhabitants and the land's. In the process, it provides a new view of Japan, tied not just to defining terrestrial features like volcanoes and earthquake fault zones, but also to the equally influential Pacific currents and migrations that intersect the spaces of the archipelago.

ONE

SEEING FROM THE SEA

A Whale's-Eye View of Japan

ONE OF THE BIGGEST PROBLEMS IN RE-CREATING A HISTORICAL moment before the modern whaling industry decimated whale populations is finding solid information about these animals: where were these large populations, how large were they, why did they appear where they did? Even for the species that swim near coastlines populated by humans, much of a whale's life happens outside human view. While whales have to come to the surface for air, waves of only a few feet high make it hard to see more than the vapors of their breath. When swimming at night, diving for food, or moving too far away from the coast or ship traffic lanes, whales' lives become invisible to us. Before the introduction of radio and satellite tagging in the late twentieth and early twenty-first centuries, the best way we could trace the movement of whales was to follow whalers. Molecular genetic analysis is now starting to help us refine estimates of whale population sizes, but apart from that, historical whaling records are our best source for numbers and locations of whales before the twentieth century.[1] Thus, the human understanding of the history of whales is irrevocably linked to our histories of whaling.

Many different kinds of whales were likely to appear along the Japanese coast in the early modern period, some of which were particular targets for whaling groups to bring ashore for processing. Some basic whale biology is helpful to understand why they appeared where they did, particularly the aspects most likely to influence behavior, such as the coastal migration routes that brought them within reach of humans. Unfortunately, there are still large gaps in our knowledge of the natural history of many whale species today, so it is nearly impossible to completely re-create the historical behavior of different whales in the Pacific even at the species level.[2] Therefore, this discussion will necessarily be somewhat speculative and based partly on modern behavior, even though current population sizes are dramatically smaller than they were from the 1600s through the mid-1800s. However, contemporary whale biology can only offer a starting point for thinking about historical whales. Whether today's smaller populations behave in different ways than historically more robust populations is unknown, but migration routes in particular are likely to have shifted as smaller remnant populations became isolated subpopulations rather than corners of a broad habitat area filled with whales.[3] As marine historical ecologists recognize, understanding population decline is particularly fraught because of the problem of shifting baseline syndrome, where measurement of changes in the marine ecosystem are based on norms shaped by scientists' personal experience, so that each new generation sees a smaller population as the norm to which conservation efforts should be returning, rather than using objective norms rooted in a longer than twenty- or thirty-year historical reality.[4] Thus, any historical evidence that can speak to past populations can be more useful than current observations of whale population dynamics or behavior, but since the historical evidence and the current biology are both patchy, each must be carefully used to supplement the other.

Biologists today classify all whales as part of the infraorder Cetacea, which is further divided into two parvorders of baleen whales (Mysticeti) and toothed whales and dolphins (Odontoceti). Some classification systems still refer to them as belonging to the order Cetacea, with the baleen/tooth distinction at the level of suborder; since the advent of molecular genetics, many taxonomic categories are in the process of being reclassified. The important distinction between toothed and baleen whales remains, whatever classification label is used. Baleen whales have baleen plates growing from their jaws that are composed of keratin (the material in fingernails, hooves, and hair), and baleen serves in place of teeth to strain out food from seawater. Toothed whales, as the name implies, have teeth instead, and therefore are behaviorally different from baleen whales, particularly because they tend to hunt prey in much deeper water. Toothed whales are generally found in more pelagic (open-ocean) areas.

BALEEN WHALES IMPORTANT IN JAPAN

The baleen whales most important in early modern Japan are today known as the North Pacific right whale (*Eubalaena japonica*, Jp. *semi kujira*), the gray whale (*Eschrichtius robustus*, Jp. *ko kujira*), and the humpback whale (*Megaptera novaeangliae*, Jp. *zatō kujira*).[5] Occasionally whalers would also catch faster whales from the rorqual family, the largest and most streamlined baleen whales, including fin (*Balaenoptera physalus*, Jp. *nagasu kujira*) or sei whales (*Balaenoptera borealis*, Jp. *iwashi kujira*). However, these whales tend to be more pelagic, and therefore most would not have been in reach of coastal whalers. The three species of nonrorqual baleen whales were far more common targets for coastal whalers than any of the rorquals, and therefore we have more information about them (figure 1.1).[6] All three of these species migrate long distances through the shallow waters of the continental shelf, spending a portion of their lives passing near the coast of Japan.

Generally, these whales in their Western Pacific coastal migrations followed the path of the Kuroshio Current and its lesser western branch the Tsushima Current. These currents are the Pacific's equivalent of the Atlantic Gulf Stream: strong warm-water currents that flow northward and come quite close to the western shores of Japan (map 1). The Kuroshio breaks off into the Pacific about halfway up the coast of the main island of Honshu, while the Tsushima Current passes through the strait between Korea and Japan where the island of Tsushima is located. Migrating whales likely used these currents both as markers to guide them from summer breeding grounds to winter feeding grounds and back again, and as a source of food along the way, since both currents are rich in organisms such as larval fish and squid transported from warmer equatorial waters.[7] Thus, migratory whales following these currents would be seen more frequently in the western half of Japan than in the eastern and northern portions, and areas closest to these currents were, unsurprisingly, where the coastal whaling groups of the Tokugawa period operated.

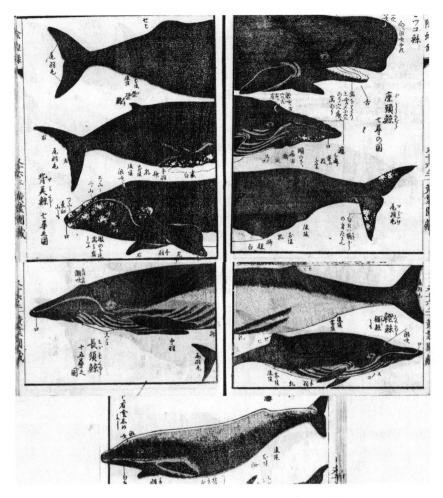

FIGURE 1.1. Major whale species found near Japan. From top to bottom: sperm, humpback, right, fin, sei, and gray whale. This is a composite created by the author from three pages of Ōkura Nagatsune's *Jokōroku*, 23–25, doi:10.11501 /2536205. Courtesy of the National Diet Library of Japan.

Right, gray, and humpback whales are approximately the same size (maximum lengths of fifty-five, fifty, and sixty feet respectively), but their different food specializations affect their summer behavior. Right whales feed by skimming zooplankton out of the water at the surface, gray whales dive down to scoop small amphipods out of the mud in shallow waters, while humpback whales feed in a wider range of the water column for krill and small fish. In the winter, baleen whales move to their breeding grounds and focus on calving rather than feeding, so in their migrations between warm-water winter calving grounds and summer feeding grounds in the Arctic, all three species were not likely to feed much, if at all. Humpback whales in Hawaii today, for example, rarely feed during the winter calving season, living off their blubber reserves instead. The timing of the coastal whaling season put whales near Japan in the winter, when all three species would behave more similarly than during the summer feeding season.

In reconstructing historical whales' lives near coastal Japan, the feeding specializations of the three different species thus do not matter nearly as much as their speed and intended destinations on either end of the migration. Right whales were the favored prey of Japanese whalers until their population began to be heavily targeted elsewhere in the Pacific by American whalers in the mid-nineteenth century (thus severely diminishing the available numbers near Japan as well). In part this was because they are the slowest of the three whales, often leisurely moving through the water at less than one nautical mile per hour (knot) and not more than three knots during regular travel, which is still a speed easily obtainable in a small open rowboat.[8] In comparison, humpback whales have been measured swimming an average around two knots when migrating past Australia, with a range of somewhere between two and 7.5 knots (a maximum speed probably unattainable in a whaleboat) when not swimming at their fastest, and gray whales on the eastern coast of the Pacific migrate at a steady three-to-four knots with a range of 1.7 to 5.9 knots regular swimming speed.[9] This is, in human speeds, a slow walking pace for right whales and a fast walk or slow jog for gray whales. At this speed, they could be using visual cues of the coastline or continental shelf to help them navigate between feeding and breeding grounds, as well as following the temperature differential and flow of the currents, although it is not yet known how exactly whales navigate.[10]

We know the regions where migratory whales were most often seen, since these are where whaling groups operated. After finishing their summer feeding, baleen whales would head south from the Bering Sea and the Sea of Okhotsk. They had two possible paths when they reached northern Japan. The first was to swim through the Japan Sea, either close to the Asian mainland or close to Japan's west coast (see map 2). As the waters narrow between Korea and Japan, some whales would come closer to a section of the northern coast of the domain of Chōshū (today's Yamaguchi Prefecture) on the main island of Honshu, and pass among the many scattered, mountainous islands off the northern and northwestern coast of Kyushu, an area known as the Saikai (Western Sea) region and warmed by the northward-flowing Tsushima Current. Whales swimming more toward the east would first pass by either Tsushima or Iki islands, the two largest islands between Japan and Korea in the strait. Iki is the smaller of the two and closer to Kyushu, with a few harbors where whalers were based around the rim of the island. If hugging the coastline, whales would also pass Ikitsukishima on the northwest corner of Kyushu, a long thin island whose diagonal orientation points toward the Gotō Islands to the southwest, a tight grouping of around 140 islands whose name means "five islands" because there are five large ones making up the bulk of the chain. The Gotō Islands are about forty to sixty miles from the port of Nagasaki, depending on whether one is going to the northern or southern end of the chain. Although they are at the margins of modern Japan, they were part of a lively fishing and trading network during the early modern period, with traffic from China and the Netherlands coming into the strait between the Gotō Islands and the Kyushu mainland while headed to Nagasaki.

The water here over the continental shelf is relatively shallow, although it drops off steeply south of the Gotō Islands. Baleen whales adapted to foraging in shallow waters could, of course, swim through deeper water on their migrations, especially if they ate very little along the way. However, they appear to prefer staying in the shallower water used during the summer feeding season. Even if constrained to shallow waters, either side of these various islands where the Tsushima Current flows would be available. Boat traffic may have shaped the details of their favored routes through this area more than geographic features. Certainly, by the time whaling groups began in the Tokugawa period, whales would have needed to avoid particular harbors and whaling bases, as well as the tracks of cargo ships or fishing boats. Whaling group locations varied over time, with shifting fortunes and possibly also with the shifting migratory pathways of whales trying to avoid being targeted.[11] One piece of evidence for increased avoidance comes from observations of an American whaling ship heading north past Tsushima on their way to whaling grounds in the Sea of Okhotsk. Writing after whalers had been operating in the Saikai area for nearly two hundred years, they observed that the humpback and right whales they saw in the area were "verry wilde" (more inclined to avoid boats) in comparison to whales sighted further out into the Pacific.[12] Whales were thus not avoiding the area entirely, but at least some of them seem to have learned to flee the small rowboats used by both American and Japanese whalers and may have adjusted their migration paths accordingly.

The second major path for southbound whales was to follow the cold, nutrient-rich Oyashio Current south along the Pacific coast side of Japan. The site where that current intersects with the Kuroshio, and both turn east into the deeper central Pacific, varies from year to year. The path for the Kuroshio bends east somewhere along the Izu Ridge, an underwater formation that trails southeast from the city of Tokyo (formerly Edo), marked by a scattered chain of very small islands extending over six hundred miles all the way out to the Ogasawara (Bonin) Islands (see map 1). When they reached this ridge, migrating whales would come closer inshore, skirting the western edges of the Kuroshio that flows north as they head south. They may have used the Kuroshio as a kind of landmark, but it is equally likely that they were following undersea depth contours, which the current also follows.[13] Because the continental shelf drops off close to the shore from the Izu Ridge south, whales staying in shallow waters would be within a few miles of the shore beginning around the Ise and Mikawa bays, down along the Kumano coast (most of which is now Wakayama Prefecture, then known as Kii domain).

The shoreline here is often rocky and steep, except in a few sheltered harbors like Taiji, Miwasaki, and Koza, which became whaling villages in part because they had a sandy shore to haul whales up onto (map 3). From the rocks on the peninsulas along the Kumano coast, one can easily see the dark edge of the Kuroshio Current, whose warm salty water is visibly distinct from the more turquoise colder water on the inland side. Whales would swim between these rocks and the dark edge of the Kuroshio past the eastern mouth of the Seto Inland Sea, between Wakayama's western shore and Shikoku's eastern one, where a large number of ships came in and out on their path between the major merchant city of Osaka and the thriving shogunal capital of Edo. Some may have swum through this passage into the busy Seto Inland Sea to join up with whales coming down from the Japan Sea. However, most would probably pass south of Shikoku, close to the two peninsulas that bracket the wide and relatively unsheltered Tosa Bay where whaling villages also rose to intercept them (particularly the eastern peninsula, Cape Muroto, where deep water is much closer to shore). Past this point, along the southern coast of Kyushu, whaling groups did not form, so we have little evidence of where the whales might have gone next. Whales were seen rarely enough in the Bungo Strait between Shikoku and Kyushu that their sightings were newsworthy events, and often were strandings of single injured or ill whales—possibly ones that had been attacked by whalers but escaped before being killed, rather than migrating whales choosing a different route to their winter calving grounds.[14]

In the spring, when they were done calving and their young had grown a thick enough blubber layer to deal with colder but more nutrient-rich waters, the various species of baleen whales turned north again and reversed the route they had taken to their calving grounds. They either moved through the shallow waters along the continental shelf traced by the Tsushima Current, back through the Saikai area's many small islands to head up along the coast of Korea or the western coast of Japan, or they followed the flow of the Kuroshio up along Japan's eastern coast past Shikoku and the Kumano coast before heading away from the Japanese shore somewhere around the Bōsō Peninsula that projects along the Izu Ridge, sheltering the city of Edo. Individual gray whales migrating in the eastern Pacific will overlap their north and south routes depending on whether they set out early or late and whether they have a calf in tow, so likely the same thing would happen along the shores of Japan.[15] Whaling records do not generally note a pause in the availability of whales during whaling season, so the winter whaling season likely began with southward-bound whales, most of them shifting over to swimming north by the spring but with enough overlap between the two directions that whales would be seen through the whole season, rather than there being a peak in the beginning of winter and another returning peak in the spring.

Situating the moment of passage along the Japanese coast within the larger paths of each of these species' migrations is a much more difficult proposition. How the whales saw this archipelago in comparison to the rest of their long migration routes will never be clear, but we also do not even know what percentage of their migration passed by Japanese shores. This is because we have very little information about historical breeding grounds for the western side of the Pacific, making it difficult to trace a migration line from summer feeding grounds in the Sea of Okhotsk and the Bering Sea. The gray whale's nearly ten-thousand-mile round-trip migration route along the west coast of North America between their Baja California breeding grounds and Arctic Ocean feeding grounds is well known, but the current few remaining western North Pacific gray whales have only been occasionally sighted heading south along the Asian coast from the Sea of Okhotsk to unknown breeding grounds in winter, possibly around Hainan Island, currently the southernmost point of the People's Republic of China.[16] The difficulty in knowing where historic gray whale migrations might have been is related to population size: whaling pressure diminished western North Pacific gray whales to fewer than two hundred individuals as of 2006, so there simply are not enough whales left of this population to know if the larger historical population went to the same breeding grounds they use today, even if we knew exactly where they were.

Omura Hideo, a scholar of Japanese whaling and whale biology, has looked for gray whale bones and records of catches to try to recreate this earlier migration. He thinks that Japan's Seto Inland Sea, the sheltered body of water between western Honshu and Shikoku, may have been a calving ground for gray whales in the Tokugawa period. This might have been a subset of a population that migrated along Korean shores down to somewhere further south in Asia, one which for some reason pulled away to swim through the very narrow strait at Shimonoseki between Honshu and Kyushu to calve in the Inland Sea.[17] Given the force of the current in such a narrow strait, and the fact that this was a major path for shipping into the Inland Sea, it is unclear how many whales would have chosen this path to a calving ground that was equally busy with cargo vessels. The occasional whale seen in the

Inland Sea, which Omura takes for evidence of calving grounds, may not have been breeding there, but instead just traveling through or foraging. In any case, it is not surprising that the vastly diminished population of gray whales does not calve there today. There is strong evidence that some of the few remaining gray whales in the western Pacific may have changed their migration routes entirely to try to join up with the far larger population of recovering eastern Pacific gray whales (currently between fifteen thousand and twenty-two thousand individuals): at least two whales tagged in the Sea of Okhotsk have been found swimming all the way to the coast of North America rather than along the Asian coast. So even though we now have satellite tracking capabilities to follow whales along their formerly hidden migrations, we do not necessarily have any way to tell how closely these routes overlap with historical patterns except by scattered references to the presence of the whales in places that we do not see them migrating now.[18]

Gray whales are not the only species whose migration paths may well have changed. Historical accounts before the twentieth century rarely mention humpback whales in and around Hawaii, the location where large numbers are found wintering today, so their previous calving grounds may have shifted to Hawaii from somewhere else. Some humpbacks that feed in the Bering Sea have wintering grounds today around the Ogasawara (Bonin) Islands (not part of Tokugawa Japan's territory although they are claimed by Japan today) and Okinawa (formerly the Ryūkyū Islands and a separate kingdom in the Tokugawa period). These are most likely to have been the historical destination for whales swimming past Japanese shores.[19] And while right whales, the most prominent targets of many nations' whalers, also migrate, biologists have no idea where in the Pacific they went to calve historically or where they might calve today. This uncertainty makes it difficult to say why exactly any of these different whale species appeared near the Japanese coast. They migrated north and south, toward and away from winter calving grounds, in a manner conducive to a winter whaling season in Japan. Hints that waters somewhere near Japan (at least on the scale of the Pacific Basin) were good calving grounds may indicate the importance of Japanese whalers' impact on these migrating whales. Coastal whalers operating in small open boats did not have the same numerical impact on baleen whales as even nineteenth-century pelagic whalers like the Americans from the 1830s through the 1850s, and certainly not that of factory ships in the mid-twentieth century. But catching whales near calving grounds could have altered the reproductive success of these populations far more than catching them feeding in the summer. Tokugawa-period sources do indicate fetal whales in pregnant mothers and young calves were part of their catches. Whether because the right whale calving grounds were nearby, or because right whales were the focus of whalers' efforts, images of fetal whales are generally right whales.[20]

There may have been as many as ninety-six thousand gray whales in the Pacific Ocean before intense whaling efforts dropped that to today's somewhat recovered population of nineteen thousand (mostly in the eastern Pacific).[21] This overall population has been growing since the International Whaling Commission (IWC) began protecting them in the mid-twentieth century, but the fewer than 130 critically endangered western Pacific gray whales that feed in the Sea of Okhotsk are the last remnants of a thriving population that would have passed by Japan in numbers large enough for multiple individual whaling groups to catch half a dozen or so every whaling season.[22] Only about one thousand humpback whales are now found in the western North Pacific, out of a total North Pacific population of somewhere around twenty-two thousand.[23] The total number of right whales in the North Pacific is even smaller, somewhere around five hundred, from a historic population that had to have been larger than the thirty thousand taken by American whalers in the 1840s.[24] With such small population sizes to work with, any study of behavior and migration patterns today will not necessarily capture the historical reality of these species. Thus, whaling records and other historical information about whales are important in better understanding what these populations used to be like and perhaps explaining what a recovered population could be like. Information about these baleen whales in early modern Japan is therefore interesting not just because it demonstrates the importance of whales to the Tokugawa culture, but also because it is one of the richest historical sources to help us understand aspects of the larger historical populations of North Pacific whales that we can no longer study directly, counteracting the problem of purely modern observations potentially influenced by shifting baseline syndrome.

TOOTHED WHALES IMPORTANT IN JAPAN

Toothed whales were not targeted much by early modern coastal whalers, but many species can be found relatively near Japan. Only two types were important for whalers: sperm whales (*Physeter macrocephalus*, Jp. *makkō kujira*) and members of the beaked whale family (Ziphiidae). Female sperm whales are smaller than males, at an average of thirty-six feet to the males' fifty-two feet. The next largest toothed whales are all beaked whales (anywhere from thirteen to forty feet), and most Odontocetes are much smaller dolphins and porpoises. Sperm whales are the best known, because they were the targets of Western (particularly American) whalers beginning in the eighteenth century, and thus played a starring role in Melville's *Moby Dick* and other stories of American whaling. The beaked whale family is lesser known, in part because they were not targets of most other whalers, and also because they are usually spread out in deeper water and less likely to be encountered by people than coastal whales. The beaked whale with the most historical importance near Japan is the forty-foot-long Baird's beaked whale (*Berardius bairdii*, Jp. *tsuchi kujira*), although the Cuvier's beaked whale (*Ziphius cavirostris*, Jp. *akabō kujira*)—a much paler whale that only reaches about twenty feet long—was also recorded in lists of whale species in the early modern period.

In contrast to Western whaling efforts, Japanese whaling records and scrolls depicting whale species found in Japan contain notes of occasional sperm whales caught by whaling groups, but very few in comparison to the target baleen species. Western whalers preferentially targeted sperm whales, particularly in the Pacific. Early European and American whaling, as in Japan, required processing stations on shore to boil down blubber into oil and to process whatever other parts people wished to consume. One way around this problem once whales close in shore became more scarce was to bring the whaleboats out to sea on larger sailing ships, lowering them from the main ship to chase after a whale. If they successfully caught a whale far offshore, whalers had to tow it to the ship and cut it up there, dumping most of the carcass for sharks while keeping slabs of blubber in casks to be boiled once the ship returned to port. While whale hearts were a delicacy in medieval Europe, as Basque whalers depleted the near-shore right whale population in the Bay of Biscay, whale meat vanished from cookbooks and travel accounts outside of far northern Europe.[25] As whalers chased their targets farther from the European coast, only the blubber, baleen or teeth, and bones would keep until they returned ashore. American whalers joined in the hunt in the mid-seventeenth century with very minimal desire to eat whales.[26] Right whales produce a good quality oil, but sperm whales, with their huge heads filled with spermaceti oil, are even better. The problem was that sperm whales, as a deep-water species, are almost always found far from the coast. The first solution was to bring a portable tryworks (a set of large kettles in a brick framework built over a firebox) to set up on the nearest shore and boil down the casked blubber. By around 1750, Americans began installing a tryworks on the deck of the ship, so the whalers would not have to go ashore to transform the blubber into oil that went rancid much less quickly, and truly offshore whaling began.[27] Japanese whalers, in contrast, who were still producing both meat and oil from their catches at this time, continued to operate out of shore bases and rarely tried to catch sperm whales when baleen whales were conveniently migrating within their reach.

Some sperm whales do migrate, but not in the same way that baleen whales do: the males are found in higher latitudes and only the largest mature males migrate toward the equatorial breeding grounds. They also feed in much deeper waters than the coastal baleen whales, since their prey is squid found over a mile below the surface. Thus, they are more likely to be found on the steeper side of the continental shelf and over underwater canyons cut into its edge than they are to be close to shore. The sharp drop on the Pacific side of Japan means that people were more likely to encounter sperm whales near shore there than in the Japan Sea. The scrolls depicting Japanese whale species that do include sperm whales are most likely to have gotten their information from Kumano coast whalers or those from the Cape Muroto side of Shikoku, who were closest to deep water.[28] But they were not a major focus of most whaling groups—they were probably included more because, like the Baird's and Cuvier's beaked whales also found in these scrolls, they are the only toothed whales close to the same size as the major baleen whales found near Japan, and people out on the water saw them sometimes.

The fact that Japanese whalers continued to practice coastal whaling while other nations were moving offshore in pursuit of sperm whales makes early modern Japanese whaling seem more sustainable than European and American whaling. The Western impetus for shifting to offshore whaling came not just from the desire for the more pelagic sperm whale, but also from declining coastal populations of baleen whales hit hard by shore-based whalers like the Basques. The history of Euroamerican whaling is a long list of collapses in target populations, followed by the search for increasingly distant new whaling grounds and species.[29] But the assumption that Tokugawa-period organized whaling was completely sustainable just because Japanese whalers did not shift to pelagic whaling and new species like sperm whales and fin whales until after American whalers had decimated Pacific right whale populations in the mid-nineteenth century obscures the impacts they did have. This assumption also sets up an idealized view of Japanese whaling where early whaling groups had some kind of sensitivity to sustainable harvest that carried through to modern factory ship whaling, even though sustainability was clearly not part of twentieth-century Japanese whaling corporations' race to harvest as much as they could from the Antarctic in competition with other whaling nations.[30] In reality, sperm whales were just not the same level of tempting target for people who wanted both meat and oil as they were for those who were solely focused on high-quality oil.

The role that sperm whales played in early modern Japan was relatively minimal, but in one specialized region of Japan beaked whales were quite important, and whalers there have sustained their harvest from the early modern period through to today. Like sperm whales, beaked whales are found in deep waters along the continental shelf break or further out to sea. The only two places in the world where people consistently hunted any species of beaked whale are the Faeroes in the North Atlantic and the Bōsō Peninsula in Japan, which is near the deep Sagami Trough, a major tectonic plate boundary zone. Baird's beaked whales were the target species for Japanese whalers in this area. Because no other region in Japan hunted these whales, and they were not targets of other nations' whalers, this particular shore-based whaling practice has continued into the modern era. In that sense, Bōsō whalers have been able to sustain their historical whaling practices, mostly because they are small-scale enough to not deplete the population as a whole, and have not been not part of a larger global competition for the same whales.

Most of the Edo-period records for whaling on the Bōsō Peninsula have been lost, but some period scrolls that illustrate the different species of whales (and other strange fish like hammerhead sharks) include beaked whales in their listing of whale species. Since these whale scrolls generally were compiled with information from whaling groups in the Kumano area, an assortment of beaked whale species might appear in them—more likely from incidental catches or sightings than from a concerted whaling effort like that of the Bōsō Peninsula. Because deep waters past the continental slope are not terribly far from these whaling areas (although farther than the distance to the Sagami Trough from the shore of the Bōsō Peninsula), some beaked whale sightings could be expected even from villages focused on hunting shallow-water baleen whales. Some Kumano coast whale scrolls include both a *tsuchi kujira* (Baird's beaked whale), and also an *akabō kujira* (Cuvier's beaked whale).[31] Another scroll explicitly stating it came from a visit in 1721 to the two Kumano whaling villages of Taiji and Koza also includes Baird's and Cuvier's beaked whales among the whale images.[32] Because these scrolls also depict killer whales and pilot whales, which were not major targets of whalers in that region, as well as sometimes including interesting sharks or strange fish, the fact that beaked whales are in them does not prove they were ever specifically hunted by Kumano whalers, and other records do not indicate they were targeted.[33] The most famous source discussing the details of whaling in the Saikai region of Kyushu does not include any toothed whales at all, so it is likely that most toothed whales were hunted only on the Pacific coast side of Japan, and much less frequently than baleen whales were.[34]

Beaked whales were rarely targets of whaling outside of the Bōsō Peninsula because, like sperm whales, beaked whales do not have the same coastal migration patterns that made baleen whales tempting targets. They appear to arrive in the deep waters of the Sagami Trough in the spring and head for Hokkaido in late summer, returning in the fall before vanishing to unknown wintering grounds, but in places without canyons or trenches their movements are less clear. They are found in much deeper water on the continental slope than baleen whales, as their prey is found at the bottom in waters between 0.6 and 1.2 miles deep. That fact, along with their more northerly range, limited the area in which they were specifically targeted to the Bōsō Peninsula during the early modern period.[35] Therefore, although the practice of hunting these whales was part of the history of whaling in the period, it was a side project far less connected to the network of whalers and whaling in areas further south. While the Bōsō whalers were an exception in the practices of the Tokugawa period, they may still have been connected to fishermen on the Kumano coast, an area where whaling was quite important. A particular style of shore-based net fishing for sardines in the Bōsō area developed from a singular contact with an outside expert washed ashore sometime around 1247 in what is now Chiba Prefecture. In a similar fashion, one specific contact in the 1590s with a famous Owari-based harpooner Mase Sukebē taught local Kantō-region fishermen how to catch whales. This seems to have developed in isolation into harpooning beaked whales, because there was less frequent and regular contact with whalers from other areas afterward.[36]

CATEGORIZING WHALES IN GENERAL

Tokugawa classification of whales ignored the two modern categories of baleen and toothed whales and focused more on size to determine what was a whale and what was not. However, since sperm whales were only occasionally targeted by early modern Japanese whalers, most of this book will focus on the baleen whales that made up the bulk of the interactions between people and whales in this period. The very general category of "whale" is one that resonates not just today in the English-speaking world, but also in contemporary and historic Japan. All of the whale species found in Tokugawa-period sources are referred to as some kind of *kujira* (whale), whether baleen (e.g., *semi kujira*, right whales) or toothed (mostly just *makkō kujira*, sperm whales). I am therefore not artificially lumping the targets of Japanese whaling together just for the sake of an argument about the importance of whales in general. Whether called a whale or *kujira*, the people of Tokugawa

Japan found commonalities across these species of cetaceans that make it worth referring to them as a whole. Since these names are still used today, the less scientific category of "whale" is also used by contemporary Japanese speakers. The usefulness of such a general term is its common-sense impression of whales as a particular type, an impression that has continued to shape common understanding of these animals even after the introduction of Linnean scientific classification: while all whales are cetaceans, not all cetaceans are whales.

While some Japanese scrolls illustrating whale species also contained dolphins and even less-related fish like sharks, these nonwhale inclusions were labeled with names distinguishing them from the larger whale species, all of which the artists marked as *kujira* of some type. If "whale" is a common-sense category for large cetaceans across cultures, the line that separates whales from dolphins is less uniform. In general, whether one asks an English speaker the difference between whales and dolphins or asks a Japanese speaker the difference between *kujira* and *iruka*, the average person would say that dolphins are much smaller than whales. However, there are many lesser-known small whales that are very close to the same size as other species known as dolphins. Dolphins are of the family Delphinidae, but so are killer whales (*Orcinus orca*, Jp. *shachi*) and pilot whales (*Globicephala spp.*, Jp. *gondō kujira*), which—as is obvious from the names—are both generally considered small whales in English but not necessarily in Japanese. The difficulty of making the distinction between a smallish whale or large dolphin is clear in a comparison of the similarly sized Risso's dolphins (*Grampus griseus*; up to thirteen feet), and the Beluga whale (*Delphinapteras leucas*; thirteen to sixteen feet).[37] Risso's dolphins in Japanese are *hana gondō*, relating them to pilot whales, while beluga whales (unknown to the people of Tokugawa Japan) are *shiroiruka* (white dolphins). It is not merely a problem of dividing the two at approximately thirteen feet long: melon-headed whales (*Peponocephala electra*) only reach nine feet.[38] In contemporary Japan, *kujira* are whales, including toothed whales of the family Delphinidae over about 16 feet long, whereas smaller Cetacea are considered *iruka* or dolphins.[39]

For my purposes, the fact that neither "whale" nor *kujira* is a strictly defined category means that, when I refer to whales in general, I mean larger Cetacea. I am considering here the interactions with a broad category of animals rather than one particular species, so the fact that there is not exact overlap between Japanese and English definitions, or even the fact that there is often no consensus between scientific and lay understanding of what is included in the category of whale or dolphin, is not a problem. Because the ambiguous size division between small dolphins and large whales holds for both the early modern period and today, and because whales are by far the more influential, I will leave dolphins out of my discussion and focus on whales rather than all forms of cetaceans.

One of the more interesting things about whales is the difficulty that they pose for people trying to figure out where they fit in the natural world. This difficulty may explain why people have paid so much attention to whales and been so curious about them. Even when they were included in the category of fish rather than mammals (something that did not change globally until the nineteenth century), it was clear that their need for air and their production of milk for their young made them a very strange type of fish, never mind their immense and impressive size.[40] In fact, the bafflement of scholars trying to place whales and other difficult organisms into their classification system of the natural world helped to drive the development of the Japanese scholarly field of natural history (honzōgaku) in the Tokugawa period (see chapter 4).

Terajima Ryōan's Wakan sansai zue (Illustrated Sino-Japanese encyclopedia), published in 1712, placed whales in the category of scaleless oceanic fish. This was a rather catchall grouping for weird types of marine "fish" like whales, sharks, and eels. It also included some scaled fish whose less typical features apparently overrode the consideration of whether they had scales or not, such as swordfish.[41] The Illustrated Sino-Japanese encyclopedia combines information from a wide variety of sources in describing whales and their uses, so it is probably the most comprehensive source for answering the question of what a whale was to people in the Tokugawa period. In this work, Ryōan begins with a brief description of whale folklore, which says that a great whale lives in a hole in the ocean floor, and by moving in and out of this home it produces tides.[42] But after this introduction to legendary whales, Ryōan moves on to the best understanding of natural history scholars in his day, and focuses on the different parts of whales, followed by descriptions of the six main Japanese whale species. All six of these were targets for whaling, as reflected by his inclusion of whale parts in each species' description. He also indicates how good a target each was, beginning with the favored right whale which produced the most oil.[43] Even including the legends, his is a very practical way of considering whales: what do they do that might affect people, and how can they best be used by people?

WHALES AND PEOPLE IN COASTAL WATERS

The fascination with whales and their possible uses is a major part of the interaction between people and whales in this period. Of course whalers interacted with these animals directly, but it is important to realize that whale-human connections merely began with that meeting out on the water. According to one early nineteenth century whaling text, *Geishi* (Whale chronicle), at least ninety different whaling groups were in operation at that time, and other villages may have had whaling groups that had already failed or moved by that point.[44] The minimum size of a whaling group, including both the whalers out on the water and the people required for processing on shore, was around three hundred people, and some were much larger. But even if there were only around twenty-seven thousand people hunting whales and processing their carcasses, whales reached into the lives of far more than that fraction of a percent of the population of Tokugawa Japan.[45] From sources left behind by scholars, administrators, merchants, and sightseers, we know that there was a lively fascination with whales among people who lived far from the whaling villages. Whaling was just the mechanism by which these animals were brought out of the marine environment and into that of the people of early modern Japan.

While the following chapters of this book will focus on the different parts of Japanese society and culture affected by whales, it is useful to first think about what the experience of whales in the coastal environment might have been like. Beyond the danger of being chased down by people in small boats wielding harpoons and lances, whales swimming in coastal waters would also encounter people out on the water for other reasons. Many other forms of marine life also thrived along the Tsushima and Kuroshio currents, allowing coastal villages to support themselves off a variety of fishing practices depending on the season. In fact, whaling villages relied on many denizens of the ocean for their survival: these villages generally are found out on the ends of peninsulas and on steep islands far from the areas of intensive rice farming that literally formed the financial basis of the Tokugawa economy, since the major form of tax was paid in rice. Often, little arable land could be found in whaling regions, with steep mountains running right to the shore constraining both buildings and fields. However, they were able to turn a variety of fisheries into cash to buy the food they could only minimally grow themselves, and they were thus tied into the mercantile network of the period. Fishermen in these villages had the maritime equipment to travel along the shore and to major port cities like Osaka and Edo, but even if they didn't travel that far, they exchanged the products of their catches with merchants in such city centers and could buy not just food but also other goods like popular books in return. With the lively coastal trade of the Tokugawa period, no one living on the coast was all that isolated from the broader urban-centered culture developing from the movement of people into and out of the growing city of Edo.

Over the course of the seventeenth century, new fishing villages appeared all along the coast because of the Tokugawa peace. After the constant upheaval of the Warring States or Sengoku period (1467–1603), when warlord daimyo were all fighting among themselves for territory and loyal followers, a progression of three major warlords consolidated power into what became the Tokugawa shogunate. Oda Nobunaga, Toyotomi Hideyoshi, and Tokugawa Ieyasu in turn gradually consolidated power until Ieyasu finally took the position of shogun over a pacified Japan, with political control over the approximately 250 daimyo, who each still ruled as lord of his own domain (a political category replaced by a smaller number of prefectures in modern Japan, the equivalent of American states or Canadian provinces). The Tokugawa peace enforced by Ieyasu allowed for wartime energies to be diverted into other pursuits. Specialized fisheries began to develop as part of this redirection of energies, particularly because new policies of shogunal control of foreign trade and restriction of foreign travel by Japanese people confined those with experience on the water to areas close to shore.

Further into the period, specialization and refinement of new fishing techniques led to complex new fisheries all contributing a particular catch to the thriving commercial marketplace. A plethora of marine products (particularly foods and fertilizers) came from adapting particular fishing techniques to specific conditions and locations. Tokugawa specialized fisheries targeted not just whales, but also bonito or skipjack tuna, cod, herring, flounder, mackerel, salmon, eel, shrimp, octopus, squid, abalone, and various seaweeds.[46] As the marine environment became an important supplementary source of resources for the restricted terrestrial area of early modern Japan, more and more people could be found out on the water, making the winter migration of whales through these highly productive waters increasingly crowded with people even when they were not hunting whales.

It is clear that whales were swimming through waters rich with many species of fish and with fishermen chasing a wide variety of prey. But they also would have encountered even more people on ships that were simply traveling along the coast hauling cargo and passengers. Even after the Tokugawa shogunate made efforts to restrict foreign trade to specific ports under their control, such as Nagasaki and Hirado, coastal shipping was an important avenue for getting rice tribute and other goods to Osaka and Edo, a thriving city of over a million people by the early eighteenth century. Much of this shipping passed through the Seto Inland Sea from Kyushu, Shikoku, and the far western parts of Honshu to the merchant center of Osaka, where some of it was then transshipped to the shogunal capital of Edo. In his analysis of coastal trade statistics, Louis Cullen argues that the Tokugawa-period coastal trading fleet "was probably almost as large as the entire fleet engaged in both the coastal and foreign trade of England and Wales," which is a significant amount of shipping.[47]

In fact, during this era of highly restricted foreign trade, coastal trade boomed to an extent that may well have exceeded the volume and value found anywhere else in the world at the time, although discrepancies in the focus of record-keeping make that difficult to prove. What we do know is that records of trade in and out of Osaka, and the trade into Edo, show a huge volume of shipping flowing through the waters near Japan's shores. Four or five thousand ships passed through Osaka's offshore anchorage every year (the waters closer to the city were too shallow for massive cargo ships, so smaller lighters would take their goods the rest of the way in to port and bring exports out to the anchorage). Over seven thousand arrived in Edo annually.[48] These were the largest but not the only ports involved in the coastal trade, since ships were designed for short legs from port to sheltered port rather than long offshore routes where they would be more likely to hit disastrous weather. This is why the Seto Inland Sea was a particularly busy thoroughfare, offering more sheltered travel than on the Japan Sea or Pacific coasts and also providing more ports in and among the scattered islands along its length than were available for much of the less sheltered coastline.

The sea was inextricably linked to travel, especially for people coming from the islands of Kyushu or Shikoku to the major cities of Osaka, Kyoto, or Edo (all on the island of Honshu). There was a strong network of roads, including five main trunk roads developed by the shogunal government and many smaller roads maintained by local lords from their castle towns at the center of domains linking them to these roads. But the steep interior of Japan made it more reasonable to ship cargo by sea than by land, especially since there were few vehicles beyond hand-carried palanquins, and most cargo was loaded on pack horses. Even people planning to travel mostly on land had to spend part of their journey crossing rivers, large lakes, or sections of coastal ocean. While travel by boat was quite dangerous, even for ships that stayed in port until the weather was promisingly calm for their next leg, travel entirely by land (when possible at all) took much longer. With a strong and well-maintained road system and the ability to ship a large variety of consumer goods by sea and land, and the spread of peace and the economic growth that followed it, the Tokugawa period was one of mobility and travel from the late seventeenth century onward.[49] Pilgrimage, samurai requirements of alternate attendance in Edo, and the rise of recreational travel and tourism were all part of the growth of a distinctive culture of the Tokugawa period, which relied not only on a particular terrestrial infrastructure but also on access to the nearshore marine environment, filling the waters through which thousands of whales migrated with thousands of ships headed up and down the coast.

CONCLUSION: RETHINKING THE MARGINS OF JAPAN

With all of this lively movement up and down the coasts of Japan's islands, whether of migratory whales, fish, or people, it is surprising that there has not been more discussion of the importance of the near-shore waters in the history of the Japanese archipelago, particularly in the Tokugawa period. From the perspective of whales, of course, the land was something they passed by rather than chose as a destination, and only those unfortunate enough to be killed by whalers or stranded in shallow water would visit the terrestrial portions of the archipelago. However, the people who helped bring them and other marine denizens ashore lived not on the outer edges, but rather in an important intersection between the maritime and terrestrial portions of Japan. By following whales, we also follow the people who were out there with them, and we can see that the coastal villages were not isolated from either the land or the sea.

Reconsidering the importance of the tens of thousands of whales that used to swim in nearshore Japanese waters is necessary in part because of modern experience and perception: today, these places lie on the far edges of the transportation grid. The Kumano coast has one slow local train line, which occasionally has to suspend operations due to high winds or landslides. The whaling village of Muroto on Tosa Bay lies within the one remaining section of Shikoku's coastline without rail service. The only way to get there is by car or bus along the single road linking a chain of former fishing villages into the current Muroto city designation, an administrative area covering the whole peninsula on the eastern side of the bay, with a population of less than fifteen thousand people. Northern Kyushu's Saikai whaling villages are on islands accessible only by infrequent ferries and, in the case of the Gotō Islands, Iki, and Tsushima, light aircraft (map 2). Since the construction of a bridge in the 1960s, the former whaling village of Kayoi in Yamaguchi Prefecture can be accessed by bus from the station in Nagato city (to which it technically belongs), but it is far from the center of town, and Nagato itself is not a major travel destination. If the old whaling areas are so difficult to get to today, in the modern high-speed transportation era, it is easy to assume they have always been difficult to get to, off the beaten path and therefore not particularly important.

However, these modern-day impressions of marginality should not color our ideas of these spaces too strongly. While road access to whaling areas was not simple, even with Tokugawa Japan's well-managed system of roads, coastal waters formed another type of road whose utility is often overlooked. If we refocus our view of the space of coastal Japan to include sea access, whaling and other fishing villages become far more interconnected, an integral part of the lively coastal transport and trade system between the cities of Osaka and Edo and these supposed hinterlands. They could be, and were, visited by people on their way to somewhere else, as well as being destinations in and of themselves. On the Kumano coast in particular, whaling villages were on major pilgrimage routes to Kumano Nachi Shrine and Ise Grand Shrine. People along this coast were connected not by roads through the steep mountains that rose rapidly from the shore, but by boats, leading to the development of cooperation as well as competition between the three major whaling villages of Taiji, Kōza, and Miwasaki.[50] In the Saikai area, trade networks with the Asian continent and foreign ships were less busy than they had been before the Tokugawa restrictions, but they still connected the people all around the islands near Nagasaki and Tsushima where foreign trade continued.

Despite government policies nominally trying to keep people in one place (especially rural villagers who needed to provide tax rice from each domain to fund their domainal lord's castle town and also the shogunate), villagers moved a lot during the early modern period. Not only did fishermen leave a particular village to head out on the water to fishing grounds, but they might also leave one village to go live in another, for a season or permanently, in search of better fishing grounds. Kyushu fishermen, making use of their strong historical background in maritime trade, tended to migrate up along the Japan Sea coast.[51] In the same period, on the other side of Japan, migrant whalers from the Kumano area travelled both to Tosa and to the Saikai area. In some cases they settled there to found new whaling groups, and in other cases they worked for a few years in distant waters before returning home. Whalers thus did not work in isolated villages, nor were they tied to a particular domain. The same trade routes that shipped goods between northern Kyushu and Osaka, and the relatively direct sea-route between the southern Kumano coast and Tosa, proved equally useful for whalers moving between successful whaling areas in the early modern period. The interconnectedness of this era becomes much clearer when we include the maritime realm in our picture of Japan, not just the roadways and the political structures of domains that have been the focus of previous scholarship.[52]

The impression of marginality does not arise solely from a modern misperception of spaces whose importance has shifted over time. Scholars during the Tokugawa period also tended to ignore fishing communities in favor of discussing the peasant farmers that fit into the framework of proper government and civilization copied from the Chinese model. The Manchu-led Qing government (1644–1912) turned inward and focused on their Inner Asian frontiers rather than their maritime borders, and this geocentric view was echoed by Japanese scholars' perceptions of the land as central to civilization.[53] Meanwhile, the products of specialized fisheries like whaling moved far inland, tying these coastal peoples and their work into the society of early modern Japan even when scholars did not focus on them. The land, in this period, cannot be separated from the marine resources that supported it. The movement of whales, their parts, and stories and information about them throughout Tokugawa society, created resonances and interconnections far inland and even into all-important agricultural practices.

Even though we still know relatively little today about the majority of whales' lives, we can extrapolate from bits and pieces of information to try to understand whales throughout the northern Pacific. The scattered remaining sources that talk about historical whales in and around Japan—images of different species, records of the meat and oil produces from their bodies, records of the interactions between whalers and their prey, stories and broadsheets, and speculation about whales—all show that whales were a powerful presence throughout early modern Japan. Apart from bringing back into focus a part of the history of the archipelago that had been relegated to local histories and specialists only interested in the business and culture of whaling itself, a consideration of whales in early modern Japan also helps us recenter that history to include overlooked but important maritime spaces.

This shift in perspective necessarily highlights Tokugawa whaling's cultural importance, which might seem to support the contemporary prowhaling argument about a traditional whaling culture within Japan as a reason to continue hunting whales far offshore. However, clarifying the scope and wide-ranging impact of this early coastal whaling actually shows just how different this practice was from today's pelagic factory whaling, how much more imbedded in local culture and society it was, and how it was far from a monolithic tradition within an unchanging set of cultural practices even within the Tokugawa period, never mind across the transition into the twentieth century. The far greater numbers of whales swimming through coastal waters while these groups were operating meant that whales must have had a greater influence on humans in the Tokugawa than modern observers of today's minimally whale-populated sea near Japan would assume. The evidence for the variety of ways that people hunted, consumed, and thought about whales in early modern Japan discussed in the following chapters is not just a product of a particular cultural perspective about whales. It is also evidence for the greater number of encounters between whales and humans before the modern collapse of whale populations under commercial hunting pressure.

TWO

BRINGING WHALES ASHORE, WHALERS OFFSHORE

Coastal Networks and the History of Whaling

IN 1840, AN OBSERVER DESCRIBED THE WHALING GROUP IN OGAWA-
jima, a small island off the coast of northern Kyushu, as full of bustling
activity every winter during the whaling season. Although Ogawajima
is currently home to only about 550 people, in the mid-nineteenth century around eight hundred men crewed the whaleboats based there,
and another three hundred day laborers, both men and women, worked
onshore processing whales.[1] Whaling was not limited to this set of over
a thousand people on Ogawajima, but rather was spread throughout
coastal villages in western Japan. Each of the hundreds of whaling
groups active from around 1600 to the end of the nineteenth century
required similarly large numbers of boat crew working in concert on
the water, and hundreds more on the shore to help process the whales
they caught in the twenty-four hours or so before they began to spoil.
During the Tokugawa period, organized whaling became a big business
all along the coast from Ise down to Kyushu, employing tens of thousands of people.

Japanese whaling did not appear from thin air in the late sixteenth
century, but it was something quite new. Archaeologists have discov-
ered signs of some kind of cetacean hunting, mostly involving dolphins,
approximately five thousand years ago in the Jōmon period. Unfortunately, there is little evidence for what prehistoric behavior matched

the artifacts and bones found, and the practices did not continue beyond the prehistoric era.[2] Some beached whales were opportunistically harvested in the intervening centuries, but the numbers were likely to be quite low, reserving any harvest for a fortunate few people. There was clearly a major change beginning in the late sixteenth and early seventeenth centuries, resulting in the rise of an active, coordinated whaling enterprise on a much larger scale than previously seen. Because "old-style" or "traditional" whaling (*koshiki hogeigyō*), the term used in Japanese whaling histories for Tokugawa-period practices, does not indicate which "tradition" and how far back it stretches, I have chosen to refer to early modern whaling practices as organized whaling, in contrast to opportunistic harvest of beached whales performed by people who were not otherwise specialized whalers. Specialized, organized whaling groups are something that we have little to no evidence of in Japan before the late sixteenth century.

The first organized whaling groups went out in small open rowboats that could hold a crew of around ten to thirteen men, seven or eight of whom were rowers. This is slightly more than the six men (five rowers, one of whom became the harpooner, and one man on the steering oar) who crewed American whaleboats in the eighteenth and nineteenth centuries. While both types of whalers used rowboats, the Japanese whaleboats were propelled with sculling oars, which allowed for more men to stand closer together than in whaleboats with long sweep oars that require room to pull. However, with these extra men on board, Japanese whaleboats did have to be built larger, at just under thirty-five feet long and seven feet wide, in comparison to American whaleboats, which were twenty-seven to thirty-one feet by about five feet wide.[3] They had a sharp bow but squared-off stern like most Japanese boat designs. The Japanese boats were not lowered from a larger ship, but instead launched from a whaling village's shore base and coordinated with signals from shore. On Japan's mountainous coastline, it was easy to find a height near the water from which the boats could see smoke signals and flags (figure 2.1). This made for a much more coordinated whale hunt than that practiced by American whalers, who were limited to the maximum of five whaleboats carried on one ship unless they agreed to share the catch with another ship. Japanese whaling groups

FIGURE 2.1. Flag and
smoke signals from a
whaling shore post. Ōtsuki
Heisen, "Geishikō" (1808),
3:35, doi:10.11501/2575477.
Courtesy of the National
Diet Library of Japan.

could have as many as forty boats on the water at once, all working in
concert and coordinated from shore (figure 2.2).[4]

Over the three centuries of coastal whaling in Japan, two major techniques developed.[5] In the first, beginning in the 1570s and the only technique used for the next century, whalers chased down a whale with a
number of boats and harpooned it (figure 2.3). Their harpoons had a long
wooden handle and an iron end with two asymmetrical points on either
side of the tip, much like the early version of European and American
whale harpoons, although likely independently developed (figure 2.4).[6]
The Japanese did not use anything like the toggle head innovation first
used by Arctic natives and then adapted to American iron harpoon
heads by a blacksmith in 1848, at least not until the end of the nineteenth
century when struggling whaling groups tried to adopt modern (foreign)

FIGURE 2.2. Coordination of a whaling group around Ikitsukishima. Note the signal and lookout post in the lower center of the image. Oyamada Tomokiyo, *Isanatori ekotoba* (Edo, 1832), 2:18, doi:10.11501/2576169. Courtesy of the National Diet Library of Japan.

whaling practices. Japanese whalers would throw many harpoons into one whale in the hopes of slowing it down, but the kill was made with a hand-held lance wielded by the *hazashi* or harpooner. Once the whale had slowed from blood loss and exhaustion of dragging the boats, the *hazashi* would leap onto its back to stab it, making this by far the most dangerous role in the whaling group (and thus the one which had the highest prestige; figure 2.5).[7] Once the whale was dead, it was lashed between two boats, making a sort of raft which was towed by the rest of the boats in the whaling group to the beach for processing.

As right whale catches began declining, whalers developed a new technology in 1675, one which sets Japanese coastal whaling apart from that of any other culture. The differences between early shore-based American or European whaling and the first style of Japanese harpoon group whaling rest mostly on divergent boatbuilding and rowing traditions, as well as minor differences in tools. But the introduction of nets reshaped Japan's organized whaling into something found nowhere else. Net whalers supplemented the chaser boats used by harpoon groups with net boats of the same length but around twelve feet wide, to provide more room for a huge pile of net dropped into the open water

FIGURE 2.3. One of the most lavishly illustrated images still extant of a whaling group harpooning a whale. The speckles above and below the central image are gold leaf. Anonymous, "Illustrated Scroll of Whaling (*Geigeiki mokuroku*)," eighteenth century, 1985.647, bequest of the Hofer Collection of the Arts of Asia, Harvard Art Museums/Arthur M. Sackler Museum. Photo: Imaging Department, copyright President and Fellows of Harvard College.

within a few miles of shore and held by a semicircle of boats. This net made a kind of open-water fence into which the chaser boats could drive the whale they were hunting (visible around the head of the whale in figure 2.5). This open-water net whaling entangled the whale, slowed it down, and helped keep it from escaping while the harpooners worked—especially necessary for targeting species faster than right whales. With the additional boats, these groups were often quite large. Without the shore-based coordination made possible by the particular coastal environment of Japan, net whaling probably would not have been possible. It was not even adopted by the Bōsō Peninsula groups that caught beaked whales, because these whales spend far less time on the surface and would simply dive deep when harassed rather than swimming away near the surface like baleen whales.

Both plain harpoon groups and net whaling groups operated in the same areas, even at the same time in the early transition between techniques from 1675 to around 1685. While the specific geography of whaling areas varied, they all had high places to set up lookouts on shore, waters that were shallow enough for migrating whales to come within a few miles of that shore, and harbors with sloping beaches onto which the whale carcass could be winched up, with large windlasses to peel

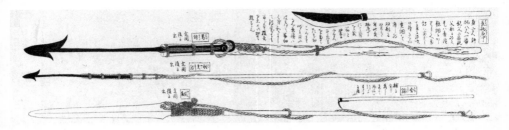

FIGURE 2.4. The long-handled knife at the top was used by a harpooner on the back of a whale. The two harpoons and lance below it were thrown at the whale first to wound it and slow it down. Oyamada Tomokiyo, *Isanatori ekotoba* (Edo, 1832), 3:11, doi:10.11501/2576170. Courtesy of the National Diet Library of Japan.

off massive sheets of blubber and bring them into nearby sheds to be boiled down into oil. Net whaling groups began in the Kumano area, including the Pacific coast side of modern Wakayama Prefecture and adjacent parts of Mie Prefecture, an area under the governance of Kii domain in the Tokugawa period and near to the coastal path of the warm Kuroshio Current followed by migrating whales. After fierce competition between groups within this area, some whalers moved to new whaling areas on the east and west sides of Tosa Bay, which makes up the southern border of Shikoku and is within modern Kōchi Prefecture (formerly Tosa domain; see map 3). They also migrated only a few years later to the Saikai (Western Sea) area of northwestern Kyushu, including the Gotō Islands, Ogawajima, Ikitsukishima, Iki and Tsushima (under the management of various prefectures today, and various domains in the early modern period), where the Tsushima Current branch of the Kuroshio brought migratory whales and other species into the Japan Sea. The last area to adopt the new technology of net whaling was close to the Saikai area, just to the east on the tip of the island of Honshu around the village of Kayoi, on the Japan Sea side of Yamaguchi Prefecture (then Chōshū domain; see map 2).

Cooperation among whalers could be found within an individual group, but also between nearby whaling villages and between the four whaling regions as well. This level of cooperation or at least networking (sending crews to different whaling areas for a season or a few years, sometimes to compete with other groups in those areas) was possible because the regions were all closely connected along common shipping

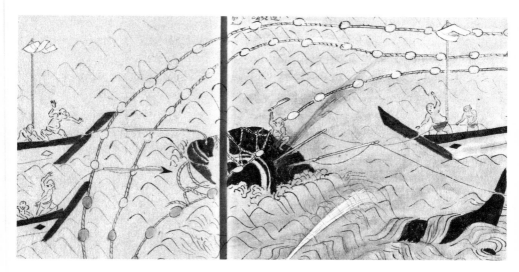

FIGURE 2.5. A harpooner (*hazashi*) from a net whaling group leaping onto an entangled and wounded whale to deal it a death blow with a long-handled knife. Note the harpoons being thrown from the left and the lances thrown from the right. Kizaki Morisue, "Shōni no rōgei ikken no maki," in *Hizen Karatsu hogei zusetsu*, 12, doi:10.11501/2537195. Courtesy of the National Diet Library of Japan.

routes. Whales thus brought people together within whaling villages scattered along their migration routes, and they also helped strengthen ties between villages as much as six to seven hundred miles apart on different islands of the archipelago. Day laborers and local villagers from a broad area around the whaling village worked for whaling groups in the processing sheds, making stronger regional ties for people who were not out on the water as well.[8] Furthermore, some whales also strayed off the usual routes, whether because they were avoiding whalers, had been injured by whalers but escaped, or because they were sick and disoriented. Discussions of the rare whale ending up in places like the Shinagawa River in the middle of the city of Edo, considered in more detail in chapter 4, show that knowledge about whaling groups and their products circulated more widely than just within whaling areas. The mobility of migratory whales was echoed by the movement of whaling groups and also by the spread of interest and information about both the whales themselves and the people who hunted them.

One of the drivers for development of specialized whaling groups right around the same time as the start of the Tokugawa peace was the availability of people who could be whalers instead of fighters serving warlords, since whaling was a martial and masculine occupation. Women were involved only in the less skilled processing work or, in some cases, were the exclusive producers of nets in the off season. But a further impetus for whaling was the need for new resources to support a growing population no longer limited by war and its accompanying hardships. Environmental historian Conrad Totman notes that the near doubling of the Japanese population in the seventeenth century, at the prosperous start of the Tokugawa peace, led to resource depletion and to associated searches for "ways to maximize the biosystem's immediate utility."[9] Some of these new resources were marine resources, whether consumed as food directly (whale meat, bonito) or used as fertilizer and agricultural support (whale bones and oil, sardines and herring). Totman argues that the restriction on foreign travel under the Tokugawa rule, along with shifts in land use and coastal shipping, was what led to an increase in specialized fisheries.[10] The search for new resources was thus the impetus for the expansion of the early modern Japanese resource base out into the ocean, and the reason why it is important to include the coastal waters as part of our conception of the territory of Tokugawa Japan.

Japanese whaling practices changed significantly over the course of the early modern period because they needed to adapt to shifting availability of different species. While the literal decimation of Pacific whale populations by American whalers in the 1840s and '50s was a rapid and obvious impact of particular whaling practices, the effects of Japanese whalers on migratory whale populations were more subtle. Within a century of the founding of the first organized whaling group, as right whale numbers were diminishing, net whaling developed to take advantage of species like the humpback and gray whales that plain harpoon groups had targeted less frequently. Then, by the end of the nineteenth century (around two centuries after the start of net whaling), most organized whaling groups had collapsed, although some of their whalers transitioned to modern whaling companies operating in new areas farther from the coast—in part, but not entirely, because of the impact of American whaling on Pacific whale populations. The more detailed examination of Japanese whaling practices that follows will show how and when they had the most impact on local whale populations. It will also begin to tease out the environmental changes that occurred as a result of investment in maritime space during the Tokugawa period. The picture that results is not one of unbroken whaling traditions smoothly carrying forward from their instigation into the modern era, but instead shows complex and dynamic practices succeeding and failing with changes in whale presence—some of which must be blamed on overfishing by these early whaling groups.

THE RISE OF HARPOON WHALING GROUPS

Harpoon whaling arose in the 1570s in the interconnected Ise and Mikawa bays, where fishermen from the village of Morozaki on the tip of the Chita Peninsula between the two bays formed the first recorded whaling group. This is before the end of the Warring States period, so the arrival of peace and expansion of the population into new areas was not the first impetus behind the development of whaling in Japan. While there is evidence that the practice spread to groups in Ōsatsu by 1592 and down the coast to the Kumano area by 1596 (see map 3), no direct source material from this practice remains, so their motivations are unclear. It is possible that there were other early whaling groups for which the evidence is now lost. Even nineteenth-century authors seeking the origins of organized whaling had to rely on the patchy survival of the first groups' records, because as one chronicle written in 1808 noted, by that time there were no longer professional whalers in the Ise Bay area to interview.[11] While there is thus not much detail available about what these groups were doing, or what inspired them to start whaling, records of the Imperial court indicate that gifts of whale meat were regularly sent by people living on the shores of Ise Bay for many years between 1582 and 1625.[12] These gifts show that at least some of the whales were intended for consumption by people of high rank, a delicacy sent as tax or tribute, possibly as part of carving out a safe space for the whalers in an era of political chaos.

The semienclosed geography that made it so much easier to begin whaling in this area also made it much easier to quickly impact the whale population. Not all whales struck with harpoons made it in to shore, and many could have died from their wounds even if they escaped the whalers. Overfishing most likely caused whaling in Ise and Mikawa bays to die out sometime before 1800, even though whaling in other areas such as the Kumano coast and northern Kyushu prospered longer. Unlike later whaling groups, Ise whalers may not have depended as heavily on migrating whales. Their target may have been a population that sheltered in the bay for a time during coastal migration, or even stayed there year-round.[13] Pressure on this constrained population soon led to the center of whaling in Ise to shift in search of more whales: the practice began in villages along the Ise coastline, but migrated gradually south to be centered along the Pacific-facing Kumano coast by the 1630s. By this time, instead of (or in addition to) sending whale meat to the imperial court in Kyoto, whalers in Owase, just south of the bay, were sending whale products to the shogunal capital of Edo.[14] The shifting location of whaling villages indicates that people who had honed their skills hunting whales in one place had to continually move to find new sites where whales were abundant enough to catch, having removed or driven away all the readily available whales from earlier sites. Whalers began by focusing on a population consistently localized in the bay. The numbers of whales there quickly began to decline, either through overfishing of a relatively static population or through whales beginning to avoid the area where they were in danger. Expert whalers were left with the choice of giving up whaling entirely or trying their hand somewhere with an untouched target population. The trajectory of whaling groups moving southward over time therefore supports the idea that pressure on Ise Bay and Mikawa Bay whales was unsustainable: both in the economic sense, as groups could not afford to continue without a certain yearly catch, and in the ecological sense, as the lack of catches shows that viable whale populations no longer lived within or moved through the bays (although they may have moved elsewhere rather than dying off).

Such a rapid decline in available whales, while the most obvious initial impact of whaling, may not have been limited to just the area inside the bays. For example, there is some indication that Kii's domain-managed whaling in the Owase area, which had begun in 1754, was shut down in 1770 due to lack of whales.[15] Whaling historian Kondō Isao, speaking about the dynamic early stages of organized whaling, noted that "it seems the whale [stocks] were gradually becoming exhausted" in the Ise area, and thus these harpoon whalers, "consequent to the decline in whale resources, groped for new fishing sites."[16] Possibly some of the movement down the Kumano coast to the more southern whaling regions was similarly driven by declining whale populations, or at least populations that under whaling pressure changed their migration patterns to not hug the shoreline as closely as they used to.

If these practices had truly been sustainable, the Ise Bay whaling enterprise could have continued indefinitely. At the very least, if it really were sustainable, this small-scale whaling should have continued through the end of the Edo period, as foreign competition for the whales in this population was limited until the mid-nineteenth century. Instead, the small enclosed population could not support the practice that developed there, and the men who had become experts in whaling had to move out of the bay and down the coast. While there are no records of the specific numbers of whales caught in Ise and Mikawa bays, there were 192 total whalers from four different groups going out onto the water in 1758 from the Owase area, about sixty miles to the southwest of the bays.[17] Whatever basis for comparison is used, even Owase's records indicate that whaling in this area outside the bays had vanished by the mid-Edo period (likely before 1800) due to a lack of whales. It was clearly too large-scale an effort to be sustainable even in a more open area that did not have any kind of resident whale population.[18]

MOVING WITH WHALES:
HARPOON WHALING IN NEW AREAS

Even as whalers reduced whale numbers or pushed them further offshore and out of reach of coastal groups, whales were also influencing the behavior of whalers. The networking and mobility seen in whaling groups echoes the highly transitory and variable movements of whales from season to season, and helped connect different regions together as they followed the same species up and down the coast. Other coastal ties also aided in this process. For example, there were strong trading ties between the people of Kii and those in northern Kyushu and Tsushima, which linked them to trade networks with China and Korea.

Whalers moving to the Saikai area were part of a larger movement of people between these places, bringing their locally specialized expertise such as net-making and net-handling with them. One fisheries and folklore scholar suggests that the rise of organized whaling as a men's specialty coincided with the rise of abalone diving as a women's specialty, because the area around Ise and Mikawa where harpoon whaling groups first appeared was a place where there were many divers as well. When divers collected abalone and other products for trade with China in the otherwise remote and inconvenient islands of northern Kyushu, the men who came with them were often employed in whaling groups.[19] Thus, it should be noted that whaling was not an independent fishery, but rather tied into other fisheries depending on what resources were available, and linked to migrations of people for other reasons than just following whales. The seasonality of whale migrations helped increase that mobility, since no one could operate within a whaling group for the whole year, and thus some whalers became other types of fishermen the rest of the year, or found other seasonal occupations.

Whaling along the Kumano coast involved at least some of the Ise Bay whalers moving to begin new groups there. In Taiji, the first organized whaling group was founded in 1606 by Wada Chūbei Yorimoto, with the assistance of a harpooner from Morozaki named Denji. His other founding partner was Iemon, a man from the merchant city of Sakai (near Osaka) who was a rōnin or masterless warrior with experience supervising fleets. This story offers further proof that Ise Bay whaling had caused a shortage of whales. Local historian Takigawa Teizō noted that both Iemon and Denji were part of a group ferrying lumber for Toyotomi Hideyoshi's castle in Osaka when they were wrecked and washed ashore with three other men on the Taiji Peninsula.[20] The fact that Denji had moved on from whaling to working in marine transport would seem to indicate that he was not specifically searching for new whaling opportunities, but rather had been forced to give up his earlier whaling practice. Since he turned his hand to whaling again in Taiji after being wrecked there, it seems he did not lack motivation for whaling. So it should be noted whaling practices moving gradually down the coast to the Kumano area from Ise and Mikawa bays was not necessarily a conscious or organized shift. Rather, chance meetings and connections seem to have had an important influence in where and when different whaling groups would appear. The paucity of sources about Ise whaling makes it difficult to determine how much the expertise of whalers there traveled to other places in the accidental manner of Denji's shipwreck instead of more active attempts to move whaling grounds. In either case, after Yorimoto began harpoon whaling in 1606, a strongly linked set of groups arose along the Kumano coast, based out of Miwasaki, Taiji, and Koza villages. The success of these villages inspired others to pick up the technique and found groups in Shikoku and northern Kyushu.

The social position and visibility of whaling group managers at least partly motivated others to copy their techniques and start their own groups. Whaling in the early Tokugawa period was partly an outgrowth of the naval forces of the Warring States period. Wada Yorimoto descended from a warrior lineage (possibly with some connection to piracy). His father had been killed in Hideyoshi's disastrous invasion of Korea while commanding a group of retainers, and Yorimoto himself began in the service of a samurai who had been awarded a fief in Kii for services rendered to Tokugawa Ieyasu at the battle of Sekigahara that marked the end of the Warring States period. By the time Yorimoto organized the first professional whaling groups, he was a local elite with a manor, in charge of collecting taxes for twenty villages.[21] As was the case for many of the former samurai who chose to turn in their swords and settle down to farming, his family remained high-ranking village elites even after he began his peaceful lifestyle in the country.[22]

In a similar fashion, the founder of the first whaling group in the Tosa domain on Shikoku in 1624, Tada Gorōemon, was a local elite with naval experience during the Warring States period. Although people took whales in some fashion before this point, possibly just a stranded whale here and there, clear evidence of organized whaling in Shikoku appears with Gorōemon's Tosa whaling group, eighteen years after Yorimoto began his whaling groups in Taiji. He, like Yorimoto, was a warrior who settled down as village headman once the Tokugawa peace began. He was given his position by the younger brother of the daimyo of Tosa domain, in part because his prior experience crewing boats during the Warring States period made him a good protector of the Tosa coastline. On the basis of similar military experiences, it would be difficult to claim a totally independent origin for his whaling techniques, since both founders were likely adapting their prior military training to harpoon techniques and strategies.

Whether they originated independently or not, there was a strong interconnection between Tosa and Kumano whalers later in the century. Gorōemon's group ceased operations in 1641, after the numbers of passing whales had diminished too much to support the enterprise of over two hundred fishermen.[23] Ten years later, a samurai from Owari was installed as governor (*daikan*) of a district in Tosa. Seeing a number of whales swimming off the coast, he contacted his relative Oike Shirōemon, who quickly came to Tosa with six whaleboats and began operations there. They only stayed for six years before returning to their own domain, but this example does show how, in some cases, entire groups from the Ise Bay area and northern Kumano coast moved elsewhere when they heard of better possibilities.[24]

At least some of the whaling groups operating in the islands on the northern edge of Kyushu had strong ties through longstanding coastal trade with Kumano area whalers. There were a few groups operating in this region just before the Tokugawa period, for example a group in Arikawa on the Gotō islands starting in 1598, which had expanded to ten groups by 1605.[25] While some of these efforts may have arisen independently, records show that sometime between 1624 and 1644, Fujimatsu Han'emon from Kii brought thirteen whaleboats to Hirado domain, while in 1625 another Kii whaler, Yoshibē, brought twenty boats to another area of Hirado to found a whaling group.[26] Another whaler from Kii became head of the whaling group in Arikawa in 1626, while yet another partnered with the head of Arikawa village to begin a harpooning group in the same year.[27] So, as harpoon groups were developing in Ise and Miwasaki bays, as well as in villages along the Kumano coast, some whalers took their chances in the rather more distant Saikai area of Kyushu rather than competing within their home region. This is a sign of not just the intensity of competition in Kumano, but also of the close trade relationship between that region and the islands north of Kyushu. By 1650, there were whaling groups operating in seventy-three different locations in northern Kyushu, at least some of whom had direct ties to whalers in the Kumano area.[28] During the period from 1636 to 1661, a total of twenty-five harpooners and two crew members from the Kii whaling village of Miwasaki alone worked for different whaling groups in the waters around the Gotō Islands in Kyushu, although individuals tended to work for only a few years each.[29]

Founding a whaling group required more than just gathering people with the ability to row offshore to catch whales, because groups also needed a space on the coast where they could bring those whales back to the beach and haul them ashore for processing. This meant a space to build processing sheds, as well as sheds where the whaling equipment could be repaired between seasons. Sometimes these buildings were dismantled and rebuilt in other sites, and they were not always specifically used solely for processing whales.[30] The success of whaling in Taiji led to many other villages with a good beach space in the Kumano area taking up whaling operations; by 1675, the demand for whaling forced Wada Yoriharu to gather together village administrators from seven of the villages in the region to make an agreement to reduce confrontations over whaling sites.[31] This was also the time and place when the next major development in whaling practices appeared.

SHIFTING TO NEW WHALE SPECIES: NET WHALING

While historians of whaling often frame the transition to net whaling simply as a technical improvement, this technique arose from the need to expand target species of whales. Both the cycles of boom and bust in particular whaling groups like Tada Gorōemon's, and the conflict that arose over whaling sites in Kumano and elsewhere, show the intense pressure on migratory whale populations passing the Japanese coast in the early seventeenth century, as more and more people tried to hunt whales. Whaling communities throughout Japan, with the exception of Bōsō whalers, focused on similar species. During the early stage of organized whaling, as with other whaling communities in Europe and America, the preferred target was the right whale. Other whales of similar size, the gray whale and the humpback whale, swim slightly faster and tend to sink when killed, making them more difficult targets. The new net whaling technique, whose development is usually credited to Wada Yoriharu of Taiji in 1675, slowed down all targeted whales, but also kept dead gray and humpback whales from sinking. While some species other than right whales had been taken by harpoon whaling groups, this new procedure made it much easier to catch whales that had not previously been worth the effort of chasing when plenty of right whales were available.

The technique of entangling whales in nets was not developed solely in Taiji: the earliest evidence for the use of nets is in the village of Kayoi on the Japan Sea in 1672. However, in Kayoi they used a method that involved setting a large straw net across the mouth of the bay, into which they chased the whales and then harpooned them.[32] The technique developed in Taiji used hemp, a stronger and more expensive material that stood up better to the force of whales. Taiji whalers also set the nets from dedicated net boats, rather than a specific fixed location.[33] Kayoi's straw-net whaling took advantage of the fact that their peninsula formed a bay that migrating whales could be driven into as they passed along the coast. A similar form of fixed-net whaling developed in 1656 in Ineura, on the northern coast of modern Kyoto Prefecture. Whales would sometimes follow sardines into the bay, and three villages there drove these whales away from the mouth of the bay, where whalers would then set nets to close off escape. Using this method, they were able to take not only humpback and right whales, but also the much faster fin whale. They caught an average of two whales a year, with a maximum of eleven in one year.[34] Unlike Taiji's net whaling, neither of these set-net types of whaling spread to other locations.

Because the method developed in Taiji was less dependent on the local landscape configuration, it was the one that more easily spread to other whaling areas. Kii fishermen had a leading role in the history of Japanese fisheries, setting nets and hauling them offshore rather than from the beaches long before fishermen in other regions, which may explain why the new net whaling technique developed there.[35] Furthermore, straw nets were only strong enough to entrap right whales and gray whales, whereas hemp could withstand the force of humpbacks as well. This new technique opened up two new species as regular targets for whaling even in areas without narrow bays.

By 1680, the numbers of gray and right whales—the easiest whales to catch—were diminishing. The peak catch of ninety-five whales in one season for Taiji whalers occurred in 1681, after which numbers gradually fell.[36] It is no coincidence that the net whaling technique spread outward from Taiji after 1681: whalers trying to replicate this success moved to new grounds that had not depleted or driven off local whale migrations. The new technique spread within a decade from Taiji to Tosa in Shikoku (1683) and the Hizen domain in Kyushu (1684), and from there along the Japan Sea coast to Chōshū.[37] They also sent the net whaling technique back up the Kumano coast to the region around Owase, probably because villages within the entire Kii domain were sources of whaling labor for places like Taiji and thus tightly interconnected.[38]

Given the numbers of whalers from various parts of the Kumano region who had gone to Kyushu for whaling since the 1620s, it is likely that news of the net-whaling technique arrived quickly in Kyushu. However, there is little direct evidence indicating how the new technique was taught in this region. With the great demand for people employed in large whaling groups, local populations were often supplemented by extra-local specialists. Thus, the workers in the shore processing stations were often local laborers, while the more specialized harpooners tended to be migratory fishermen from outside of Kyushu. The crew of the boats, the net and oar makers, and other experts were often seasonal laborers from the Inland Sea. General developments in the use of nets for fishing there meant an increasing number of fishermen with expertise in net handling and other ship-specific tasks available to go elsewhere for things like whaling. Unlike many fishing industries, whalers were given rice rations every day whether they caught a whale or not, which added to its appeal even for fishermen who did not have harpooning expertise.

Including people who worked in the whaling groups and also those who worked only in other kinds of fishing, thirty to forty thousand people from the Inland Sea came to fish off of Kyushu every year, searching for better catches than they could find at home.[39] Fishermen thus increasingly required resources from the Pacific Basin as a whole, not just those confined to near-shore waters. The mostly enclosed Inland Sea would have had a more limited population of various fish species under heavy and growing fishing pressure than would be the case for the waters near other coasts of Japan, which were open to wider maritime spaces like the Japan Sea and the Pacific Ocean that could restock the local populations of target species. A Tokugawa Japan able to subsist purely off local maritime resources would not have seen such large numbers of migratory fishermen leaving the Inland Sea for better opportunities.

Catches in Saikai did not show the same peak and decline that they did in Taiji after the introduction of net whaling. For example, the yearly catch for the Arikawa whaling group in the Gotō Islands between 1691 and 1727 did not fall below twenty whales, with totals between sixty and eighty whales in the 1690s and again in 1710 and 1725. Admittedly, the best years were in the 1690s, after which peak catches were smaller and for fewer years at a time, so there was some change in either whale population size or their ability to evade capture. However, this one group consistently managed twenty to forty whales per year for a thirty-five-year period, in an area with the highest concentration of whaling groups in Japan. Technique alone was thus not a determining factor in how badly whale populations would be impacted by whaling groups. There may have simply been more whales in the Saikai area than along the Pacific coast of Japan, so these regular high catches had less impact than the smaller catches along the Kumano coast that prompted whaling groups to keep moving in search of better whaling areas. Alternatively, the Saikai whales may have continued to swim within reach of shore-based whalers because of a lack of better options for their migration paths in the narrow strait between Korea and Japan, in contrast to Pacific whales with the option to move further out to sea, out of range of whalers, while still following the Kuroshio Current.[40] It is not always clear from whaling records whether a lack of whales in a given area is indicative of a diminished population or just a movement of that population somewhere else, and the Saikai groups' heavy whaling pressure for decades seems to indicate that level of catch did not necessarily lead to population collapse. Perhaps Taiji-based net whaling did not reduce local whale populations so much as drive them away to other areas.

THE SUSTAINABILITY OF NET WHALING GROUPS

In considering the effects on whale populations of the main whaling technique used from 1675 through to the end of the 1800s, it is important to note that the groups that employed net whaling were often not very long-lived. As with harpoon groups, net whaling groups in a particular location did not form an unbroken line of whalers, but rather tended to last for a short period before going bankrupt and being revived by someone else. The ways that whales moved through a given area and the changes in whale populations caused by whaling pressure influenced this dynamic aspect of whaling. Even in areas where whaling was more or less continuous, the many short-lived attempts at successful whaling groups within that continuity show that the presence and availability of whales was not constant, making sustainability tricky to measure. This is true of both types of whaling: the first harpoon whaling group put together by Wada Yorimoto in Taiji in 1606 only continued until 1614. Whaling was restarted in the next year, but only for two years before it too was suspended. Such turnover was common because there were high startup costs to gathering the equipment and people necessary for whaling, and not enough whales could be caught every season to pay back these costs. Adding nets and net boats only added to these initial startup costs. People continued trying again mostly because, when the whaling season was successful, it could be very profitable. Furthermore, most of the whaling areas did not have many better options for making a living. These issues raise difficult questions about the relationship between the population dynamics of whales and the economically driven dynamics of whaling groups, given the fact that all our information about whales from this period is filtered through whalers' experiences and records.

Groups did not rise and fall independently from other whalers. Kukiura, on the Kumano coast about seven miles southeast of Owase, had village-managed whaling in 1683, during the early stages of net whaling. They came under Kii domain management at a point when they were prospering, in 1754, as part of the institution of a domainal whaling office, and so became more closely tied to other whaling groups. After some years where they caught as many as two or three whales in one day, they could not catch any in the 1760s. The domain's whaling office (and Kukiura whaling with it, apparently) closed by 1770.[41] This closure provided Koza whalers with a source of equipment that they recorded as having "borrowed" from Kukiura in 1770, including nets, rope, knives, and at least one boat, which of course was unlikely to have been returned to a defunct group.[42] The record of the equipment transfer, sent first from the headman (shōya) of Kukiura to regional headman (ōshōya), and then from him to high-ranking officials of Kii domain, shows that the domainal government had a hand in regulating whaling not just through taxes or tribute payments but also in providing access to whaling gear. The use of the honorific in referring to the equipment in their records may indicate that it was thought to belong to the domain rather than to the villagers.[43] This passing down of equipment to Koza was also part of the gradual shift of whaling's focal point southward along the coast, facilitated in this case by the fact that both villages were within Kii's extensive territory.

Groups also shifted across domainal boundaries. This movement could promote the rise of new groups in the area left open by a departing group. After the Oike group moved from where they had begun whaling operations in Tosa back to Owari, the local people who had participated as crew and as processing help lost a major source of livelihood. Within a few years they became so destitute that they talked about moving elsewhere, perhaps to Kyushu. Even though two previous whaling enterprises had already folded between 1625 and 1657, the situation was so dire that the village headman of Ukitsu and the local elites, including the Tada clan who had moved away from whaling to become headman of the region (ōshōya), petitioned the domain to be allowed to revive whaling. With the arrival of net whaling in 1683, the locations of the whaling group bases shifted, operating out of sites in Shiina and Kubotsu in the winter but recombining to become one large group in the spring whaling season.[44] This first net whaling group did not last much longer than the earlier harpoon groups had, and a history of Tosa whaling written in the late nineteenth century blames its suspension on the fact that whales became rare.[45]

Although two groups situated near each other in Tosa managed to coordinate during spring whaling, the competition between neighboring groups could be quite fierce. Legal disputes arose over the definition of territory and who could, for example, claim a whale that had been injured by a whaling group offshore, but escaped only to die and wash up on someone else's beach. When the net whaling method was invented in Taiji, the other groups in the area that still practiced harpoon whaling petitioned the domain to force net whaling to stop. But they lost their petition, and net whaling became the dominant method, requiring either retraining and new equipment for old groups, or simply the dissolution of those old groups and the construction of new ones by other backers.[46] Such disputes were most complex in the crowded Saikai whaling area.

PEAK WHALING IN SAIKAI

Although the main techniques were first developed in other whaling regions, nearly 80 percent of all the whaling groups in the early part of the Tokugawa period operated within the Saikai area of northwestern Kyushu. The Gotō Islands, Ikitsukishima, Tsushima, and Iki Island were all well-positioned along whale migration routes, and there were numerous beaches onto which whales could be hauled for processing.[47] This region was also historically at the center of a far-flung and lively trading network. When the Tokugawa shogunate instituted tighter controls on shipping, whaling offered seasoned boat-handlers another option for making a living.[48] Unlike whaling in Kumano (almost entirely under the control of Kii domain), Shikoku (under the purview of Tosa domain), or the Japan Sea side of Chōshū domain, Kyushu whaling was not confined to just one domain's territory or management. This led to a more complex system of compromise over territorial access and regulation between groups than in the other regions. These whaling groups also demonstrate that a large domain with a long coastline exposed to whale migration routes was not a requirement for successful coastal whaling. The large numbers of whaling groups that coexisted in the Saikai area likely benefitted from the fact that they were within a cluster of islands of different sizes. In the other three whaling areas, mountain lookouts had to be placed along the shoreline, but in Saikai they were often situated on different islands, covering a broad cross section of water surrounding the shore processing station (figure 2.4).[49]

This variety of geographical possibilities may also explain why net whaling did not smoothly and completely replace harpoon whaling in Saikai. The second Fukazawa Gidayū, leader of the largest Saikai whaling enterprise of the mid-Tokugawa period, introduced net whaling learned from Kumano whalers in 1678 at his group's site in Arikawa in the Gotō Islands. It was introduced in two of their other whaling sites in 1683 and 1684. Even though this large group managed to shift relatively smoothly to the new technique, not everyone followed suit. At least one of the Saikai villages continued harpoon whaling as late as 1735.[50] Whaling historian Sueta Tomoki's analysis of this delayed shift is that the practice of net whaling was far more expensive in capital outlay than harpoon whaling, so if groups could not get outside support to finance the acquisition of nets and other required equipment, they were forced to continue harpoon whaling. Furthermore, even after the introduction of net whaling to the area, new groups did not always begin with net whaling techniques. The Masutomi group, which eventually became the major player in this area in the latter part of the Tokugawa period, began harpoon whaling in Ikitsukishima, Hirado domain, in 1724. They did not shift to net whaling until 1733. Before this point, they found their steady catches of twenty-two whales per year begin to decline to seventeen, sixteen, then fifteen whales per year. Thus, perhaps due to some worry about this trend, perhaps because they had been simply biding their time and building up capital to be able to move to a better site for net whaling, they moved whaling sites in 1727 further north on Ikitsukishima and switched to net whaling.[51]

Eventually, the groups run by Masutomi moved south into Gotō domain areas and took over these groups. The Gotō groups then began to specialize in spring whaling, because Hirado domain's groups caught whales in winter as they swam south before they arrived in Gotō territories. Even so, the richness of the whale populations in this area meant that this competition was not fierce enough to force Gotō groups to collapse. Over the course of 142 years, Masutomi group records indicate they earned over 3.3 million ryō.[52] This group became famous for becoming rich off of whaling, with that fame boosted by influential manuscripts that described their whaling to a broad audience outside of Kyushu. But they were famous because they were exceptional.[53] The success of the Masutomi could not be easily replicated outside the specific conditions in northern Kyushu. This was proven when the shogunate, based on the recommendations of Masutomi whalers, tried and failed to set up whaling stations in northern Ezo (now Hokkaido), where the climate and oceanic conditions were colder and harsher for whalers, without the warm-water currents that brought whales close to shore in the south.[54]

Unfortunately, there is no direct evidence for the sizes of whale populations before the nineteenth century, when we know that populations declined rapidly. Thus, I have inferred an early decline in whale populations in Ise Bay, or at least a decline in availability of right whales that caused the shift to net whaling to make use of new target species in the late seventeenth century. With the only records of population size coming from whalers' logs of number of whales caught, it is difficult to see overall population trends unless catches drop precipitously along with records of similar or increased whaling effort, as is the case in the mid-nineteenth century. Catch data from American whalers' logbooks shows a rapid and negative impact on right whale populations (and likely also sperm whale populations) after they became a target of American Pacific whaling efforts in 1835. Within a decade and a half, American whaling north of Japan, in the whales' summer feeding grounds, decimated the Pacific right whale population.[55] This sudden intense pressure on right whale populations was felt by Japanese whalers in the mid-nineteenth century, although some whaling groups were clearly having trouble maintaining their catch before this point. Because whales were not harvested on nearly the same scale by Japanese coastal whalers as by American pelagic whalers, the drop in whale catch they caused was more subtle than the 90 percent decrease in American catches, especially for species less preferred by American whalers. However, since both industries targeted the same migrating populations, continued Japanese whaling on stressed and shrinking numbers of whales may also have contributed to the decline.

Whatever the exact response of whale populations to pressure from American and British whalers in the Pacific, Kumano-area whalers in the nineteenth century certainly were having problems. In fourteen of the twenty-one years between 1823 and 1844, the Koza Whaling Office operated with a deficit, for a cumulative deficit of 191,224 monme of silver (about 3,824 gold ryō at government standard conversion rates, or the entire yearly wages of approximately 145 tradesmen).[56] By the 1860s, the lack of whales was severe enough that the two-year deficit from 1864 to 1866 exceeded one hundred thousand silver monme (about two thousand ryō), and in 1866 the Koza Whaling Office published a notice indicating possible foreclosure. The 271 whalers belonging to the office had to petition to borrow rice from the domain that year to prevent starvation. At that point they also began to experiment with borrowing money from merchants outside of Koza.[57]

On top of these difficulties, there was a major earthquake in 1855 that affected villages all along the Kumano coast. The tidal wave that hit Taiji after this earthquake destroyed the whalers' homes, the processing sheds, and much of their equipment. It also washed away the sheds and equipment belonging to the Koza whaling group.[58] The money for reconstruction came from funds that had been put aside to pay taxes, which only increased the poverty of Taiji inhabitants.[59] Apart from this large-scale natural disaster, more localized problems increased their hardship, such as the 1830 fire that destroyed all of the Koza whaling sheds and equipment.[60] Two records written in 1844, supposedly as a memorial to the four humpback whales caught after a long dry spell in 1827, show the pressure whalers felt in these conditions. Koza whalers reported to various domainal regulatory offices for fisheries until 1808 or 1810, when they had to go on hiatus, having exhausted their means of support. The histories complain that this led to starvation as the price of rice increased, and even though they became desperate enough to try whaling again in 1823, Koza whalers failed to catch anything until the whales whose catch they celebrated in 1827.[61] These problems show difficulty catching whales along the Japanese coast even before American whalers arrived in the Pacific.

Environmental factors beyond whale population sizes and availability contributed to Koza's problems. They had few agricultural or local forest resources to make a living with apart from sardines, which were not available from the tenth month to the third month (when, conveniently, whales appeared in good years).[62] The villagers had to beg for aid so much that their repeated petitions lost weight. They even received one reply that, instead of worrying about continuing whaling to support themselves, they should open up the sandbanks in the middle of the river mouth on which Koza was built and turn them into fields. They did not find this to be a reasonable solution, since they would have to buy farming implements and learn farming techniques from elsewhere. Their hardship continued until they were finally granted permission to go out whaling in 1824.[63] The suggestion to try farming was locationally specific, but it does point out the way in which domainal officials would consider more land-based solutions to their problems rather than trying to work within the context of finding ways to make the villages' maritime endeavors more profitable or sustainable.

The Pacific whale population crash affected whale migrations through the Japan Sea as well as those on the Pacific coast of Japan, so that any effect of the intense pressure of Saikai whaling efforts on whale populations must be teased out from underneath the larger collapse brought on by American whalers. The catch records for four different groups under Masutomi management in Saikai from 1764 to 1778 were variable but did not show an overall decline in whales.[64] However, between 1805 and 1823 there was a sharp drop in whales taken, from a total of nearly 140 per year to less than twenty by three groups under Masutomi's direction.[65] The Masutomi group was an umbrella management for a number of smaller groups in different territories in the waters from around Iki and Tsushima down to the Gotō Islands. One of the important families in this enterprise was the Yamagata family, whose records contain a number of cases bemoaning the lack of whales "recently," without, unfortunately, including a year. Still, many of these were signed by Tatamiya Seiemon. Other instances with dates that note this name in the Yamagata family records include two from 1797 and 1803, then a larger set from the years between 1833 and 1854.[66] Since the majority of the reports come from the mid-nineteenth century, it seems likely that they felt the greatest hardship and lack of whales around this time, with declining catches from the drop noted in 1823 onward through the following three decades. In Chōshū as well, the total catch by decade of around fifty right whales dropped from 1851 through 1860 to only twenty, and then in the following decade to nothing, even though the catch of fin whales (not a target of American whaling efforts in the mid-nineteenth century) rose.[67]

Whether or not Japanese whaling efforts were contributing to the lack of whales along the coast in the nineteenth century, after the mid-century crash it became increasingly clear to whaling groups that they would again have to try changing techniques to deal with the changing availability of whales. This time, they began looking to foreign whalers for new ideas. In 1875, Nagaoka Moriyoshi, a diplomat, peer, and influential member of the government, claimed that "knowledge of the use of whales drives the wealth and power of the nation."[68] In other words, the development of a modern Japanese whaling industry would go hand-in-hand with the development of a strong, internationally competitive Japan in the new Meiji era (1868–1912). This was not just a concern about the economic success of whalers, but also showed a new perspective entirely on the role of whales and whaling in Japan. The ideas about new whaling industries included some ineffective attempts at leveraging the power of armed coastal whalers as naval defense against foreigners, and some attempts at founding American-style whaling, which had already proved ineffective after the 1850s due to the lack of whales. Finally, Japanese whalers joined other modern whaling nations in adopting Norwegian Svend Foyn's invention of bow-mounted harpoon guns on catcher boats, paired with factory ships in the open ocean for processing. The engines in these catcher boats made it possible to chase faster whales like fin whales generally found farther offshore. The shift to what the Japanese call Norwegian-style whaling (essentially the same commercial whaling techniques as all other major whaling nations of the twentieth century) was successful. However, it required an entirely different environment and species, so it spelled the end of local shore-based whaling and forced an accompanying shift in the place of whales in an also dramatically changing Japanese society.

Despite all of these collapsed groups and retrenching of whaling villages, there is some continuity of whaling and whalers between the Tokugawa period and modern Japan. In 1877, a man named Moroki Sennosuke took some of the Taiji whaling group's boats, equipment, and men and set up a net whaling base in Busan, Korea, similar to the one that had been operating in Taiji on and off since the late 1600s.[69] This shift was part of a recognition by Japanese whalers that their catches in and around Japan's coastal waters were declining. But various whaling companies that tried to develop modern whaling techniques in Japan at the end of the nineteenth century were only intermittently successful. In the 1870s and 1880s, corporations began forming to hunt whales with the new technology of the bomb lance, a shoulder-mounted exploding harpoon gun.[70] A functional exploding harpoon had been in development for over a century, but the first successful version was patented by American Thomas Roys in 1861.[71] Ultimately, none of the versions of bomb lance, American or Japanese, were particularly effective, in part because aiming from the shoulder standing on the pitching bow of a small whaling boat was nearly impossible. It was not until Svend Foyn developed a mounted harpoon gun for use on larger, more stable ships that such weapons became successful and revolutionized whaling techniques around the world.

A Japanese steamship equipped for whaling in the Norwegian style managed to catch a total of three fin whales in their inaugural cruise around Tsushima in 1899, but failed to catch any when they tried the fishing grounds around Tanegashima (Kagoshima Prefecture), around Yobuko (Saga Prefecture), or around Busan in Korea. In 1906 off the southernmost peninsula on the Kumano coast, near the village of Kushimoto, another ship operated by the Tōyō Gyogyō company managed to successfully catch fin whales. Their success was perhaps in part because this company was not connected to any of the whaling groups with a long history in the four main regions of organized whaling groups, but rather was run by a Yamaguchi Prefecture native named Oka Jūrō, whose company made a point of hiring a Norwegian gunner for three years to teach them how to operate the equipment.[72] In other words, the most successful whalers became the people who were less attached to the old coastal whaling areas and instead were able to shift to a new offshore environment chasing new species of whales.[73]

CONCLUSION: TRACING IMPACTS AND CHANGE

The exact impact of whaling efforts on whale populations in the early modern period is difficult to trace, but Japanese whalers certainly did not have the same large, rapid impact as American Pacific whalers. In comparison to this sudden collapse in the span of less than two decades, any whaling efforts lasting two centuries seem much more sustainable. Still, Japanese whaling was not a small-scale or even necessarily sustainable enterprise in this period, as some have claimed.[74] Even before the mid-nineteenth century, there were definite signs that Japanese whaling groups were changing the whale populations they hunted: right whales were not as available, humpback and gray whales began to be targeted more closely by net whalers, and the yearly catches of whales varied widely enough that many whaling groups could not last continuously for more than ten or twenty years. Because the only solid information we have about whale populations in this period comes from records of how many were caught, it is difficult to say whether lower numbers of whales available to whaling groups were due to smaller populations or to whales moving further offshore or finding new migration routes to avoid Japanese whalers. Over centuries, it is possible that baleen whales adapted to deal with the impact of whaling in ways that they were not capable of doing when hit hard in one decade by pelagic whalers. But similarly, it should be remembered that whalers were also adapting to changes in availability of whales and began to use different marine spaces as coastal waters proved less productive. With the dramatic shift between the culture of Tokugawa Japan and a rapidly modernizing Meiji Japan, the place of whales perforce shifted as well, so continuity is very thin between the organized coastal whaling groups and their modern counterparts operating in Antarctica and the far northern Pacific, despite prowhaling arguments emphasizing the cultural importance of "traditional" whaling in Japan today.

The four major centers of organized whaling groups considered in this chapter were also not the only places with whaling groups in the early modern period, but they were the largest and therefore had the greatest impact on whale populations. As noted earlier, a small-scale form of net whaling (using fixed nets rather than those set from a boat) lasted in Ineura in Kyoto Prefecture from 1657 through sometime in the 1910s.[75] There were also areas such as the villages on either side of the Bungo Channel between Kyushu and Shikoku (in current-day Oike and Ehime prefectures, respectively) that erected monuments to the occasional whale, usually a stranded or otherwise weakened whale rather than as the product of organized whaling efforts.[76] Whalers on the Bōsō Peninsula near the city of Edo performed an unusual form of whaling for beaked whales, and this was the only area where whaling groups operated steadily through the transition into modern Japan. The fact that beaked whales are not generally a whaling target in other places may have contributed to the ability of Bōsō whalers to continue their hunts, as there was far less pressure on their total population of target animals than on the populations of right or humpback or gray whales, which were also hunted by British and American whalers and by many whaling groups along the coast of Japan.

As for the impact of whaling groups on humans in the early modern period, although fishing and whaling villages tended not to fit well into the ideal, farming-centered status system of Tokugawa Japan, it should now be clear that they still had a major role in the Tokugawa economy and in the subsistence of a large number of people up and down the extensive coasts of the archipelago. The whaling industry was one of the largest and most interconnected specialized fisheries that developed during this period, and in some cases made managers quite rich. However, the influence of other fisheries also reached inland to the more agricultural areas of Japan. As David Howell shows in his study of the herring fishery in Ezo (later Hokkaido), the new specialized fisheries of the Tokugawa could be central not just to local economies but to a whole regional system, from the fishermen themselves to the farmers using their catch as fertilizer.[77] Further research on other major fisheries is necessary to provide a full picture of the ways in which the coastal marine environment was integrated into early modern Japan, but the interconnections between whaling villages and the additional ties that they had with merchant and government sponsors at various levels show that coastal villagers were not simply a marginal curiosity within Tokugawa Japan.[78]

Even if we confine our attention to the coasts, whaling was linked to the rise and success of other new fisheries and to growing coastal trade networks. Without other forms of fishing, for sardines or bonito or other summer species, whalers could not survive on the agriculturally difficult coasts, since whaling was seasonal rather than year-round. Coastal traders and the movement of ships and thus people all around Japan were also a necessary part of the evolution of a whaling network responsive to new innovations and changing conditions outside of a single group's experiences. Coastal trade also provided a connection for whaling groups to urban markets and merchants throughout Japan. Finally, those who depended on this bounty from the sea may not have ventured very far out into the open ocean, but whales and other migratory species brought some of that Pacific into contact with Tokugawa Japan. The knock-on effects of American whaling are one of the clearest touches of broader Pacific events upon coastal waters of Japan, but even before the existence of such influence, some of the variability in success of whaling groups depended on dynamics of whale populations also shaped by natural forces like changes in food availability in the North

Pacific feeding grounds, or on conditions in the more southerly breeding grounds not directly felt within Japan. There is no way to isolate Japan's coastal waters from the wider Pacific Ocean, when people were pursuing organisms whose habitats stretched across large swaths of the Pacific Basin.

As long as coastal whale migrations continued, Japanese people had access to a far broader resource base than just the nearshore waters they rowed and sailed through. Our only vector for information about these whales is the presence or absence of different species of whales in the records of specific coastal villages, which does not include any knowledge about the whales' experience in the rest of the Pacific. So at first glance, the history of whaling in early modern Japan looks like a purely coastal enterprise confined to within sight of land. But no matter how close Japanese fishermen stayed to their shores, the movements of whales and fish made them part of a larger Pacific environment. An important consequence of the development of specialized coastal fisheries, including whaling, was that a small human expansion out into the marine environment could take advantage of the wider ranges of marine organisms to provide replacements for nutrients no longer available purely from agriculture. These marine nutrients were not as finite as the terrestrial nutrients bound up in the rather limited space of the Japanese islands, because they were collected in the bodies of organisms that travelled thousands of miles in the Pacific. The high productivity of northern waters literally swam past whaling and other fishing villages.

Whales as targets of whaling groups offered not just basic nutrients in the form of meat and fertilizer, but also sometimes offered products with whole new effects, reshaping the culture as well as the consumption habits of the period. In the following chapters I will look at how the efforts of whalers to make the most of their new resource influenced the material, intellectual, and religious culture of a broad area of Japan during this period of intensifying organized whaling, as whales and their products were brought ashore and shipped to nonwhaling areas. This impact is important not just in considering the complex and dynamic role of the marine environment in the society of early modern Japan, but also in showing the specificity of that role to the conditions of the early modern era.

THREE

MOVING WHALES FROM COASTS TO MOUNTAINS

The Circulation and Use of Whale Products

IF THE FASCINATION WITH WHALES TODAY IS IN PART BECAUSE OF their rarity, one might expect that whales would have been less fascinating in an earlier era of abundance, when people could more frequently see them in Japanese coastal waters. The response of thousands of people in the summer of 1798 to the unusual sighting of a stranded whale in the Shinagawa River in the bustling city of Edo (now Tokyo) shows that other ways to define rarity resulted in just as much fascination. While there were many whales swimming past the coasts of Japan, they did not usually swim directly into harbors and up the rivers that fed them into major cities. This fifty- to sixty-foot whale was unusual in bringing itself ashore, or at least within reach of one. But even playful descriptions of this Shinagawa stranding, such as the text "Kujira bōsatsu hyaku hiro kōryū" (Whale-bodhisattva one-hundred-fathom monument) by a man named Toboke, show an acute awareness of and interest in the ways that whales more usually came ashore along the coast of early modern Japan: at the hands of harpoon-wielding whalers, in order to convert them into cold hard cash. Looking at the stranded whale, he mused, "Shouldn't it already have become money?"[1] Toboke's question highlights the popular assumption that whales were most important as a commercial item. In fact, the potential profits of whaling were so well-known during the Tokugawa period that this otherwise unknown writer, who spoke about a whale seen where no whaling groups were based, made an easy assumption about whales' essential nature as money-making commodities. Whaling was a big business, commodifying not just the whales, but also the necessary human labor, just like other growing early modern industries often referred to as protoindustrial or protocapitalist (although neither of these terms should be taken to imply that the early modern Japanese economy was destined or guaranteed to become capitalist).[2]

Urban residents of this city of over a million people rarely had a chance to see whales in person, but they had many opportunities to interact with the products of whaling. First, Edo was a major destination for whale oil. The city of Edo barely existed as a village before the Tokugawa shogunate made it their government seat, but its rapid growth as the shogunal capital brought a sharp increase in the demand for lamp oil, to the point that whale oil was shipped there from over 750 miles away in Kyushu.[3] Furthermore, Edo residents may not have eaten much whale meat, since even salted meat could only travel so far in the days before refrigeration, but the rice they ate and which samurai-class residents relied on for their stipends was protected by whale-based insecticides. Through such products, the bodies of whales were divided into more manageable pieces and moved from coastal waters into the agricultural plains and steep terrain of Japan's islands. In this way, people who lived far from the whaling villages that directly interacted with migrating whales also relied on the marine space of the archipelago. Far from being the kind of small-scale and often reverent harvest of just enough whales for local needs implied by the conflation of "traditional" whaling with subsistence practices of aboriginal whaling groups, organized whaling of the Tokugawa period was a business centered on making a profit for its managers.[4] Whales were therefore an influential part of a money-based economy that increased the environmental impact of Japanese society over the course of the early modern period.

The story of whale products highlights the expansion of Japan's resource base out beyond terrestrial boundaries, along with the sardines, bonito, herring, and seaweed that made a thriving society possible in this geographically constrained area, even with limited trade with other countries.[5] The narrative of modern industrialization tends to focus on market-driven societies outstripping their available resources, driven to expand colonial possessions to provide such resources.[6] In contrast, the decidedly circumscribed boundaries of Tokugawa Japan, where the shogunate controlled the few ports open to international trade, would appear to be a society that must have used its domestic resources sustainably since the population neither collapsed nor expanded territorial boundaries to replenish diminished resources.[7] From this perspective, strict controls on foreign contact "forced the Japanese to consider their lands *and natural resources* as finite and limited" (emphasis mine).[8] While the terrestrial spaces of the archipelago were finite and limited, the natural resources they had access to were less so when the ocean is included. In reality, one of the major colonization or expansion projects of early modern Japan was out into the coastal waters that brought nutrients from throughout the Pacific, whether they were eaten directly or became part of increasing the yield of agricultural products that were then consumed by people. As the easiest to access portions of this new resource base were tapped out, there was some initial territorial expansion into areas like Ezo (modern Hokkaido) where resources that were formerly traded for could be better controlled by the Japanese.[9] Before this point, the booming, incredibly urban population of the Tokugawa period relied on a less visible form of resource expansion than that of co-opting existing human territories. Instead it connected with the large nutrient cycles of the Pacific Basin through marine organisms like whales. Just as Western Europe (particularly England) leveraged their colonial landholdings to break through eighteenth-century ecological limits, adding the productivity from these "ghost acres" to their per capita resource supply in the imperial center, Tokugawa Japan began to leverage their connections to the Pacific's marine environment to supplement scarce terrestrial resources.[10] The result was not as dramatic as the European Industrial Revolution, but it may add to our explanations of how Japan successfully and rapidly modernized right after the end of the Tokugawa period.

The thriving market economy that led to Toboke's assumption about the stranded whale's value arose from new developments after the institution of peace, in particular urbanization and agricultural growth. The Tokugawa shogunate's restructuring of society had the unintended consequence of massive urbanization, along with a national economic network to supply those growing urban centers. The samurai portion of the population was required to live in castle towns in each domain and/or the city of Edo itself. Enforcing the peace required an ability to keep a close eye on warriors, which meant having them in castle towns rather than in the more distant countryside. Furthermore, the shogunate controlled the power and wealth of the daimyo by requiring them to live in Edo on a set schedule of alternate attendance, whose processions back and forth from their domains to live in the city for a year at a time drew down the coffers of rivals to Tokugawa family power.[11] As a result of these policies, as much as half the population in castle towns could be samurai, even though they only made up about 6 percent of the overall population. Furthermore, Japan was more thoroughly urban than most other early modern states: by 1721 Edo had grown to over a million people in an urban network of more than thirty cities of over twenty-five thousand inhabitants, while London, for example, was both the only city of any size in England and also only about half the size of Edo.[12]

Such intense urbanization was supported by equally intense agricultural development to supply urban markets, including both greater production of staple crops and also increased growth of cash crops. While rice was the theoretical center of the economy, as the major taxes financing the government and samurai stipends were paid in rice, peasants generally ate dry-field crops such as millet and barley. They also grew mulberry trees to feed silkworms and expanded into other cash crops like sugar and ginseng by the mid-eighteenth century.[13] With a rise in cash crops, there was a concomitant rise in other natural products that could supplement rural incomes, including marine products not consumed directly by their harvesters. The various specialized fisheries from this period like whaling and northern herring were part of this agricultural expansion and economic shift in production.

The institution of peace both directly and indirectly affected agricultural development. First, the daimyo warlords could no longer increase total harvest under their control by simply taking over more land from others as spoils of war. Instead, they worked with the productivity of the land whose boundaries were codified in the restructuring that came with the Tokugawa peace, finding new ways to profit from the natural resources available within their domains. With an initial doubling of productivity through conversion of abandoned fields back into rice paddies, the ecological and geographical limits of intensifying cropland productivity were quickly reached—the steep mountainous interior of Japan means only a maximum of 35 percent of the land is actually available for human use.[14] By the eighteenth century, farmers were looking to technological innovations and fertilizers such as fish-meal to improve the productivity of depleted fields. Technological inno-vations such as winnowing machines also increased the efficiency of farming staple crops, which gave farmers time to grow cash crops as well, and thus put pressure on an even broader set of resources.[15] To fully understand the thriving peacetime economy of early modern Japan, we thus have to consider the marine environment as well as the terrestrial one, because expansion out into maritime spaces was one of the major ways that nutrients could be added to the agricultural cycle in such an intensely farmed and intensely urbanized setting.

Sardines and herring were major marine inputs for Tokugawa agri-culture. Both of these small fish were used as fertilizers, particularly in the rich cash crop area around Osaka and Kyoto on the Kansai Plain. Because catches of these fish could be far larger than what people could eat before they spoiled, processing the extra as fertilizer meant nothing went to waste. Osaka was a merchant city, so it was relatively easy for farmers in the region to coordinate with merchants to get these inex-pensive fish fertilizers shipped from elsewhere—at first, from local fish-ermen who travelled up to the coast near Edo to bring sardines back to the Kansai area, then from even farther away when the early modern trade network linked northern herring fisheries with the central mar-kets in Osaka.[16]

Such specialized fisheries developed for fish and whales in part because they were tied into a complex cash economy, where fisher-men could afford to focus on catching as much as possible of only one type of organism in order to make the money to buy everything else they might need to survive. Whaling required large investments in gear, but had the potential for even larger profits. As a commercial fishery, it had very little connection to prehistoric whaling practices, which is why I do not refer to this form of whaling as traditional whaling but instead as organized whaling. It was a new practice developed within and made possible by the particular setting of the Tokugawa merchant economy.

This chapter explores how early modern Japanese whaling was a commercial enterprise that also tied people more closely to dependence on and awareness of the marine environment. Whalers made use of as many different pieces of whales as they could to maximize profits. Whaling groups sold muscles and some sections of skin and blubber (particularly from the tail flukes) for consumption as whale meat. They boiled blubber down into oil, and sometimes also boiled the fat out of muscle and bone for the same purpose. Skin became leather, tendons and intestines became gut strings, bones became fertilizer and sometimes construction materials (see the beginning of chapter 5), and baleen was shaped into a wide array of products such as sword hilt wraps, folding headrests, clothing stiffeners, and springs. Furthermore, the body of even a single whale could be transformed into an incredible amount of each of these different products.

Whales also provided in one body an array of natural resources not found in any other species. Therefore, Japanese whalers produced and sold plenty of meat, but also sold many other whale parts. This is quite different from the way that commercial whaling developed in the West. For the offshore commercial whalers of Europe or America, meat was not a product after the medieval period.[17] American whalers, in fact, specifically preferred not to eat whale meat when any other options were available.[18] These pelagic whalers focused on the production of whale oil, used for lighting (candles and lamp oil, including for street lights and lighthouses) and for lubrication in such places as factory cotton spindles.[19] In Japan, whale oil was also used for lighting, although only in lamps. Just as whale oil lighting was replaced in Europe and America with gas lamps and kerosene, whale oil did not light Edo homes for the entire Tokugawa period. As Japanese farmers developed technologies for producing plant-based oils, the more foul-smelling whale oil fell out of favor with people who had the funds to purchase more pleasant options.[20] Whale oil lamps were also used extensively in mines, such as Besshi on Shikoku, until rapeseed oil replaced it as an inexpensive yet effective light source.[21] In contrast to Western whaling, other whale products and uses were far more influential in Japan than lamp oil.

People living away from the shore might not have much opportunity to see an entire whale in person, but they were quite likely to encounter some of the parts of whales that circulated far beyond coastal whaling villages, especially by way of the peddler women who carried products from fishing villages and houseboats up into the mountains and helped bring the marine environment inland.[22] Furthermore, people who had never been near a whale or whaling group still knew that someone could become fantastically rich from hunting and processing whales. This likely increased their fascination with the production of whatever whale parts they were buying, and led to some cases where it was useful to market a product as whale-based even when it was not. This chapter will consider these different aspects of the sale of whale products to show how the whaling groups discussed in the previous chapter fit into the broader Tokugawa economy.

WHO PROFITS FROM THE BUSINESS OF WHALING?

A great deal of money was tied up in whaling groups, and the general public assumed vast wealth was in the hands of the whaling group managers. One early social commentary by popular seventeenth-century author Ihara Saikaku, in a book of short stories about the rise of merchant wealth, includes a story focusing on a (fictional) former harpooner in Taiji who made his fortune extracting every possible product from whales, including processing the bones for extra oil he could sell.[23] Illustrated whaling scrolls also circulated for different groups, showing the process of breaking down an individual whale in great detail, possibly as a way of explaining to investors what they were buying into (figure 3.1). Images like these certainly helped promote the idea that whales could make someone rich, but the reality of whaling groups' economic influence is harder to determine.

The few remaining business records from individual whaling groups show the magnitude of the sums involved, even if overall economic impact of the groups as a whole cannot be directly calculated. Koga Yasushi's analysis of the Tsujikawa family's management on Iki Island (map 2) provides one of the most detailed looks at whaling group finances. This whaling group came under the broader management of the massive Masutomi group in the 1830s. The funding for whaling in

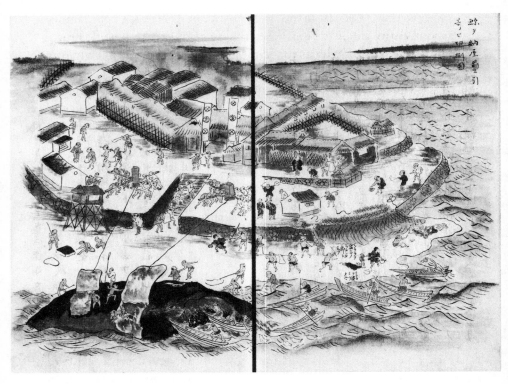

FIGURE 3.1. Processing a whale on shore. The workers are using large windlasses to pull the sheets of blubber off the whale, and carrying all the parts into the sheds in the background for further processing. Kizaki Morisue, "Shōni no rōgei ikken no maki," in *Hizen Karatsu hogei zusetsu*, 14, doi:10.11501/2537195. Courtesy of the National Diet Library of Japan.

this area was complex because of this split management. The Tsuji-kawa family were members of the *konaya* (managers of onshore whale processing), but they were also sake distillers and mid-size cargo shippers. The *ōnaya* (whaling group members) were the professional whalers, with part of the processing farmed out to the group of merchants in the *konaya* association who had the capital to buy shares of the whales caught by the *ōnaya*'s whalers. This divided management system arose because whaling required immense startup capital. Operating a whaling group could cost as much as five thousand gold ryō per season, including maintenance costs for the boats and nets every year.[24] For comparison, an average farmer's yield from one year's cash crop was approximately twelve ryō, and an average carpenter's yearly wage was approximately 26.5 ryō.[25] This high operating cost led to complex investment networks, and the potential for both large profits and large debts.

Over 142 years of operation, the Masutomi family paid 770,000 ryō in assorted taxes and fees to the domains in which they operated—the closest we have to a measurement of what kinds of profits they might have collected.[26] Furthermore, they donated 15,000 ryō outright and loaned 240,000 ryō to these domains in the same period.[27] Revenue streams in the Masutomi whaling group flowed between: the domain and the whaling group; the whaling group and wholesalers in Osaka, Shimonoseki, and elsewhere; the whaling group and the konaya merchant association; and between the merchants in the konaya. As with their merchant investors, the Masutomi family was diversified, with investments in tuna and other fisheries along with whaling. Some of their costs included taxes and fees that helped domains to gain a share of the profits: whalers had to pay a fee or tax to the domain in order to secure the fishing rights for their whaling areas, and also transport taxes on the products they sold.

In some cases, money could flow in the other direction: whaling groups could get a loan from their domain, if the management could not fund the group normally (in times of crisis, for example). Wholesalers would pay an advance to the whaling group based on whale products that might be acquired during the upcoming season. The konaya also bought shares in the parts of whales to be caught in the upcoming season. Sometimes, this meant providing up to half of the whaling group's operating funds. The flow of funds within the konaya was determined by how much each merchant had paid upfront: their shares, contributed in the beginning of the season, determined the proportions of profit and loss that they would bear at the end of the season. For the konaya, whaling was an investment opportunity rather than their main business.[28] Thus, whaling was embedded in the rest of the market economy and the finances of the domains that had whaling groups, an essential cog in a complex economic machine.

The records from the Hirado-based Ōsakaya group suggest the amounts that people below the rank of managers and investors might have earned. In 1857, this whaling group spent 30 percent of its operating budget on paying various laborers, and another 23 percent of the budget on daily rice rations given to each worker. The ones who benefitted most were the harpooners and boat crew, who had to be paid before the season started to convince them to join: while some boat crew were from the local area, many were hired in from other places and presumably could be hired by someone else instead if they got a better offer. In 1857, harpooners in the Ōsakaya group were paid 187 silver monme each, while the most that regular crew were paid was 116 monme. The crew of ten local chaser boats earned only thirty-nine monme apiece because they had obligations to their local government that they were repaying with service to the whaling group. In comparison, an average yearly cash income for an early nineteenth-century farmer, who also would not have food expenses, was 720 monme. Thus, none of these whalers were likely able to subsist on this work alone.[29] All of the pay for crew together took up 17 percent of the group's total operating budget. Another 9 percent was paid to the permanent workers in the processing sheds, such as the managers who coordinated the work, and only 1.6 percent of the total was divided among the one hundred to two hundred day laborers who did most of the processing. The manager of the group actually operated at a loss at this point, despite the large amounts of money flowing in and out of the group for supplies and sales of whale products.[30]

Account books for a Tsujikawa group's whaling season show that there was a one-sided payment made from the *konaya* to the whaling group that they never recovered. This payment was the cost of being able to buy into potential profits. But apart from this *fugin*, which at least in the 1855–56 season was about 20 percent of the total funds provided by the *konaya*, they paid for shares of a given total catch. If there was a lower total catch for that season, then the remainder of their prepayment was carried over into the next season. In the 1855–56 season, the Tsujikawa paid a total of 28,275 monme in four installments before the season started, based on an estimated catch of twenty right whales.[31] The number of whales actually caught was only fifteen. The calculations of shares of whale parts also included a weighting for different species, where right whales counted as one whale, but a less desirable humpback whale was counted as only 0.7 of a whale. Therefore, the 1855–56 season's catch was only 10.38 right whales' worth of catch. Since the whaling group had to carry over the rest of the prepayment for the 9.62 whales they failed to catch, they operated at a loss of 2,405 monme, despite the relatively good season of fifteen whales with sales totaling 41,439 monme. In the following season, after catching only six whales, they lost over 19,000 monme (after expenses much higher than the total sales of 16,048 monme). The profit that they finally brought in in 1857–58 of 10,347 monme off of a catch of nineteen whales and total sales of 44,631 monme was thus still not enough to make up for the previous years' losses.[32]

The Saikai area, with the densest concentration of whalers, may have been the place where the largest amount of capital was tied up in whaling efforts; however, similar problems with estimating yearly catches and thus earnings applied elsewhere as well. In the Kumano area (map 3), Kasahara Masao's calculation of Koza whalers' net profit took into account a category of "assorted expenses" and one for trade commissions. Average expenses and trade commissions both appear to have increased slightly in the middle of the nineteenth century, whereas the number of whales caught did not. To calculate net profit values, he subtracted both expenses and trade commissions from an income that must have included not just money from selling whale parts, but also loans or other sources of money for the whaling group. This is the only way to explain how there were significant incomes of 92,000 and 233,000 silver monme in 1865 and 1866, respectively, even though in both years no whales were caught. Therefore, the ability of any whaling group to remain profitable was not influenced solely by the number of whales caught, and the economic records of these whaling groups are not a source of direct information about catches, although fortunately the same groups' records often contain numbers of whales caught as part of their bookkeeping.[33]

The prices of different whale parts could also vary based on many different factors, including not only perceived quality of the products, but also seasonal variations.[34] With whale products provided to distant and local marketplaces, the price varied depending on what the merchants thought each market could bear, and how much of the product was available that season. For Masutomi whale oil shipped to markets outside of Kyushu, for example, prices were set based on a comparison to sardine oil or other competitors, based on how much oil could be provided for the market in what timing. But they also had to consider the competition, because if they set prices too much higher than other nearby whaling groups, no one would buy their oil.[35] As reliable supply diminished with declining catches in the mid-nineteenth century, prices rose. For example, the price for whale oil in the northern Kyushu domains of Higo and Chikuzen rose from around 100 monme per container before 1830 to 165 monme in 1843 after years of no or low catches. There were long deliberations between the Masutomi group and their sellers on whether they should set the price at 170 or 175 monme after this, so prices continued to rise later in the century.[36]

In the Masutomi system, *onaya* whalers needed the *konaya*'s funds to start the season and enable them to produce the oil that they sold. They acquired the financial support of these local merchants by promising them unwanted whale parts. In other areas, funding from partners outside of the whaling group often came from the domain rather than from local merchants' associations. Therefore, the sale of whale parts could be an important part of local merchant economies and investment opportunities, as well as providing products to distant markets in Shimonoseki and Osaka, or it could be an important part of domainal finances through taxes and repayment of loans from the whaling group.

The difficult balance between whaling group finances and their creditors' expectations of yearly income is clear in petitions between whaling villages and Kii domainal officials, especially during periods of whaling group crisis. These crises for Kumano and other whaling groups included not just poor catches, but also local crop failures and social unrest beginning in the 1780s. For example, one major complaint which appeared in an 1865 series of negotiations between Taiji whalers and higher authorities was that, due to the overall economic situation of the area, commodity prices were going up.[37] Even when whalers were not able to catch many whales, they still needed to buy new equipment to replace destroyed or worn out gear, and such maintenance was becoming more expensive along with everything else. Many whaling groups also relied on manpower from surrounding villages for processing their catch, which could become less available during times of unrest.

For some areas, the uncertainty of whaling income was simply an aspect of the business that had to be managed along with everything else. In good years, the profits of the Koza Whaling Office were sometimes a useful source of cash for paying assorted forms of taxes, as in

1805 when 1,642 monme of silver were borrowed from them to pay taxes the village owed to the government.[38] Unfortunately for the whaling group, it took an entire whaling season to regain this amount of money.[39] Later in the century, the Koza Whaling Office suffered from severe deficits, possibly because of the need to use their funds for taxes, as well as the increasing rarity of whales from which to profit. Because there was no other fishing to support the village in the winter, both the government and the villagers themselves made a serious effort to keep whaling operations going after bad years. For example, in 1823 the villagers and the domain together contrived to raise enough loans to revive whaling after the previous year's failed season.[40]

The economic difficulties of whaling groups came not just from an unpredictable catch of whales, but also from both predictable and unpredictable outlays to maintain the whaling group. Above and beyond daily rice rations for workers who had to be fed even when they weren't catching any whales, there was a strong welfare-style system set up to support those who had become too sick or old to work, or those who were family of dead whalers.[41] Therefore, it could be difficult for whaling groups to remain solvent. Large amounts of money may have been raised to support whaling in all the major whaling areas, which certainly was important for their local and sometimes more distant economies, but these large investments did not always provide a steady return. The visibly rich whalers like the Masutomi influenced a public perception of whaling as a lucrative industry, and someone seeing gross income from a whaling season without knowing how much of that money was already owed elsewhere might assume that whaling was an easy way to get rich. But the tribulations of failing or indebted whaling groups throughout the period show that, while a lot of money flowed through the whaling industry, it was not always easy to keep hold of any of it.

HOW TO EAT A WHALE:
THE CULTURAL ROLE OF WHALE MEAT

One might assume from prowhaling discussions today about the importance of whale meat in Japanese food culture that most of the profit for Tokugawa whaling groups would come from selling whale meat, but the specific roles that whale meat played in this period do not easily map onto the role of whale meat in modern Japan. Furthermore, the fact that the whalers themselves in the ōnaya in Kyushu reserved the rights for sales of oil and gave the meat to the local merchants' association to sell makes the importance of meat less clear. Were the investors given the best share of the whale, or was that reserved for those who did the hard work of hunting them? In reality, the division of products may not have reflected their importance so much as the practicality of their sales. The local investors may have been given the products that had to be sold near the processing sheds because of rapid spoilage, as an acknowledgement of the market connections they already had, for example, as sake brewers. In any case, whale meat did have a much greater presence in Tokugawa society than it does in modern Japan. But an investigation of the ideas about whale meat and how it should be consumed in the period also fails to support modern ideas that its role in food culture reflected a particular reverence for animal lives or a moral concern that might be part of restricting whaling's scope to a sustainable practice.

The most obvious lack of restrictions on whale meat consumption is the fact that whale meat (geiniku) was a rather broad term. It applied not just to the whale muscle that is equivalent to other meats (niku) like beef and pork, but also to blubber and skin attached to that muscle. "White meat" (shironiku) was actually fat, pure blubber with sometimes a thin strip of skin attached, so the type of food that could be seen as whale meat was highly variable. It was so variable, in fact, that it included "mountain whale" meat, which did not come from whales at all, but rather from wild boar. The application of the name "mountain whale" to other game meat shows that there was a cultural cachet to eating whale even when it wasn't actually whale. This may have reflected limits to the availability of true whale meat, or it may be an indication of a desire to eat whale beyond the capacity of whaling groups to provide the unspoiled product (at least to locations too many days' travel from the processing sheds).

It should not be surprising that whale meat had social importance as a desirable food item before the rise of whaling groups, when access to whales was limited to occasional and unpredictable strandings. There are some scattered references to whale as a delicacy eaten by members of the Kyoto court or high-ranking samurai before the Tokugawa period, generally in soup, which might have contained meat or some other part of the whale.[42] But what about after larger amounts of meat were made available by the new, organized whaling efforts of the Tokugawa period? The only real evidence we have for how people might have consumed whale from these whaling groups comes from cookbooks, particularly one called *Geiniku chōmihō* (Whale meat seasoning methods). This book was published in the nineteenth century as a supplement to the Masutomi group's *Isanatori ekotoba* (Illustrated whaling), a description of whaling techniques and processes, and was part of a genre of literature that was less about specific cooking instructions and more about public interest in the product. It therefore tells us more about the commercialization of food in general in the Tokugawa period than it does about specific habits in cooking and consuming whale meat, particularly in the context of the development of cookbooks as a genre over the course of the period.

The earliest known book to contain instructions about basic, daily cooking procedures was a work called *Ryōri monogatari* (Stories of cooking), which first appeared in 1643. By 1664 it had gone through multiple printings and two editions. Its original title may have been *Ryōri hiden shō* (Excerpts of secret transmissions on cooking), a title that better indicates how it was related to a number of similar works exposing trade secrets that began appearing within the burgeoning print culture of the period. While its anonymity makes it difficult to determine how widespread the readership of *Stories of cooking* was, the work does contain information about whale meat in the chapter entitled "The art of cooking and preservation."[43] There is also a recipe for whale soup, which made use of preserved whale meat.[44] Wherever this cookbook was originally written, it does not appear to be directed at people purchasing fresh whale meat. Most likely, it was part of the cooking tradition for members of the court in Kyoto, who expected feasts with unusual delicacies.

A new kind of cookbook appeared after about 1750 that was based not on the practical aspects of cooking, but on the famous places that different foods were associated with. These kinds of cookbooks capitalized on people's interest in travel and local specialties. Cookbooks devoted to only one type of food, like *Whale meat seasoning methods*, were an outgrowth of these tourist books rather than of practical cooking manuals. This whale meat cookbook was thus of interest because many of its whale meat dishes were unique, strange, or unknown to the book's audience.[45] As a supplement to the book *Illustrated whaling*, with its extensive description of one of the largest and most successful whaling businesses in the Edo period, *Whale meat seasoning methods* could even have been intended as an advertisement for the products of the whaling group. The book explains the different parts of the whale and the method or methods best used to cook them, but it does not contain very detailed descriptions of the actual process of cooking. For example, most entries are vague about not just the amounts of ingredients, but also the time taken to boil, fry, or otherwise prepare the food. If this whale cookbook was not really intended to be a practical guide to cooking whale, then it is not a very good guide to how people ate the whale meat that they bought, although its wide circulation does indicate how far an awareness (if not practice) of consuming whale meat might have spread.

One of the most surprising and popular ways that people ate whale seems, in fact, to have been by eating something that was *called* whale without it actually *being* whale. *Yamakujira* or "mountain whale" was the specialty of increasingly popular small restaurants in the nineteenth century.[46] The origins of this meat were not a secret, as one of Toboke's vignettes talking about the Shinagawa whale stranding shows: "Now, when it heard the whale had come to Shinagawa, a boar [came] from the mountains in the surrounding countryside, and other fish chastised that visiting boar: 'This is the ocean! Why is a beast living in the mountains coming here?' They rejected it. The boar was greatly angered, and putting out its arms with the sleeves rolled up [ready to fight], said, 'Hey! I'm not entirely a stranger! I am also a mountain whale.'"[47]

If people knew that mountain whales had nothing to do with actual whales, why did they refer to the meat of wild game such as boar, deer, or rabbit as if it were a terrestrial cousin of whale meat? We now categorize whales as mammals, and thus in the same category as the wild game species that might be called mountain whales in Tokugawa Japan. But at the time, whales were thought to be fish, in Japan and elsewhere.[48] So, the label *yamakujira* could have been meant to disguise the fact that people were eating meat instead of fish, by referencing the type of fish that it most closely resembled. A common explanation for meat taboos in Japan relies on religious proscriptions: either Buddhist moral objections to killing, or Shinto concerns with pollution related to contact with blood or death.[49] But while a religious explanation fits neatly with the modern idea of a small-scale, sustainable whaling tradition and also with demonstrating that tradition's importance in supporting unique characteristics of Japanese culture, it does not entirely explain why someone would disguise one meat under the name of another.

In fact, there is some evidence that Buddhist prohibitions against meat eating during the Tokugawa period were important not because they involved animal death, but rather because meat had aphrodisiac qualities that clergy should be avoiding. The arguments for Pure Land Buddhist clergy being allowed to eat meat focused not on any link to death, but rather on concerns about their also being allowed to marry. Since this was the most popular Buddhist sect in the period, their lack of strict prohibitions on meat eating would indicate that Buddhist moral concerns about killing were unlikely to have driven the practices of the majority of the populace.[50] And although one scholar of the history of food in Japan argues that the early Tokugawa period was when the restrictions against meat eating were strongest, this argument seems to rely more on the frequency of prohibition than on an analysis of whether the prohibitions were effective.[51] References to meat-eating in diaries cannot be found between 1688 and 1736, after which there are increasing numbers of such references, especially beginning around the 1830s when there are many references to meat-based shops, but this could be a trend in what people felt worth recording in diaries rather than proof of not eating meat.[52] Another scholar argues that the supposedly foundational seventh-century Buddhist proscriptions against eating meat in Japan were intended to be temporary ritual abstentions as part of efforts to ensure healthy crops. They were not based on ideals of compassion or other moral objections to meat-eating, nor were they permanent or year-round.[53] Additionally, if Buddhist morals—against killing or for some other reason—were behind the pretense of not eating wild game meats, there surely would be better options than disguising the meat as another form of meat, even if the supposed fish (whale) the meat came from was a lower animal in the Buddhist hierarchy of being.

Shinto theories of ritual pollution are likely to have had more of an influence on people's eating habits and on the use of euphemisms like *yamakujira.* Consciousness of spiritual pollution from contact with death or blood within a Shinto framework did have an influence on whether people could eat meat, but managing this pollution did not require total abstention. Instead, people who had eaten meat were considered ritually defiled for purposes of entering shrine grounds for specific periods of time. The amount of time that the pollution held generally varied based on the type of animal: the most polluting animals were large domestic animals with legs, particularly what we would call mammals. Birds—smaller and with fewer legs—were less polluting, and the legless fish were least polluting.[54] Although whales were definitely at the top of the size category, they were otherwise at the bottom of the pollution hierarchy with the other fish. Replacing a commonly eaten form of wild game like boar and venison, which tended to carry the longest pollution penalties, with the name of a fish would make sense if you wanted to eat game meat but were nominally concerned about the issue of ritual pollution and wanted to shorten its duration. Whale, rather than other forms of fish, may have been the chosen label because whale meat was most similar to wild game meat.[55] Of course, plausibility was not always necessary to rename meat as something else entirely: other labels for different presentations of meat included boar as tree peony (*botan*), cows as plums, horses as cherries, deer as maple leaves, rabbits as a feather, and so on.[56]

While religious proscriptions did exist, and in the case of ritual pollution could well have guided the logic behind replacing the name of one kind of animal with another before eating the meat, they should not be given too much weight in prohibiting meat entirely. Tokugawa-period commoners were unlikely to follow such prohibitions, which became more important the closer one was to the emperor. Until the Meiji reorganization of Shinto, village shrine grounds could be found right next to gravesites, so the concern about separation from contact with death was not particularly strong.[57] Similarly, the renaming of game meat into a kind of whale meat probably did show some concern about eating some animals, but it certainly did not stop people from eating their meat. Given how much more accessible to inland villages wild boar and deer were, this mountain whale might have been the most frequently eaten and widespread form of "whale" meat in the late Tokugawa period. Unless they lived within one of the whaling areas, it is likely that those who read specialty cookbooks about whale meat would have to slake their appetite for the meat by finding a local shop to sell them some mountain whale. But this euphemism does show the cultural and religious centrality of at least the idea of whale meat as food, lending some weight to the idea that it had a special role in Japanese food culture of the Tokugawa.

WHERE TO EAT A WHALE:
FROM PRODUCTION TO CONSUMPTION

If whale cookbooks were not really a practical manual for how to consume parts of whales, and many people were actually eating mountain whale rather than whale itself, what happened to the meat harvested from whales? Distance from the processing sheds where whales were dismembered into component parts was an important factor determining what kind of meat would be available to consumers. Fresh, untreated meat could not travel very far or very long before spoiling. Salted meat and the scraps of meat that were left after having the oil boiled out of them would be available to a wider geographic audience, including people as far from Kyushu whaling groups as residents of Kyoto and Osaka: although residents of these cities could acquire whale meat from the Kumano area or from Shikoku, records indicate that the Masutomi group did ship preserved whale meat at least as far as the Kansai area.[58]

Outside of cookbooks that may have been more entertaining than practical, only a few scattered references provide details about whale meat consumption in the Tokugawa period. One Kii domainal official traveling in the Kumano area in 1717 noted: "On the way [to Taiji] I saw a rustic old village wife carrying a bamboo winnowing basket with some small packets.[59] Inside all of these was whale meat. I asked her, and she said that the other day in Taiji village, they succeeded in catching two large whales."[60] However, this is all the information he gives about whale meat in his description of the village's whaling enterprise. Clearly, people who were local to whaling villages were able to get whale meat to eat, but this type of record does not show just how far it might have been distributed. He does not say where she was taking the meat, but whale meat was definitely sold in Kii's castle town of Wakayama, which is not far south of Osaka, so it is likely that whalers took advantage of the merchants in nearby Osaka as well (map 3).[61] Beyond references like this, the extensive business records of whale meat sales from the Masutomi whaling group in northern Kyushu are currently the best evidence for what could be done with large amounts of whale meat. Since it is clear that there was regular contact between the whalers in the Saikai area and other whaling areas, there should be some similarities in their production of whale meat and other parts. Although there were differences in the details of how the sales and distribution were organized, due to the differences in roles held by the local domains' governments, a closer look at Kyushu whalers' sale of whale meat is our best stand-in for the possibilities in Japan as a whole.

Whaling historian Koga Yasushi argues that oil production rather than the consumption of whale meat was the original motivation behind whaling in the Saikai area. This is supported by the fact that the custom of eating whale spread only after net whaling started to bring in larger numbers of whales to be disposed of. The focus of much of the scholarship on Saikai whaling has been on this lucrative oil trade and its marketing in Osaka. As Koga points out, however, this does not diminish the importance of the local whale meat trade. He focuses on the extensive business records from Iki Island, where the processing sheds belonged to the Masutomi whaling group, to build a picture of whale meat markets. The local market for whale meat was somewhat distinct from the whaling group's long-distance market for oil and other parts. The ōnaya whaling group management took approximately 60 percent of the whale, and gave the remaining portion to the konaya merchant investors. In the case of the Masutomi group, at least, the konaya was the division that produced and sold most of the whale meat, while the ōnaya focused on oil.[62]

Our best information about demand for fresh whale meat comes from the prevalence of theft as the whaling group processed whales on the beach. The konaya did offer immediate sales on the beach as the whale was taken apart. However, some Kyushu whaling scrolls hint at the local popularity of free whale meat rather than purchases from the konaya. In these crowded pictures of the final stages of a whale hunt, once the carcass has been winched ashore, there is often a small scene with an armed guard or two chasing off meat thieves (figure 3.2).[63] In at least some cases, locals felt they ought to be entitled to some of the meat, but the members of the whaling group would drive them off. One explanatory text for such scenes notes that "when the island's adults and children, carrying newly-sharpened knives, cut and stole meat [off the whale], this was called *kandara* and was a customary practice from long ago."[64] By customary practice, they likely meant the way that people had historically dealt with stranded whales, which would appear on the beach without human interference. The whaling groups in Kyushu paid taxes to their domains for the rights to go whaling in a specific area of water. Therefore, when local people who were not part of the whaling group happened to haul ashore a dead or dying whale, they were supposed to give it to the whaling group whose territory it was in. The custom of claiming meat from any whale that had appeared on the shore did not sit well with the whaling groups, who specifically went out to capture the whale and haul it up onto the beach, without the help of the locals who came in to take their "customary" share. Whaling groups also worried about workers inside the processing sheds stealing meat. The Masutomi group even employed a guard to patrol their sheds, checking that the paid day laborers were not taking any meat. In other groups such as the Tsuro group in Tosa, the whale parts apportioned to different members of the whaling group were determined by individual jobs (and presumably shared by the individual's whole family, some of whom likely helped process the whale), so that a form of institutionalized distribution of "free" shares of whale cut down on this concern.[65]

Salted whale meat was often marked down in the same category as raw meat in the Iki account books, so it is difficult to say how much of the meat bought from the *konaya* was preserved in salt first to keep it from spoiling. The vast majority of what they sold was meat in either of these two forms. They also boiled some of their share of the whale (presumably the lowest-quality pieces or those that were not immediately auctioned off) to extract oil, just as the whaling group management did. Once the oil extraction was finished, the boiled scraps were sold. The boiling was a form of preservation, and the scraps were shipped out to be sold in places as far as a week's sail away from Iki.[66]

The amount of the whale that was sold directly as either raw or salted meat versus the amount from which oil was extracted, leaving oil and scraps to be sold, varied over the course of a whaling season. The calculation of what to ship out was based on the local market value

FIGURE 3.2. A close-up showing *kandara* thieves being chased away from a whale being cut up on the beach. The whale is off to the left. Kizaki Morisue, "Shōni no rōgei ikken no maki," in *Hizen Karatsu hogei zusetsu*, 14, doi:10.11501/2537195. Courtesy of the National Diet Library of Japan.

compared to what the *konaya* could get if they sold it further away. Koga's analysis of the shipping records for the Tsujikawa *konaya* on Iki Island in the 1850s shows that red meat's value in particular declined over the course of the whaling season, as the whales thinned and thus had less fatty meat. As its value went down, the meat was more likely to be shipped out to be sold rather than sold locally. The market for whale meat also varied by year. A total of twenty-two tons of whale meat was sold on the beach in the 1857–58 season, but a year earlier, over 70 percent of the whale products sold by the same group were shipped out as oil and preserved meat. The decision of where and how to sell the whale meat also seems to have been influenced by the species and numbers of whales caught in a season, and from which whaling grounds they were taken.[67] This was a much more complex calculation than the one performed by Western whalers, who did grade the quality of their oil based on species, but only had one main product to worry about selling at the end of the voyage.

CONSUMING WHALES INDIRECTLY:
WHALE PARTS IN AGRICULTURE

In the Tokugawa economy, before the invention of synthetic fertilizers and pesticides, whales were a natural resource capable of supplying food twice over: directly, as meat, but also indirectly, by promoting successful crop production. The same dual purpose could also be found in the case of fish such as herring, which could be eaten or used as fertilizer, but whales are a special case. For one thing, because of their sheer size, meat and other agriculturally relevant products like oil and bonemeal could all be produced from a single whale in large quantities. Fish considered effective as a fertilizer were often ones that were poorer quality food and were thus inexpensive because of a lack of other demand.

An 1840 agricultural treatise by Satō Nobuhiro, *Baiyō hiroku* (Secret notes on cultivation), demonstrates the wide variety and importance of fertilizers, not just to prevent crop failure and famine in marginal areas, but also for the economy. Nobuhiro was a mid-nineteenth century nationalist writer who promoted economic growth and military power to defend against the increasing pressure from Western ships trying to open trade with Japan. Part of his program for strengthening Japan was "the development of natural resources, which formed the basis of his economic rehabilitation program," based on family expertise in agriculture, horticulture, forestry, and mining.[68] The fertilizers discussed in *Secret notes on cultivation* include the waste of humans and domestic animals, as well as terrestrial and marine animal products. He recommended dried sardines and sardine oil as the best marine fertilizer for rice, followed by whale oil, then other dried fish and oils.[69] Whale bones, because of their oiliness, were also a necessary additive to promote bountiful cash crops such as sugarcane, indigo, tobacco, hemp, and ramie.[70] Thus, having whales and other marine species available in the environment of early modern Japan was necessary for the successful production of the staple crop of rice, and also in the diversification of agriculture into cash crops. These agricultural developments would not have been possible if the boundaries of Japan during this period stopped at the shoreline. Marine products like whale-based fertilizers were not used just within the coastal whaling areas, but also in distant domains without whaling groups of their own, including ones that likely bought it from markets in Osaka or Edo rather than dealing directly with whaling group merchants.[71]

Fertilizer was only the beginning for whale-based agricultural products, as whale parts were also instrumental in the production of Japanese cotton. Something referred to as whale tendons or sinew (*suji*) could be boiled, softening them back up for eating in soup, but they were more likely to be turned into bowstrings. Such strings were essential for the cotton-beating bow, an instrument used in the processing of cotton. This tool was developed for use in Japan at the end of the eighteenth century in Nagasaki, based on Chinese models. Instead of the more common cow-gut strings used in China, these bows used whale-gut strings. The term used for the animal part that could be turned into any kind of string—for shamisen, bows, or even in the more modern era in tennis racket strings—is most commonly "gut" in English. But this product did not always come from a whale's gut or digestive organs. The term used for this part in Japanese is *suji*, which can refer to tendon, sinew, or muscle, but this is also not the best description of the anatomical source. This type of gut or *suji* came most commonly from processing thin strips of skin or intestines, and possibly also tendons, soaked in water and scraped clean before hanging them to dry.[72]

While cotton grew best in Kyushu, the materials for the bows used to process the crop were available from whaling groups outside this area. However, Kyushu cotton growers felt the whale tendon or gut processed outside of Kyushu was of lower quality. According to Okumiya Nizaemon's 1809 comparison of gut from Tosa and Kyushu, the lesser quality of the Tosa gut came from the fact that Tosa workers were less careful about preservation, taking the strips out of warm water and putting them directly into the sun, instead of putting them in the shade for half a day first as they did in Kyushu.[73] Perhaps the better quality of whale gut produced in Kyushu was related to high demand for quality products necessary in processing the cotton grown extensively there. But it is also possible that better processing of whale gut came from Kyushu farmers' close contact with information about Chinese methods of string production through their foreign trade ports like Hirado, Nagasaki, and Hakata. In this case, the overlap between cash crop development and high numbers of whaling groups in the same area may have facilitated the success of cotton as a cash crop in Kyushu. While farmers could grow cotton without whale products, their reliance on whale-gut strings to process their crop meant that the overall success of this crop depended on access to whale parts.

Both the example of fertilizers and that of the cotton-beating bow show roles of whale products in agriculture that could also be filled from other sources. There were plenty of other fertilizers used in Japan, and whale-based fertilizers are thus just one example of new marine sources of nutrients. There also were at least potential alternate sources of gut strings for cotton processing, since in China these implements were based on cow parts (although cows were more common in China than in Tokugawa Japan). However, there was one whale product that truly was the most effective option in its particular agricultural role: whale oil insecticide.

PREVENTING NONHUMAN CONSUMPTION OF CROPS: WHALE OIL INSECTICIDE

Since humans began cultivating particular plants for their own use, they have had to fight off other organisms also trying to consume them. Insect pests have long been one of the most prominent agricultural enemies, and insecticidal substances were developed before the advent of modern chemical pesticides. For example, American farmers began using pyrethrum (derived from chrysanthemum flowers) as an insect repellant in the late eighteenth century.[74] In Japan, one of the first recorded insecticidal treatments developed for agriculture was whale oil.[75] This treatment involved scattering oil over the surface of the rice paddies and knocking insects off rice stalks into the oily water to suffocate and drown. While any oil could potentially coat the carapace of insects and block their ability to breathe, whale oil seems to have been more effective and faster-acting than plant-based oils that were developed later. Modern scientists studying the spread of polychlorinated biphenyls (PCBs, a category of manmade halogenated compounds) and their decomposition products tested the chemical composition of early twentieth-century whale oil. They looked at a sample of whale oil held in the New Bedford Whaling Museum that had been processed before the manufacture of PCBs, and found in it complex halogenated compounds that bore a close resemblance to the artificially made pesticide DDT.[76] While the study did not then test this chemical's effectiveness as an insecticide, it does show that reports from early modern Japanese farmers that whale oil worked faster and more effectively than rapeseed oil could have some basis in the chemical composition of the oil.

Whale oil was particularly effective in killing *unka* (ricehoppers or planthoppers), which destroyed 90 percent of the rice crop in central and western Japan in 1732, triggering the disastrous Kyōhō famine. Some agricultural improvements of the period harkened back to Chinese sources, and oil extracted by boiling from either whales or seals appears to have been used as lamp oil in China as far back as over two thousand years ago. However, there are very few references to pesticides developed from oil in Chinese agriculture.[77] Whale oil was therefore most likely developed as a pesticide independently in Japan and more than once, with unrelated instances recorded in the seventeenth and eighteenth century in various counties in at least two domains in northern Kyushu.[78]

Whether or not it was the first or most important discovery of the insecticidal properties of whale oil, the most well-known origin story is the one provided by Ōkura Nagatsune, one of the most famous and prolific agricultural authors of the Tokugawa period. He published this description in a treatise entitled *Jokōroku* (Record of eliminating locusts) in 1826. He credits a Mr. Yahiro in Mikasa County, Chikuzen, for discovering whale oil's effect on planthoppers, when he was filling shrine lamps to pray for protection from insects during the massive infestation of 1732. Given the widespread use of whale oil in lamps, others had probably also observed its ability to kill insects which fell into the lamp's reservoir. However, Yahiro gets credit because he then experimented with whale oil sprinkled on the water on one of his fields, and recorded his results for Nagatsune to read a century later.[79]

No matter who started using it first, whale oil insecticide does seem to have originally appeared in Kyushu, which makes sense as this was the area with the most concentrated whaling effort by the middle of the Tokugawa period. Nagatsune's publication was probably the most widely read description of the effectiveness of whale oil, but other authors (usually ones focused on whaling rather than on agriculture) did mention it, and thus it gradually became more well known.[80] In particular, the promotion of whale oil stores for emergency insect damage prevention spread from Kyushu domains to other areas of the country after the Tokugawa shogunate became aware of local practices and ordered its use to combat insects in 1787 and again in 1796.[81] It is probably not a coincidence that the height of success for the Masutomi whaling group (one of the largest operations in Japan) came during the same period that the knowledge of whale oil's effectiveness as a pesticide propagated throughout Japan in the early nineteenth century, particularly because they had a monopoly on providing oil to at least three domains as an antifamine measure.[82]

The remarkable effectiveness of whale oil insecticide created an extensive market for oil throughout the agricultural areas of Japan. Rice production was fundamental to Japanese society in the Tokugawa period not just as a staple food, but also as the basis of the financial system, with land taxes calculated and paid in rice. Therefore, pest control in rice fields was a prime concern for farmers trying to maximize their harvest. Other insect control options like rapeseed oil did exist, but were less effective than equal amounts of whale oil. As whale oil became rarer with declining catches and thus more expensive, farmers did turn to cheaper plant-based oils, but they had to apply more of these oils to effectively ward off insects. Whale oil, good for at least a year before it started souring, was able to travel throughout the country in support of this essential aspect of life in Japan, even though entire whales would never make it that far.

CONCLUSION: WHALES AS MULTIVALENT RESOURCES

The various products derived from whales influenced different levels of society. Some of the many possible interconnections between the marine environment and people in different areas of early modern Japan are reflected in the local, regional, and interregional trade in whale parts. The movement of whaling groups embedded in a coastal and regional network that followed migratory whales was echoed by an equally lively movement of whale parts through the hands of merchants to consumers all over Japan. Focusing on a particular part of the marine environment and how some of its pieces moved through the terrestrial spaces of Tokugawa Japan makes the movement and interconnectedness of the economy more apparent. This is not to say that marine resources moved more freely than everything else, but rather that they were embedded in a highly urbanized economy where all products were forced to circulate as freely as marine products, since at some point in the transport chain everything moved by water.[83] The fluidity of movement is more obvious in the intersection with the ocean, which then reminds us that the natural resources ecosystem of the period extended from the deep mountains down to the cities on the plains, but also between coastally linked cities. In a parallel of (rather than a contrast to) the movement from mountains to plains, Tokugawa society relied on resources coming from deeper ocean waters inshore and inland, building up a reliance on outside natural resources that eventually drove the modern Japanese empire into colonial possessions to supply the needs of an even larger population.[84]

Interestingly, the agricultural role of whale oil has not been emphasized in Japanese whaling histories. Perhaps this is because it invites too close a comparison between Japanese whaling and the industrial whaling of countries such as the United States and Great Britain. Americans and Europeans did not generally go whaling to acquire meat, but instead focused on the production of oil and whalebone (baleen).[85] But as its use as an insecticide shows, whale oil was an important product for the Japanese as well, especially after the early 1730s, when it became integral to the success of rice crops in Kyushu and western Honshu. There is a widespread assumption that early modern Japan farming essentially had no farm animals, and thus the role of animals in Japanese farming is often overlooked. However, domestic farm animals were not useful merely as draft animals or as food sources. In early modern Japan, horses and oxen were most useful as producers of fertilizing manure.[86] Whales are only one of many examples that also help to counter the assumption of animal-free farming, by showing the ways that agriculture was dependent on animal inputs through the use of fish and whale parts. A view of early modern Japanese agriculture focused only on terrestrial resources is just as incomplete and misleading as the assumption that domestic animals were unimportant.

One reason for the oversight about agricultural roles of whales is that, in the contemporary debates about Japanese whaling, whale meat is usually presented as the essential product, because eating whales rather than making money off of them is a practice characteristic of subsistence whaling cultures. Groups for whom whaling is a necessary subsistence activity can legally pursue small-scale whaling practices today, even under the commercial moratorium imposed by the International Whaling Commission in 1986. In an effort to make Japanese whaling seem more like subsistence whaling, and less like a modern commercial industry, supporters try to show consumption of whale meat to be a longstanding and culturally important part of Japanese food customs. The problem with this argument is that the earlier period of Japanese whaling was not a purely subsistence activity either. The monetary importance of all whale parts, and the ways that some whale parts further promoted the production of other cash crops, negates this argument about subsistence for Tokugawa Japan's organized whaling groups.

Domainal lords as well as merchants benefitted from the sale of natural products and the monetization of crops in the Tokugawa period. Many lords recognized they would have to make the most of any resources to which they had access in order to do well, and this included not just increased agricultural production but also support of the discovery of new uses for all aspects of the natural world, including the marine environment nearest each domain with a coastline. Surveys commanded by the shogun Tokugawa Yoshimune tried to collect enough information on each domain's agricultural productivity and exploitable natural resources to enact agricultural reforms beginning in 1735, in response to the devastating Kyōhō famine of 1732.[87] Marine resources were part of these surveys, with some domains reporting the fish (and whales) available and others also including the methods through which they were caught.[88] Japanese people's relationship with both the terrestrial and marine environments during the early modern period thus was an extractive one. It was also a relationship whose monetization and market orientation by the nineteenth century was explicitly parallel to the transformation of European society into the modern era under the ideal of rational domination of nature.[89]

Whales in particular provide one of the best lenses on the roles and circulation of marine products in Tokugawa Japan because they highlight so many of the different impacts of individual products, and because they were known to be a way for individual whaling group leaders to make a fortune, highlighting the interconnectedness of the economy and natural resources. One single whale is so large that it almost has to be broken down into many different possible products, and the process of doing that tied up a large amount of capital in each group. Because of the variety of whale products, it is difficult to say which was most important to Tokugawa society, or whether any were the most important marine product in the period. Agriculture relied more heavily on other species of fish like herring for fertilizer, for example, although whale bones were also used in this role. And about half the herring catch was actually eaten directly, so the fact that whales also provided meat is not unique. However, herring were not also turned into an insecticide, or a source of light. It is possible that further research into marine products would provide other examples of resources necessary to early modern Japanese society that have not yet made it into our histories of the period, but it is unlikely that any one of them would provide so many different products from one species (never mind one individual organism). In that way, whales are a uniquely useful lens on early modern Japan's extensive reliance on the marine environment to support their economy and society.

Following whale products into the Japanese landscape shows the innovative ways that people in the early modern period were able to adapt available resources to their needs, including their need for money in a growing urban society. The circulation of whale products reflects the transfer of nutrients gathered across the Pacific Basin within the bodies of whales caught near the shore and processed into parts sold throughout the terrestrial portion of the archipelago. Even when people were not consuming whales directly as food, other whale parts added to the food production of the archipelago and helped early modern Japan to push their ecological limits. The secular, cash-focused society of the period reinterpreted older ways of interacting with the fruits of the natural world, as reflected in their lip service to spiritual traditions about different food taboos. Whale meat consumption and the popularity of mountain whale show that the religious strictures meant for priests or high-ranking court officials did not have much influence over the diets of the rest of the people of Tokugawa Japan. So if we are to acknowledge that whale meat did seem to have some importance in the food culture of the period, at least enough that substitutes were also developed, we also should acknowledge that this food culture was distinct from any traditional spiritual perspectives on the natural world.

Expansion of the resource base into nearshore waters through specialized fisheries like whaling of course supplied basic subsistence needs by supplementing food production, but it also promoted the development of complex markets. Through cash crop improvement, with new fertilizers and technologies like the cotton-beating bow, and through the systems set up to fund whaling groups and divide up shares of profit, whaling groups were a commercial enterprise heavily reliant upon and integrated with the protoindustrial economy of Tokugawa Japan. While scholars should be cautious about the teleological implications of the term, the basic idea encapsulated in protoindustrialization, that of increased rural industry tied into regional markets, aptly describes the economy of the Tokugawa period, particularly the latter half.[90] As a conceptual framework, it helps illuminate one reason why the interconnections of whaling groups and their wide distribution of various whale products are worth investigating in some detail.

Thinking of Tokugawa whaling as protoindustrial also helps to emphasize the fact that the aspects of organized coastal whaling that were most similar to modern Japanese factory-ship whaling are not necessarily any kind of longstanding attitudes toward whales or a special place for their products in Japanese culture—rather, both forms of whaling were economically driven and inseparable from the goals of profiting off animals as natural resources. The products sold by whaling groups did shape some aspects of Japanese culture, feeding not just bodies but also minds. Unlike the economic foundation of whaling, many of these aspects were specific to the culture of Tokugawa Japan rather than continuing through to the modern era. The next two chapters will elaborate on the ways that the link facilitated by whales between ocean and land could be more metaphysical than directly material.

FOUR

SEEDING STORIES

Whales as Cultural and Scholarly Inspiration

TWO MEN, NORO GENJŌ AND NATSUI MATSUGEN, WERE ORDERED BY
the government of Kii domain to visit Taiji village in 1721 (map 3). The
record of their visit shows how information moved inland from whaling
areas in a complex network of personal connections, and how people
used whales to think about the natural world more generally in new
ways. These two emissaries acquired a picture of a whale or of a hunt
drawn by whaling leader Kan'emon, which was then annotated by a
natural history scholar, Niwa Shōhaku, and passed along to the shogunal government.[1] The information spread from whalers to these traveling officials and scholars followed an important vector for ideas of
whales entering Japanese society. All of the information about whales
in this period began with someone's personal interaction with a whale:
whalers, people visiting a stranded whale, or people seeing parts of a
whale all had direct knowledge of whales. But more importantly, these
people then would reinterpret that experience for others, as Kan'emon
did for the two scholars. From initial contact with whales, information
spread outward, in second-, third-, and fourth-hand interpretations and
reinterpretations in different media, bringing whales ashore figuratively
rather than literally.

In this process of satisfying curiosity about a particular sort of
marine creature, people—whether scholars of natural history or of
medicine, or people with less academic interests—wrestled with their
understanding of the whole natural world (including the marine

environment) and the place of humans and other animals within it. Explaining these massive creatures was not a task reserved for one particular sort of person, as curiosity about them was widespread, particularly because of the association of whaling with large amounts of money. Whales, and the varied understandings of them expressed in different types of illustrations and texts, represent how Tokugawa-period people interacted with the new marine life specialized fisheries were bringing to their attention. But they also show how these people connected with and conceptualized the other living things in their environment, in both scholarly and commonsense ways that were particular to this historical era—an era of abundant whales, much larger numbers of people directly involved in whaling, and of far less specialized scholarship than today. The numbers of people who had direct contact with whales decreased with the nineteenth-century loss of large numbers of Pacific whales, and with the rapid modernization push in the Meiji era, particularly after 1880, which included a shift in whaling technologies. Therefore, the ways that information spread from that personal contact also changed, reshaping the role of whales in society and perhaps also the perception and role of the marine environment as a whole. To counter the impression of continuity of whaling leading to an easy continuity of culture related to whales, we need to start with a detailed view of the complex cultural networks of ideas about whales in Tokugawa Japan.

According to one observer at the time, the 1798 stranding of a whale in the Shinagawa River "was an unprecedented seed for stories."[2] Unusual events like this stranding of course drew attention, but people in Tokugawa Japan also talked about and drew whales without this kind of exceptional event to prompt their interest. As strange and unusual creatures, whales have captured the imagination for centuries. But some aspects of Japanese illustrations of whales show how these animals, more than other marine creatures, became particularly fascinating in early modern Japan. The stories and illustrations discussed in this chapter demonstrate the impact of public exposure to the new maritime resource base that helped to support a larger human population under the Tokugawa peace. Contemporary descriptions of whaling practices arose not just from interest in how much money whaling groups could make, but also from simple curiosity about whales as fascinatingly strange creatures. This curiosity was expressed in many scrolls and manuscripts produced between the start of organized whaling and the end of the nineteenth century. Such texts described and illustrated not only the process of whaling, but also different aspects of the whales themselves. There was (and still is) something about the idea of whales that fascinated people and made them receptive to stories, songs, and pictures about them and about the whalers who caught them, even when they could not interact with whales or their parts physically. Through these imagined whales, the broader populace lived with aspects of the marine environment even if they never went near the ocean.

In particular, whales were caught up in a major shift in views of the natural world during this period.[3] Of course, curiosity about the natural world did not suddenly appear at this point. Various aspects of nature had long been an important subject of illustration in Japan, for example in the Chinese-inspired tradition of bird-and-flower paintings, but such illustrations were often more symbolic than they were faithful depictions of the natural world.[4] As the Tokugawa peace allowed for a great flourishing in many leisure arts, new ideas about images and representation reshaped traditional illustration, prompted by contact with two new influences: Europeans and the marine organisms harvested by new specialized fisheries. Novel concepts in books and art that came from Europe through limited but influential trade, first with the Portuguese and then the Dutch, inspired new subject matters and also new ways of creating images and representing subjects.[5] Science, particularly medicine, was an integral part of this change in how the Japanese visualized the world, with whales at the center of new understandings of both natural history and medicine. Importation of Dutch medical texts helped shift the ways that Japanese understood internal medicine and the body, and new human and whale anatomical diagrams were the tools scholars used to make that transition.

What is fascinating about anatomical diagrams of whales is that other nonhuman, nonwhale anatomical illustrations did not seem to be produced in early modern Japan, in contrast to the large numbers of animal species whose dissection and vivisection were illustrated in Europe and America. Because the development of medicine in early modern Europe relied both on human cadaver dissection and on animal vivisection, scholars produced a wide assortment of illustrations of the internal anatomy of humans and other animals. While not all anatomy texts illustrated multiple species, anatomist Samuel Collins, to give just one example, published a treatise in 1685 containing illustrations of the internal anatomy of humans, cats, birds, fish, and insects.[6] However, whales were not one of the animals studied by Western anatomists, and in Japan, whale anatomical drawings do not appear in anatomy texts, but rather in scrolls about whale species. This makes the special case of anatomical whales even more puzzling. Why choose whales to focus on, and not one of the many other animals dissected in Europe and America?

The answer to this question resides in changes in natural history practices, medical knowledge, and the philosophy of relations between humans and nature in Edo Japan. Questions about the natural world, natural resources, or animals were not limited to scholars or philosophers, as the lively print culture of the period promoted breadth rather than specialization of interest. Thus, a text or image or display meant for one type of scholar could also be of interest to someone who did not identify as a scholar at all—a merchant or townsman or samurai retainer looking for entertainment could also find these sources fascinating. Widespread circulation of information about whales only took off after the development of organized whaling and the concomitant arrival of whale products in the lives of people outside of high-ranking members of the court (who had occasionally consumed meat from stranded whales as a delicacy before the Tokugawa period). As more and more people struggled to fit these peculiar, air-breathing, and milk-producing fish into their understanding of the world, in a process similar to the development of European natural history upon encountering the baffling creatures of the New World, scholars moved away from a kind of natural philosophy heavily influenced by Chinese medicine to a new form of natural history.[7] While whales, with their incomparable size, stood out as something special, a discussion of their peculiarities and the ways they were interpreted by scholars also indicates a general level of interaction with the marine environment in Tokugawa Japan, counteracting the notion of an inward-looking, isolated culture at least as far as the boundaries of the natural world were concerned.

This chapter focuses on the many interpretations of whales circulating in Tokugawa Japan to show how whales fit into people's understanding of the archipelago's ecosystem as something which held natural resources both on land and in the sea. The new forms of scholarship that developed based on study of whales in medicine, natural history, and popular storytelling were part of a flourishing Tokugawa culture that deserves interest in its own right. Culturally, the everyday lives and concerns of the modern era bear the indelible marks of modernization and industrialization, not to mention World War II and the foreign occupation that followed, all of which have transformed Japanese society and culture away from what they were during the era of shogunal rule. But because whales were hunted both in the early modern era and in the modern, a close look at earlier interpretations of their place in the world also shows how their significance for early modern Japanese people was different from the understanding of whales today.

ENVISIONING THE ANATOMICAL WHALE

One unique presentation of knowledge about whales that indicates some of the major shifts in the understanding of the natural world in this period is in the form of anatomical drawings. The 1847 scroll "Rokugei no zu" (Diagram of six whales) contains one of the best examples of a detailed cutaway view of a right whale, showing the disposition of its internal organs (figure 4.1). This image, the one anatomical diagram on a scroll illustrating the various species of whales found in Japan, is the clearest but not the only instance of this type of illustration for whales.[8] They are puzzling images because no one, not even those cutting up a whale on the beach, would have seen whales in quite this way: the processing of a whale was less a careful dissection and more a rapid dismantling of the carcass before it could begin to rot. As the only nonhuman anatomical diagrams in the period, these diagrams of whales speak to the state of knowledge both of anatomy in general and of whales in particular in early modern Japan. They are startlingly congruent with modern understandings of anatomy, but that similarity is not their most essential feature. What is more interesting is the way in which these diagrams were developed within a society with very different forms of scholarship than what underlies anatomical diagrams today, and what that can tell us about the ways that increased contact with whales forced earlier scholars to develop new frameworks to understand the natural world.

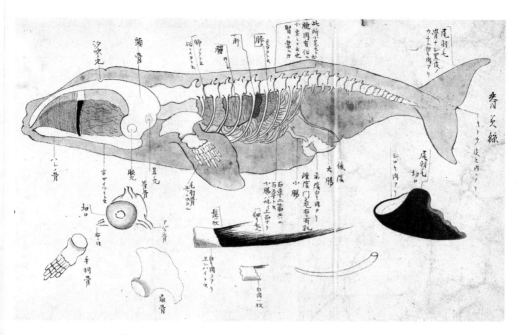

FIGURE 4.1. The internal anatomy and parts of a North Pacific right whale. Beiga, *Rokugei no zu* (1847), doi:10.11501/2543153. Courtesy of the National Diet Library of Japan.

Unfortunately, while there are multiple copies of scrolls with whale anatomy diagrams still extant, none appear to indicate the original source of the anatomy image(s). The only indicator of authorship on "Diagram of six whales" is the name Beiga, who is noted as the 1847 copyist of an earlier version, with no further information about his original source. However, the final text also references southern Kii domain. While no copy of the picture Genjō and Matsugen brought back remains, "Diagram of six whales" implies that trips to the villages in the Kumano area like theirs were how the artist was able to draw the anatomical view of a whale.[9] It is thus apparent that at least some of the anatomical information about whales came from the whalers along the Kumano coast in what is now Wakayama Prefecture. Four other scrolls depicting a right whale's anatomical image similar to the one in "Diagram of six whales" have less detailed labels and are of even more uncertain authorship and either of unknown time period or from a later date.

Their similarity in style makes it reasonable to assume they are part of a set of copies of an image that is now lost. The "Kozaura hogei emaki" (Illustrated scroll of Koza Village whaling) includes a simpler but clearly analogous image to the one in "Diagram of six whales," showing that there likely was a chain of copies being made of this striking anatomical drawing.[10] Thus, the scrolls showing anatomical whales generally seem to be related to the Kumano area, but with what little evidence remains today, it is unclear whether there was only one original drawing made in Koza, or whether this kind of image was created multiple times in the three major villages of Koza, Taiji, and Miwasaki (map 3).

One might guess that the original artist had some medical training or interests, since premodern anatomical knowledge generally arose with the development of medical knowledge. But in Japanese medicine and the traditional Chinese medicine on which it is based, the details of anatomy do not receive the same focus that they do in Western medicine. East Asian medicine did not place a heavy emphasis on being able to view and directly interact with the inside of the body, instead using a schematic or metaphorical understanding of internal organs, so medical texts were far less likely to contain illustrations looking anything like a Western anatomical diagram.[11] It is therefore reasonable to assume that the greatest influence on the production of this diagram comes from Western medicine, imported by the Dutch in the form of anatomical textbooks. However, if this anatomy was produced solely on the basis of Western medical knowledge, it should show the whale's heart and stomach and likely not show the spleen, which was much more important in Chinese traditional medicine than in Western medicine at the time. It is possible that the missing organs are hidden behind the pectoral fin or the lungs. However, the area in front of the lungs which could be either stomach or heart is not labeled as anything, so the choices of organs to label are not entirely explained by assuming a problem with the perspective. While more likely to be influenced by Western anatomical traditions, the image reflects an only partial understanding of them, or at least an adaptation of those traditions to the Japanese context.

Whoever drew the first anatomical whale, this drawing likely did not exist when Genjō and Matsugen arrived in Taiji in 1721. The field of scholarship dedicated to understanding the contents of European texts was known in Japan as "Dutch studies" because all such texts were filtered through trade with the Dutch in Nagasaki. The shogunate's close control over foreign trade makes it possible to determine when specific European ideas arrived in Japan as books. Human anatomical drawings based on European medical dissections arrived in Japan in the 1734 Dutch edition of Kulmus's anatomy textbook, *Ontleedkundige Tafelen*.[12] After physician and Dutch studies scholar Sugita Genpaku witnessed the dissection of a criminal in 1771, and compared what he saw to the images in Kulmus's text, he was inspired to produce a collaborative translation, *Kaitai shinsho*, published in 1774.[13] This was a landmark publication because the appearance of these anatomical images heralded a new way of seeing and thinking about the body and about medicine in Japan.[14]

One might assume that the increased interest in European anatomical medicine would result in the same kinds of illustrations of human and animal internal anatomy produced in Europe, but whales were never a common subject for scholarly dissection, and certainly not for the vivisection on which many of the early modern European advances were made. There is some indication that Japanese anatomists were interested in dissecting other animals. Yamawaki Tōyō was the author of *Zōshi*, the earliest Japanese text dealing with human internal anatomy from the perspective of dissection. His teacher, Gotō Konzan, suggested that he should dissect otters in order to understand human internal organs. Tōyō apparently followed Konzan's advice, but any illustrations he may have made do not survive.[15] Thus, even though some scholars in Japan did consider it worthwhile to investigate animal anatomy to understand human anatomy, there are no other illustrations of animal anatomy remaining from Japan during this period. While the introduction of Dutch medical texts was an important factor in the production of this diagram, they were therefore not the sole inspiration.

In fact, the uniqueness of these whale anatomy diagrams arises from the multiple inspirations for their production. The information derived from conversations with whalers would depend on the identity of the other person conversing with them: when scholars with an interest in natural history or traditional Chinese medicine spoke to whalers, the conversation would have focused on species characteristics and trying to classify whales within the natural order (in the case of medicine, so that they could figure out what medicinal properties whales should have). If scholars with an interest in Dutch studies and in Western medicine spoke to whalers, they might have been more inclined to ask about internal organs, which whalers understood not through dissection but through dismantling of whales. If scholars more concerned with good governance spoke to whalers, they would collect information about the contributions that whaling groups could make to domainal finances or to the security of the domain. Because scholars in this period were often interested in many different topics and types of learning, any or all of these perspectives might inform a single person's curiosity about whales. No other subject seems to have drawn quite so many different perspectives together as whales, but what looks like the unusually interdisciplinary nature of scholarly investigations is also the result of a lack of defined scholarly disciplines in this period (in Japan and elsewhere).

The fact that whales were a marine species was essential for the focus of anatomical knowledge to fall on them and not on terrestrial animals, in part because of the status of whalers who hunted them. The people who butchered land animals were *eta* or *kawata*, hereditary pariahs or outcastes considered unclean for their work with death and blood.[16] While medical or Dutch studies scholars could hire someone to dissect a corpse (human or animal) and keep themselves spiritually clean, this clearly did not happen frequently enough to produce other studies of animal anatomy. Although no sources specify why unclean or outcaste status did not fall on any of the people who worked with the massive amounts of blood and gore involved in rendering down a whale, it may have something to do with the fact that whales were considered fish, and/or that maritime spaces or the newness of the profession lent a different interpretation to these taboos. Fishing, too, was not an unclean occupation in the way that butchering was, even though fishermen killed the fish they caught.[17] Some of whalers' avoidance of discrimination also may have come from the fact that the managers of the groups had high social connections when whaling groups were first founded, long after other categories of taboo occupation had solidified into outcaste groups.

Wherever the anatomical diagrams came from, they are not purely medical and therefore could not have appeared without a more general curiosity about whales as resources produced by whaling groups. Scrolls that include anatomical diagrams of right whales, like "Diagram of six whales," also show plainer views of other species of whales. The information provided for these other whales is limited to externally visible features, and sometimes indications of the size and weight of average whales of that type. Such images are more tied to the study of traditional Chinese medicine and natural philosophy than they are to Western anatomical medicine. Their inclusion on scrolls with anatomical whales show that scholars thinking about whales were just as concerned with classifying them within a Chinese-inspired medical and philosophical system as within the Western one. Since Chinese natural philosophy became a major tool for maximizing the benefits of natural resources available within Japan during this period, this provided additional motivation for illustrations of the major whale species targeted by the specialized whaling groups contributing to the expansion of Tokugawa Japan's resource base out into coastal waters, and also shows the practical side that drove some of this kind of scholarship.

WHALES FOR THE SCHOLAR: WHALE SPECIES
AND NATURAL HISTORY KNOWLEDGE

The importance of natural history to curiosity about whales, and vice versa, is clear in Genjō and Matsugen's visit to Taiji. These and other emissaries to the Kumano whaling villages from the Kii domainal seat in Wakayama city collected information not just about the potential value of the whaling enterprise, but also about parts of the whale more relevant to studies of medicine—whether Chinese medicine focused on the efficacy of all animals, vegetables, and minerals for the promotion of human health, or for the later anatomical studies inspired by Dutch imports. The strong ties between traditional natural history (honzōgaku) knowledge of organisms and medical uses for those organisms provided scholars an easy link between interest in animals-as-products and interest in the internal workings of their bodies. Many illustrations have sparse or no text on them, but one illustrated whale scroll dated to 1764 comments on the source from which the author copied his images of whales, noting that they were originally done from life on the order of the shogunal government in 1721—in other words, when Genjō and Matsugen were sent to the Kumano coast.[18] Some original version of another, the "Illustrated scroll of Koza Village whaling," was under control of the government officials in Koza at least as early as 1726, based on the trip made by Noro Genjō and Natsui Matsugen in 1721, and copies made from that original were sent to the domain's chief retainer, with known dates of copying including 1751 and again in 1798.[19] The combination of species lists, occasional anatomical diagram, and illustration of whale parts and the products derived from them show how the official and personal interests of scholars like Genjō and Matsugen intersected in these whale scrolls. Government-mandated surveys like this one produced natural history knowledge that was for government benefit, but also provided knowledge for scholars with less economically oriented curiosity. The high economic value of whales and whaling groups therefore drove the collection of information that became critical in the development of a new field of natural history (honzōgaku) within Japan, and shows why whales in particular were such influential representatives of the marine environment.

It is likely that the earliest versions of whale illustrations were all produced by natural history scholars (honzōgakusha). Those in the lineage of scrolls coming from the 1721 trip certainly were. Noro Genjō was a honzōgaku scholar who had been commanded by Tokugawa Yoshimune to study Dutch in order to help translate two of the most influential books for natural history imported into Japan: Johann Johnston's lavishly illustrated Historia naturalis and Rembertus Dodonaeus's botanical Crujdeboeck.[20] This link to Dutch studies may have introduced some interest in whale anatomy to the trip, although the anatomical whale drawings might have come from a different source. His travelling partner Natsui Matsugen was a student of honzōgaku scholar Niwa Shōhaku.[21] Niwa Shōhaku worked on the production of medicines around the country for the government, and was later in charge of a massive survey of natural resources in each domain.[22] But the concentration of honzōgakusha on this topic was not limited to this single expedition, even though its illustrations were clearly copied and recopied extensively. The earliest known work solely about whales in Japan, Geishi, was written in 1670 by a Kii native with an interest in honzōgaku. This text, like the reports later written for the domainal government, was based on his personal experience of trips to the whaling villages of Taiji and Koza along the Kumano coast of Kii domain.[23] Clearly, *honzōgaku* scholars were important in collecting this information, and their curiosity drove frequent trips to whaling areas from scholars based in Edo or other cities. Their search for information was another way that the network of connections between whaling groups intersected with connections to people further inland in the major cultural centers of Japan and made whaling more than just a marginal occupation for specialists.

One of the most common types of whale illustration from the period is of the external view of different species of whales, sometimes only minimally labeled with the type of whale shown.[24] For the ones that do have more detailed labels, the labels indicate what the artist thought of as distinctive or unusual features. Some include interestingly shaped fish along with the assortment of whales.[25] Illustrations of this type are thus not just portraits of an individual whale, but rather long scrolls comparing different types of whales (and other strange fish). It is tempting to think that such a series of illustrations should correspond to a sort of early field guide to species that we know of today, particularly because the names for whales in the Tokugawa period match modern species names even though we now recognize them as mammals instead of fish. It is, of course, dangerous to assume that ideas of species classification from the philosophical systems in early modern Japan will overlap exactly with modern scientific understandings of species. But there is some indication in these scrolls that they were meant to at least be a kind of catalog of species of whales, if not a field guide per se. One version of the "Illustrated scroll of Koza Village whaling" has finely drawn whales with short descriptions for each.[26] They all share labels for tail flukes, pectoral fins, blowholes, and notes indicating whether they have teeth or baleen. This artist determined that it was not just the blowhole that set whales apart as interesting, but also these other bodily features that they do not share with fish.[27] The "Illustrated scroll of Koza Village whaling" also has text at the end indicating that it illustrates whales that have been caught in Koza, with their forms carefully copied in this scroll.[28] That could indicate that at least some of these scrolls originated as a kind of report on what the whalers in different areas were catching. But because these reports were at least sometimes written by *honzōgaku* scholars, they also show that the process of classifying whale species was necessary to understand both their commercial value and their place in the natural order.

The classification system used by scholars interested in the natural world in early modern Japan was originally based on the Chinese materia medica system, which classifies natural substances in reference to their effectiveness in medical preparations. This was a comprehensive system in China, where all natural substances were seen as having potential medical uses in balancing the energy within the body.[29] However, when encyclopedic Chinese materia medica texts arrived in Japan, scholars soon had difficulty matching up the contents with the natural substances found (or not found) in Japan. While such texts had existed for centuries in China, one version that arrived in Japan in 1613 was particularly influential because it had a broader focus than just medicine. This was the *Bencao gangmu* (Compendium of materia medica; Jp. Honzō kōmoku), which listed the properties of many objects and species in the natural world, including categorization of animals in some cases through habitat or similar external characteristics.[30]

After this text arrived in Japan, even scholars who could read Chinese needed to translate the substances and species in the book into Japanese equivalents, and to determine how to fit Japanese natural resources into the system if a version of them did not already appear in the text. Gradually, this led to a reinterpretation of the classification system away from purely medical uses to more broadly practical use of natural resources.[31] This was a relatively easy step to take because in Chinese medicine, almost everything had a medical use; for example, a good diet that could keep you healthy was an integral part of the understanding of medicinal substances. Anything that people ate should therefore fit into categories of natural substances found in works like *Compendium of materia medica*, but many foods eaten in Japan, including many shellfish, fish, and whales, did not appear in this text.[32] The gap between Chinese and Japanese foods is apparent in Terajima Ryōan's 1712 encyclopedia, the *Wakan sansai zue* (Illustrated Sino-Japanese encyclopedia). There are approximately twice as many fish types in Ryōan's encyclopedia as there are in the *Compendium of materia medica* or in the Chinese encyclopedia he used for his other main source. Thus, people were discovering, through the expansion of specialized fisheries that were providing new marine foods in the Tokugawa period, that the resources available in Japan's marine environment were more diverse than in the Chinese sources that up to this point were supposed to have described the entirety of the natural world.

In the process of exploring exceptions like whales to the Chinese materia medica system, the field of study known as *honzōgaku* (study of the *Honzō komoku*, i.e., *Compendium of materia medica*) expanded away from purely medical products to study the world as a whole in a similar fashion to natural historians in early modern Europe. Whales were just one of the many strange animals that came under investigation within this expanded version of *honzōgaku*, including in the surveys instituted by Niwa Shōhaku that shaped the development of natural history in Japan. Unfortunately, neither the revised encyclopedia this survey was supposed to support nor the survey data he collected for it were published, but the process of carrying out the surveys was an important part of government policy intended to increase productivity within the domains. The surveys were sponsored by shogun Tokugawa Yoshimune in an effort to prevent or mitigate famines and to boost the Japanese economy.[33] As former daimyo of Kii domain, Yoshimune was already familiar with the benefit whaling groups could bring to their local government, particularly since Shōhaku had compiled Genjō and Matsugen's report on Kumano whaling for him for Kii domain's records in 1721. By expanding this first survey of possible natural resources to a similar survey for all domains, led by natural history scholars, Yoshimune helped to spread the *honzōgaku* classification system as part of the investigation of the practical uses of the natural world. Many of these surveys included whales, so it is also clear that they were a potential resource in more than just the Kii domain, particularly in Kyushu where their use of whale oil to prevent insect damage to rice crops was a major agricultural improvement.[34]

Outside of the work done by *honzōgaku* scholars trying to classify and survey whales, and beyond the specialized anatomical diagrams that appeared in some collections of whale images, simple realistic illustrations of whale species also had a place in a kind of early scientific understanding of the natural world. Realistic illustrations of plants and animals were becoming increasingly central to natural history in Japan. The illustrations that appeared in early *honzōgaku* texts were not necessarily realistic, as this classification system relied more on matching correct names to things than to checking observations against a standard. But as this area of scholarship became more popular, it also developed from a way of finding utility in natural resources into a focus on accurate description, depiction, and classification of plants and animals, especially those whose classification needed clarification.[35] When Niwa Shōhaku was collating the information from his Kyōhō reform surveys, he would send back requests for detailed drawings of some of the species listed. Federico Marcon argues that the increasingly central role of realistic plant and animal illustrations in natural history writing by the end of the eighteenth century came from Shōhaku's focus on these illustrations in the process of compiling and editing the surveys.[36]

This trend may help explain the proliferation of scrolls showing the variety of whales and strange fish species found in different areas of Japan. Animals and plants had long been a theme in bird-and-flower painting, in both China and Japan. But until the eighteenth century, animals in this type of art (which were not limited to just birds) generally were linked to Buddhist or Shinto iconography. In the eighteenth century, artists developed a new, more inclusive style that was meant to represent realistically the different animals in the world. Art moved away from a style meant to convey the emotional impact of viewing a particular symbolic plant or animal toward more lifelike depictions. For exotic animals like the camels brought to Japan by the Dutch, popularized first in sideshows and then in published illustrations, realistic pictures became part of a complete understanding of the characteristics of a broader natural world than had been contemplated before.[37] The problem of making personal observation of difficult-to-find animals such as whales could also be solved through realistic illustration, so the drive to classify hard-to-observe whales that arose out of Chinese materia medica's lacunae also pushed the trend toward lifelike illustration and thus shaped a whole different area of Japanese culture.

EXPLAINING WHALES: DESCRIPTIONS
OF WHALERS AND THEIR PREY

Judging from the number of texts describing whaling groups that still exist today, many people were just as curious about the whaling groups who conquered whales as they were about the whales themselves.

Descriptions of the process of capturing whales and of the different villages that practiced organized whaling provided another vector for whale-related information that made the marine environment more relevant to people who did not live in whaling or fishing villages. Two of the most famous and comprehensive works about whales from the nineteenth century, "Geishikō" (1808) and *Isanatori ekotoba* (1832), combined natural history information, including anatomical and classificatory images of whale species, with details about the process of capturing whales. Both of these works show how different types of information about whales intersected and spread beyond whaling areas themselves, and how it is not possible to break information from the period down into neatly isolated boxes based on specializations that exist today (e.g., science, pop culture, art, etc.). Given the broad interests of most scholars, as whales drove unique representations of anatomy and forced a rethinking of the materia medica–based classification system, we should expect to see scholars thinking about whales from other perspectives as well. The process of writing "Geishikō" is a particularly good illustration of how networking between scholars with different training brought curiosity about whales and whalers into all kinds of conversations.

"Geishikō" describes whaling based on book research and also the author's interviews of people involved in Hirado domain's Ikitsuki-shima whaling group (map 2). The author, Confucian scholar Ōtsuki Heisen, had no real connection to the whalers there before he stopped by to collect information about whaling for his cousin, doctor and Dutch studies scholar Ōtsuki Gentaku. Gentaku's interest had been sparked by conversations with a patient of his in Edo who happened to be the former leader of the Masutomi whaling group. Thus, the manuscript shows the kinds of information that an interested outsider who was also a scholar might want to know about the process and context for the whaling industry in the early nineteenth century. It also provides an interesting comparison to the kinds of information circulating from earlier trips like Genjō and Matsugen's, whose original writing and illustration do not survive. "Geishikō" remained as a manuscript and was never published, but like many manuscripts in the period, it did circulate in hand-copied form, and some of its information and illustrations were clearly used in the production of *Isanatori ekotoba*.[38]

Because of Gentaku's ties to Dutch studies, "Geishikō" is based on both Japanese and Dutch sources.[39] The text is divided into six volumes, of which the first three focus on what we would consider today to be scientific information, including whale names and classifications, as well as skeleton and internal organ diagrams. The last three sections contain information about the process of whaling rather than about whales themselves. The anatomical diagrams are of a very different type from the anatomical whale in scrolls like "Diagram of six whales." The anatomies in "Geishikō" are laid out as a simple outline drawing in a similar fashion as a view of human organs (figure 4.2). Despite the more human-like orientation, with the windpipe at the top of the drawing and the lungs laid out on either side, with the rest of the organs below them, the labels are not always equivalent to human organ labels. For example, a simple designation of "bean" (mame) was given for kidneys.[40] It was not until the 1829 publication of Isanatori ekotoba, a book about the Masutomi's Ikitsukishima whaling operation in Kyushu, that the organ diagrams in "Geishikō" were glossed with human equivalents (figure 4.2).[41] Therefore, the knowledge that scholars were getting from whalers was not necessarily part of a comparative anatomy where people were looking for organs of similar function in different species, but these illustrations were still influenced by new understandings of human anatomy and medicine being imported by the Dutch.

Ōtsuki Gentaku's interest in whales began in the 1780s when, in his role as a Dutch studies scholar, he translated a description of a narwhal. Narwhal horns supposedly had medicinal properties, which is why he first became interested in the topic. He may have begun thinking about the narwhal based on the illustration in a Dutch book imported into Japan, Johann Johnston's Historia naturalis. This lavishly illustrated book promoted curiosity about the natural history of animals in Japan because its detailed copperplate images of animals were eye-catching even without an understanding of the accompanying text.[42] In any case, Gentaku started trying to find out more about the animal that produced narwhal horns. Since he was also working on his revised version of Sugita Genpaku's Kaitai shinsho, which translated Western anatomical knowledge obtained through dissection, his interest in anatomy merged with his interest in whales to include discussions with whalers about whale anatomy. Something similar may have been

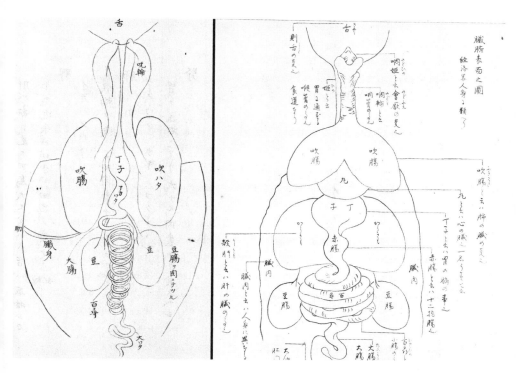

FIGURE 4.2. Diagrams of whale internal organs, with the tongue and throat at the top and the intestines at the bottom. Left: Ōtsuki Heisen, "Geishikō" (1808), 3:50, doi:10.11501/2575477; right: Oyamada Tomokiyo, *Isanatori ekotoba* (Edo, 1832), 3:11, doi:10.11501/2576170. Courtesy of the National Diet Library of Japan.

the impetus behind the production of the side-view anatomical diagrams seen in scrolls like "Diagram of six whales," but without a recorded original author, this is impossible to determine.

Gentaku's cousin Heisen was not originally interested in whales at all, but when traveling for his school he escorted Gentaku's son to Nagasaki. They visited Ikitsukishima on the way there, to collect information about whaling for Gentaku directly from the source.[43] Gentaku originally intended to take the information collected by Heisen and publish his own work on whales. But when Heisen brought back more information than he had expected about both foreign and Japanese whaling, Gentaku decided to restrict himself to translation of Western information and leave the rest to Heisen. Heisen actually ended up writing "Geishikō" for the government, as they were becoming interested in possibly setting up whaling stations in the far north to compete with Russia. This is another case, like with the domainal product surveys, where scholarship and political concerns intersected in whales. Although "Geishikō" contains whale anatomy diagrams initially because of Gentaku's medical and scholarly interests, the work itself was written because whaling promised economic, military, and political benefits to the shogunal government. This wider interest explains why, in the fourth volume, there is a global description of the places where whaling occurs, beginning with sites beyond Japan mentioned in Dutch sources (from the South China Sea to Greenland and Spitzbergen) and then focusing on a detailed listing of the places throughout Japan where whaling can be found. The final volume discusses the process of going out and capturing a whale, with accompanying illustrations of major stages in the process. Heisen chose to keep the medical and natural history information in the same manuscript as the practical details for a shogunal audience considering expanding whaling into the north as part of a territorial claim against another state. In doing so, he clearly demonstrated that the new natural history was not only driven by attempts to make sense of particularly strange creatures like whales, but also was inseparable from attempts to use control over natural resources to support political strength, whether at the domainal or shogunal level.

The production of *Isanatori ekotoba* also reflects political motives, this time belonging to the whaling group on Ikitsukishima who commissioned it. The head of the largest and wealthiest whaling group in early modern Japan, Masutomi Matazaemon, had this book produced at the peak of the Masutomi group's success, with the support and coordination of the Hirado domain's daimyo. The book stands as a demonstration of their economic power, with an audience of other daimyo and the shogunate, as the high quality and expense of its production shows. *Isanatori ekotoba* was published in 1832 in Edo, with the woodcuts done by a top-notch engraver and the text written by a preeminent National Learning (Kokugaku) scholar, Oyamada Tomokiyo. Of the twenty-four copies originally printed, ten went back to the Masutomi group and the Hirado daimyo distributed the remaining fourteen to various members of the three main Tokugawa houses and other high-ranking acquaintances.[44] Members of the whaling group did not produce it in isolation: the information came both from earlier manuscripts like "Geishikō," from scrolls describing whaling groups in the northern Kyushu Saikai area, and also from material Masutomi Matazaemon provided to his daimyo (domainal lord). This daimyo, Matsuura Hiromu, had been involved in publishing other books previously, and therefore took a central role in collating and organizing the information for the book, but he was not necessarily an expert on whaling groups in his domain. The author of the polished text accompanying the illustrations, Tomokiyo, was likely chosen for this task because both Hiromu and his father, the previous Hirado daimyo, had corresponded with him on questions of etymology, Noh, and poetry—not because he knew anything about whales or whaling.[45]

The book cost over fifty gold ryō to produce, but given that it was paid for by the Masutomi whaling group, which between 1823 and 1829 paid an astonishing 7,700 ryō in taxes alone, they could clearly afford the expense.[46] In fact, such conspicuous display of wealth seems to have been part of the point. But apart from just showing off their resources, *Isanatori ekotoba* also provides detailed descriptions of how that wealth was produced. It begins by describing the location of the fishing grounds used by the Masutomi group. It then details how whaling was done, from the preparation of nets and boats before the season started to the process of the hunt itself and its aftermath as the whales were processed on shore—focusing specifically on the whale oil that was the main portion of the whaling group's sales. It even includes information about the dance performed by the harpooners, the specific instruments used to hunt and render whales, and descriptions of whale species, anatomy, and whale-derived products. Finally, the accompanying book discussed in chapter 3, *Geiniku chomihō* (Whale meat seasoning methods), provides a series of recipes, all of which include some kind of whale part.

From the extent of the information collected in this book and the amount of money put into its production, it is clear that *Isanatori ekotoba* was meant to show the usefulness of whales as a money-making natural resource. It is not a coincidence that the book also contained information that satisfied the curiosity of a reader as to what whales were and how they fit into the contemporary understanding of the natural world, since better understanding of the natural world was a large part of more efficient and effective use of the natural resources it contained. Beyond the versions of the anatomical diagrams of whale organs copied over from "Geishikō," *Isanatori ekotoba* also includes the kind of species-identification drawings of whales found in many whale scrolls, illustrations that developed in part because of the government-sponsored surveys of domainal resources led by Shōhaku. Unlike some of these scrolls, the illustrated whales also come with brief descriptions of each species. The exact focus of each of these descriptions varies depending on the whale and the benefits that people can get from hunting them, which helps to show how intertwined curiosity and knowledge about whales as animals was with the whaling industry's exploitation of the marine environment. The cultural role of whales for people without direct connections to whaling groups or coastal villages was thus inextricably bound up in commercial perspectives on animals as resources that existed to support humans.

Isanatori ekotoba was not the only expensive text dealing with whales, just the one we have the most background about. For example, the "Illustrated scroll of whaling (*Geigeiki mokuroku*)" is an expensive picture scroll, with high-quality illustrations including gold leaf and with silver flecks decorating the back of the scroll.[47] The original provenance of the scroll and its artist and commissioner is now lost, but it is not a copy of the same information in *Isanatori ekotoba*. It starts with a story of whales coming ashore in Naniwa (one of the early capitals of Japan from 645–655 CE, now the city of Osaka). The image shows people responding with fear to this unusual event, at least until priests or monks from the local temple came to placate the whales. The table of contents indicates a more expansive story connected to this incident, but unfortunately the extant copy of the scroll has that section cut out, skipping ahead to sections 6 and 7. These pieces describe the practice of contemporary harpoon whaling. With no date, it is unclear whether this scroll was made before the rise of net whaling in 1675, or if the creator simply decided to illustrate the first style of harpoon whaling instead of net whaling (see figure 2.3). What the scroll can tell us is that someone possibly in the area around Osaka (given the reference to Naniwa), and therefore getting information about nearby Kumano whaling, may have paid for this scroll to be made. If true, it was not only

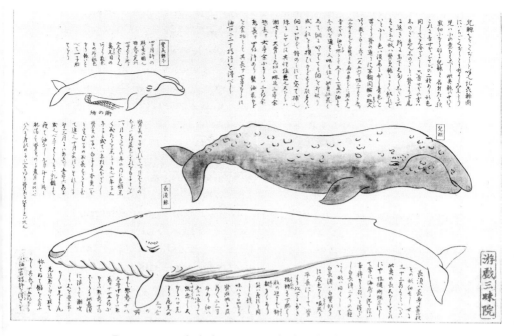

FIGURE 4.3. Description of whale species including fetal right whale (top), gray whale (center), and fin whale (bottom). The previous page included an adult right whale and a humpback whale; no young versions of other species are shown. Oyamada Tomokiyo, *Isanatori ekotoba* (Edo, 1832), 3:4, doi:10.11501 /2576170. Courtesy of the National Diet Library of Japan.

the richest Masutomi whalers from Kyushu who circulated information about how whaling worked. This might be an outgrowth of the kind of information collected by Genjō and Matsugen in the Kumano area the same way that *Isanatori ekotoba* is an outgrowth of information that Gentaku and Heisen collected in the Saikai area.

What is clear from all of the sources about whales created in this period is that the cooperation of whalers was essential in understanding these animals. Whalers were not isolated in their villages physically, since they and their products circulated widely. But they were also not culturally and intellectually isolated. As producers of important natural products and interpreters of the largest inhabitants of the maritime environment that Tokugawa Japan depended on to increase its resource base, whalers were tied into a scholarly network with visits from domainal officials and curious scholars alike. Their hands-on knowledge of whales helped shape the information that circulated throughout the country. Images of fetal whales, of the milk-producing nipples on female whales, and diagrams of the ways that whales are sectioned up on the beach all often appeared in the scrolls listing different whale species that came from *honzōgaku* surveys (figure 4.3). Until they are cut open, pregnant whales appear to be the same as any other female whale, so an image of an unborn fetus could only come from experience with incidental captures of pregnant whales by the whaling industry. Although this kind of information necessarily comes from whalers, they were not the only people who ever had direct personal experience with whales. Their experience was simply more detailed and extensive than that of nonwhalers, who might see whales swimming through coastal waters as they traveled along the shore on coastal roads or in coasting ships, but who might also see them displayed on land, not just as products like oil or meat.

WHALES FOR THE GENERAL PUBLIC: MISEMONO AND STRANDINGS

Along with classifying the wide variety of natural substances and beings found in Japan through exchanges of illustrations like those depicting whale species, scholars also shared specimens and displayed them in product exhibitions. As an outgrowth of these exhibitions, a different kind of curiosity also drove the general public to come have an in-person sensory experience, including the undoubtedly foul smell of a dead whale or its parts, at something known as *misemono*. These were the sorts of exhibitions that occasionally had rare non-Japanese animals like camels, or provided shows of acrobats, sword-swallowers, and the like. The word *misemono* translates literally as an exhibition or showing of things, but it is probably better translated as "sideshow," because like carnival sideshows these were temporary exhibits meant to present strange and unusual things for a negligible price of admission. As Andrew Markus explains, *misemono* were popular among all levels of society, and "were a favorite topic of scandal sheet and scholarly disquisition alike."[48] Their attraction lay in their novelty, as they demonstrated things that were freaks of nature or otherwise very unusual—the same attraction that brought vast crowds to the stranding of a whale in the Shinagawa River in 1798, even though that was not a planned exhibition.

Misemono were an urban attraction, profiting from large city crowds. In fact, one of the earliest records of *misemono* on the Ryōgoku Bridge in Edo is a reference from 1734 to two thirty-five-foot-long beached whales, which indicates how urban residents might still have had the opportunity to know not just what whale parts looked like, but also to see entire whales.[49] Another whole whale, this one fifty-five feet long, was brought to the shogun in 1798 (probably the Shinagawa whale), then returned to the sea. Moving a whale this size through the streets of Edo to the shogunal compound and back to the water must have been quite an endeavor, and one that proves that the plain curiosity about whales that drove these *misemono* was not limited to the lower levels of society.[50] Along with two other examples of the exhibition of whole whales, one other kind of whale-related *misemono* that Markus mentions is a whalebone sculpture, so parts of whales alone were sometimes also novel enough to end up in these shows.[51]

Misemono were generally urban, but they were not confined to Edo alone; they could be found in larger provincial cities as well. In the case of whale *misemono* it is likely that the demonstrations happened less often in major cities than in areas closer to where the whales had been found, simply because of transportation problems. At the same time, it is unlikely that *misemono* exhibitions per se occurred in and around the whaling villages, since even whales that washed ashore (rather than being actively hunted) in a whaling area would have been claimed by one of the whaling groups or villages that had experience with whaling. In Fukuoka, for example, drifting or beached whales had to be reported to the authorities so they could coordinate an auction for the bones, meat, and whatever else might remain. Some villages even got into fights over who should be allowed the whale, and theft from the carcasses was always a problem.[52]

If whales were usually too valuable as component parts for whaling villages to provide them unprocessed for sideshow displays, where did *misemono* whales come from? In some cases, such as the Shinagawa stranding in Edo in 1798, whales on display appeared in areas that did not have organized whalers able to claim the whale for their own. But they also were sometimes shown in Osaka, with its much stronger merchant ties to the relatively nearby Kumano whaling villages. An early twentieth-century account of Tokugawa-period *misemono* lists four major shows including whales: the first was a head and tail of two whales caught in the Edo River in 1734, sold and carried up to Ryōgoku Bridge to be put on display; the second was a whale caught in 1766 the Kumano area and brought to Osaka in one piece; and the last two were shown in Osaka in 1789 and 1795.[53] This is not a comprehensive list, as it includes neither the Shinagawa stranding nor another Osaka showing in 1823 for which an advertisement still exists in the Osaka Museum of History. Perhaps the whales brought whole to Osaka for shows were deemed somehow unfit for consumption or processing for oil and bonemeal fertilizer, or perhaps an agent for a show made a point of searching out whales and other curiosities and just happened to be able to offer a high enough price for a specimen that the whalers were willing to sell it whole. Unfortunately, there are very few sources that describe ephemeral *misemono* shows in any great detail, and none include descriptions of why whalers might give up a whale just to let it rot on display in the city. The description on the 1823 Osaka *misemono* flyer does note that there were six whales in the vicinity between the twenty-second day of the first month and the twenty-fourth day, presumably the period during which the whale on display was caught. Given that the flyer is dated to the second month, the whale was likely quite rotten by the time it was displayed.[54] Maybe because half a dozen whales were available at the time, one could be spared for a show in Osaka. The draw of curious crowds willing to pay a small admission fee to see the show may also have been strong enough to make this a lucrative (or seemingly lucrative) proposition.

The existence of this whale *misemono* in 1823 shows that people organizing such shows found the presentation of a whale to still be rare or fascinating enough to draw an audience nearly a hundred years after the first recorded showing of whales in Edo. The experience of the actual show is lost to us, but the choice of image on the flyer is instructive. The advertisement highlights the link between curiosity about whales themselves and curiosity about how people caught them. The central image is not simply of a whale as one might see it on display at the temple's *misemono* show. Instead, it is a dynamic illustration of how it was caught in order to be brought to Osaka, with men in boats surrounding the whale to throw harpoons at it, and signalers on shore to coordinate them. It is not a well-researched illustration, since the portion of the whale visible above the water and also the details of the whalers are not particularly realistic. The lack of realism is perhaps not surprising, since the point of the flyer was to bring people to the show rather than to be a source of detailed scholarly information about either whales or whaling. With all the other information about whales circulating at this point, it is also possible the person who commissioned the advertisement was aware that it was inaccurate but simply did not have enough time or funds to find someone who could do a better version.

Although it was not part of an organized *misemono* show per se, the Shinagawa stranding of 1798 provides the most information about public reactions to whales on display, reactions that were likely to have been similar to going to see a sideshow whale. We are fortunate in having a direct record of the experience of going to see a stranded whale, in the same way that people went to see them or their parts at regular *misemono* shows, in Toboke's "Kujira bōsatsu hyaku hiro kōryū." As is typical for Tokugawa-period literary works, puns and double-meanings are an important part of the text. The wordplay essential to the stories told in this text helps show the kinds of interrelated roles that whales could hold in someone's imagination during this period, and echoes the multifaceted roles of whale products and parts as well as demonstrating the thorough integration of parts of the marine environment into the land-based lives of people in Tokugawa Japan.

The title of the piece alone, which can be translated as "Whale-bodhisattva one-hundred-fathom monument," contains complex layers of meaning. Bodhisattva stay on earth rather than becoming Buddhas, so they can teach others how to attain Buddhahood. In the title, the whale bodhisattva's monument may refer to the way that people gathered to see the whale: the text could be honoring the death of a whale with a monument or commemoration of its presence, while also recounting the way that it drew crowds like a bodhisattva would. The reference to a bodhisattva indicates that some might have thought the whale was putting itself on display for the edification of others. However, the title given on the inner cover of the work, "Kujira no katami"

(Whale souvenir), points to an alternative explanation. The draw of the whale on display may not have been because it was equivalent to a spiritual teacher so much as because it was simply a once-in-a-lifetime fascinating spectacle. Finally, while the one hundred fathoms (*hyaku hiro*) clearly references the astounding length of the whale, this is also a term now used for a boiled and salted whale intestine dish. Leaving the spiritual aspect of dealing with whales for the following chapter, I will focus here on the text's demonstration of other aspects of the cultural importance of whales for the general public who lived far from whaling villages.

In his preface, Toboke draws readers' interest by introducing the famous place/destination (*meisho*) he was fortunate enough to have experienced. *Meisho* were famous because they appeared in well-known (often classical) literary pieces and poems, and became popular destinations for travelers during this period. By framing the stranding as a *meisho*, he implies not just a strong desire for people to go see it, but also desire for a particular cultural cachet that comes from being able to say you had been to this famous place. In fact, he describes the stranded whale as drawing people away from the other famous tourist destinations in the area. Toboke highlights the impact of the arrival of the whale in the Shinagawa River: "Vying with another, everyone went to see it—the people were standing all together like the teeth of a comb."[55] For these eager visitors, the whale was as awe-inspiring as a visit to the great sights of a local household estate or even the falconry grounds and palace of the Tokugawa shogun, at least according to Toboke's first anecdote about the stranding.[56]

After this point, most of the text does not focus on recounting the experience of going to see the whale stranding. Instead, the author uses it as a pretext for a series of quick stories laced with puns and jokes linked back to the whale from different angles. Toboke describes two stylish men he saw arriving at a nearby inn, supposedly to see the whale, but mostly to sit around chatting about the prostitutes they saw. Eventually, they call over a geisha to entertain them with whale stories. This is a good demonstration of the many ways that whales existed in the minds of people during this period. From the starting inspiration of the whale stranding, the stories presented by Toboke are not limited to unusual strandings or even to discussing the whaling

FIGURE 4.4. Roof finials in the shape of *shachi*, fire-protecting imaginary fish or dolphins, from Wakayama Castle. Photograph by the author.

industry or its products and influence. Whales had migrated much further into everyday culture than that, as shown by the many different stories the geisha tells her audience.

One story in the collection says that the stranded whale supposedly wanted to become a *misemono* in Edo, but people moved to intercept it. The whale tried to distract them by pointing out the protective fish sculpture on a nearby roof instead. Such sculptures are known as *shachihoko*, where *shachi* is also a name for killer whales. Although the forms put on rooftops to protect from fire are sometimes thought of as dolphins, they are also sometimes seen as some other form of exotic imaginary fish not much like a whale (figure 4.4). The stranded whale is thus presented as trying to get people to go see some other whale-like spectacle rather than itself.[57]

In another story, people tried all day to bring in the whale but became discouraged at how long it was taking to profit from the process. One complained that it should already have become money, and another responded with a play on the words *kujirajaku* and *kanejaku*, a cloth measure made from whale baleen and a carpenter's square respectively, by ignoring the measuring portion of the words (*shaku/jaku*): "The whale can very easily be turned into money. That is a 'whale' [*kujira*], therefore please cut and discard two inches. In that way it will immediately be made into money [*kane*]."[58] The carpenter's measure was two inches shorter than the cloth measure, so by cutting off two inches from the "whale-measure" (*kujirajaku*) the ruler would now be the length of a carpenter's square, whose name translates as "bent-measure"—but the part that means "bent" is homophonous with the word for money. Everyday objects thus bore associations with whales that were more than just similarity of words. Punning and word similarities were part of people's understanding of whales and everything else in their world, as much of the literature of this period demonstrates. These sophisticated puns relied not just on similarities of sound but also on deeper knowledge of the characteristics of the words the speaker was playing with. References to the whaling industry in other stories told by the geisha show that references to whales in puns were not limited to similar-sounding words for whale, but also relied on a complex understanding of the whaling industry and the ways that whales were brought ashore. For instance, four of the stories turn around jokes related to the word for harpoon (*mori*) punning with other words containing a homophonous *mori*.[59]

The whaling industry's products also had a role in her stories, with a layered reference to the whale oil used in lamps in one of them, and a comment about meat with a boar complaining that it was a mountain whale and therefore should be able to join a group of sea creatures visiting the whale.[60] Other versions played with the idea of whales being much like humans, with the stranded whale seen as a daughter being enclosed and protected like a young woman.[61] I have focused on this particular text because it collects and presents such a wealth of viewpoints about whales and demonstrates some of the many ways that people could have thought about them in everyday life through the types of language that were associated with aspects of the whale. However, it was far from the only work that drew inspiration from the Shinagawa stranding. Two other works written by extremely famous and popular authors also owe their inspiration to this event, and took whales even further from their physical presence into the realms of the imagination.

REINTERPRETING WHALES:
AUTHORS AND CETACEAN INSPIRATION

In the year after the Shinagawa stranding, both Jippensha Ikku and Takizawa Bakin published *kibyōshi* (illustrated comical stories) related to whales.[62] Both of these works by popular writers present fantastical stories involving a whale. Ikku's offers more anthropomorphic figures such as a rabbit, monkeys, and a blowfish-woman, while Bakin's main story has more of a tall tale flavor, talking about a merchant with an increasingly large head and his infatuation with very large things. Both brought different ideas of whales to the public who may not have seen whales themselves, tying these impressively large and generally elusive marine animals into the cultural environment of Tokugawa Japan. The timing of their publication shows that both authors were capitalizing on a particular well-known event involving a whale to drive sales of their own whale-related stories. Unlike Toboke, they did not try to frame their works within a description of personally experiencing the stranding. They simply rode the popularity of the event to sell more of their own work: as people had shown such fascination with the stranded whale, then at least while the memory of the event was still sharp, these comic authors clearly thought people were likely to pick up books that drew their inspiration from that whale.

Although the main title of Ikku's story is *Taigei hōnen no mitsugi* (Paying tribute in a fruitful year of large whales), the text begins with a brief preface "Shinagawa kujira" (The Shinagawa whale) that connects it directly to the Shinagawa stranding of the previous year. The story itself is a way of explaining how the whale might have gotten to Shinagawa in an entertaining fashion, and some of its elements show the assumptions that people made about whales and their place in the world. The main character is a monkey who was originally abducted and brought to the Dragon King's Palace under the sea, where they were planning to use his liver to help with a young princess's sickness. But the clever monkey manages to not only escape death, but also steal some of the Dragon King's treasure before fleeing into the blowhole of a whale. The monkey wants to go back to the Kumano mountains he was abducted from, but as they approach the shore, they are threatened by whalers with harpoons and cannot get close enough for the monkey to go ashore.[63] Instead, the whale swims into unfamiliar waters and ends up in Shinagawa in Edo, where people walk across his back as if he were a bridge. Then, after some adventures the monkey has with his stolen treasure and monsters from the mountains, he and the whale end up bringing riches to Edo in the form of money sprayed out of the whale's blowhole. This is the "paying tribute" from the title. Ikku's story shows how the arrival of a whale in Edo could bring great monetary value and also was similar to the regular journeys that people had to make to Edo to pay their taxes and respects to the shogunate.[64]

The value of the whale in Ikku's story was expressed in showers of gold and silver coins. Real whales' monetary value required a bit of processing first, so what sort of value would Ikku have meant? Whales' value might come from payments to see a stranded whale being shown as a *misemono*, but the inclusion of whalers in the story shows that Ikku also knew whales had value as hunted animals, not just as curiosities. The treasure coming from whales in *Paying tribute in a fruitful year of large whales* is thus most likely a reference to the amount of money earned by managers of whaling groups and the merchants who sold whale products. Ikku in this popular comedic work references not just whales as animals or monsters, but also whales as natural resources and bringers of wealth. A purpose (if not the entire purpose) of whales' existence in the world was as a resource that brought humans profit.

Takizawa Bakin's work, *Kujirazashi Shinagawa baori* (Whale-scale Shinagawa jacket), shows that one should not discount the interest that readers of comic tales might have had in more difficult scholarly works like natural history texts. Much like the easy movement of fish and whales along the coastal currents that enriched the shores of Japan, information and what we consider to be different types of scholarship were not tightly segregated but rather flowed and intermingled.

Individual scholars might be trained in a particular field like Confucian studies or Dutch studies or natural history, but there was nothing stopping them from also reading texts produced by scholars of another type. Bakin's book is a comic novel, a genre meant purely to entertain rather than to educate scholars, but he assumes that his readers have some familiarity with the conventions of scholarly texts in setting up his joke. After a short prologue advertising the book, there is foreword written in the scholarly language of *kambun*, a format showing that it is (at least supposedly) highly educated information about whales.[65] This quick summary defines whales as "large fish in the ocean," then gives the names for male and female whales as well as different names used for whale in the past. Bakin cites real reference works that talk about whales, including the traditional Chinese reference work *Compendium of materia medica*. The humor of the preface arises from the contrast between this section and the ones that follow, after the essay has set up the idea that this will be a proper scholarly work. The next sections provide a sudden shift in tone, as Bakin stretches the classification of whales far beyond accepted boundaries. The fact that the reader is expected to recognize this format and find humor in the contrast is indicative of the penetration of natural history texts into circles beyond natural history scholars, and the playfulness central to the literary culture of the period.

The four single-page segments that follow the first section talk about different interpretations of "whales" that are not actually whales at all. The first one is for *yamakujira*, which literally means "mountain whale," but more colloquially referred to wild game meat, particularly boar.[66] Bakin makes the description sound as if the boar in the image is supposed to truly be a whale type (figure 4.5). The parallel to whales includes not just a name overlap, but also a reference to a case where someone who harpooned one made seven villages profit: while this was a common saying about whales, it is far less likely to be true for one single boar. The next segment is for something called *namekujira*, which is a pun on *namekuji*, the slugs shown in the accompanying image. Since whale names were generally of the form (description)-*kujira*, adding a *ra* to the word slug makes it sound much like *semi kujira* (right whale), *zatō kujira* (humpback whale), and other real whale names. The reference to these slug-whales includes the fact that they are supposedly vanquished by

FIGURE 4.5. A mountain whale, otherwise known as a wild boar. Takizawa Bakin, *Kujirazashi Shinagawa baori* (Edo: Tsuruya Kiemon, 1799), 13–14, doi:10.11501/9892879. Courtesy of the National Diet Library of Japan.

"rain-harpoons."[67] Then, the next page introduces a *goshō kujira*, depicting an old man crouched down on bedding with his jacket making him look like a whale's back. The rest of the description leans more heavily on the old man part than the whale part, talking about how terribly diseased and lecherous he is.[68] Finally, Bakin introduces the *mimikujira*, literally ear-whale, a word that references a poorly-made article like a sword or knife hilt with a profile vaguely resembling a whale.[69] Only after these short pieces does Bakin turn to the longest and central story, about a harpooner who made a living hunting whales, and therefore wanted to make himself and everything he owned large, just like the whales he hunted. In his rapid transitions between types of not-quite-whales, Bakin relies on his audience's sharing and understanding of whales that fits the new natural history scholarship of the period. Studies of whales likely did not singlehandedly drive *honzōgaku*'s new image of the order of nature, but they certainly were inextricably tied to the public understanding of natural history.

This quick look at the different ways that the Shinagawa whale inspired comic writers shows the multifaceted nature of the popular knowledge that the stories' humor relied on. By looking at such stories, we can infer something about what people thought should be linked to whales. As Bakin's introductory section shows, whales were seen in the framework of scholarly classification even by readers who were not necessarily natural history or medical scholars themselves. Members of the reading public could be expected to fit sideshow whales at least partly into the context of Chinese-inspired writing. But the other parts of these stories show that ideas about whales were not limited just to the philosophical realm. The treatment of wild boars in a description as if they are really "mountain whales," especially juxtaposed with the following section describing slug-whales based on wordplay of the names of both creatures, shows the ways that people categorized animals for more than just essential philosophical definitions of the universe. The classification of animals and other parts of nature could be used as play, as well as for serious scholarly pursuit. Parts of the marine environment in particular were a good focus for literary play and jokes because they occupied a liminal space, partly familiar but partly strange, offering the potential for a number of surprising (and thus funny) juxtapositions.

Whales are striking animals that fit uneasily into simple categories. They are the largest living creature that anyone in Japan would have ever encountered, something that is impressive and unusual enough that size alone would drive some desire to see them in person. But unless a whale became stranded or was brought ashore for processing by whalers, most of the animal would not be visible to observers—whether they were on a boat or on land. Descriptions and illustrations could actually provide more comprehensive views of a whale than personal experience with one could, at least for people who were not involved in whaling. Even in cases like the Shinagawa stranding, people thought about how whalers would deal with the whale even as they wondered why the whale had appeared there. Thus, whalers came to provide not just substances derived from whales, but also expert knowledge about what these animals were. This expert knowledge was especially important for scholars interested in the natural world in general, because whales were one of the more difficult parts of nature to classify.

The rise of organized whaling did not solely and directly drive the rise of natural history (*honzōgaku*) as a field, but it was an important contributor. In Europe, natural philosophy and later natural history were originally part of a religious understanding of God's creations.[70] In Japan, the need for a thorough understanding and classification of the natural world arose from the Chinese understanding of medicinal properties that theoretically belonged to every substance, living or not. In the same way that the European discovery of new lands and species through voyages of exploration shook their understanding of species, Japanese attempts to fit their native plants and animals into Chinese materia medica shook their faith in the comprehensiveness of those sources.[71] Whales were one of the exceptions that demanded further study to fit into a truly complete understanding of the natural world, since Chinese sources said very little, if anything, about them. If whalers had not already been deriving material benefits from whales, it is doubtful so many *honzōgaku* scholars like Noro Genjō, Natsui Matsugen, and Niwa Shōhaku would have produced whale images and manuscripts discussing what these animals were, how people could catch them, and what their bodies could be turned into.

Whales were interpreted within a variety of scholarly contexts, including both the developing Japanese natural history of *honzōgaku* and the later version influenced by Western Linnean categorization methods. Medicine was closely tied to that science, both in the understanding from Chinese materia medica in *honzōgaku* and in the influence of Western anatomy. Furthermore, scholars whose areas of interest did not overlap with what we might think of as the natural sciences today had access to and included this type of information about whales in their interpretations of the animals. All of these scholars were also people who could be just as drawn to the more spectacle-driven curiosity of the *misemono* shows and wildly exaggerated stories that were popular with the general public.

The knowledge circulating about whales was grounded in whalers' experiences, but it was translated through different media to influence different areas of Japanese culture: scholarly texts, art, displays of whale-based curiosities, wordplay, and comic stories all made use of some aspect of whales. Although much of the connection between *honzōgaku* and the classification of whales likely was prompted by concerns about maximizing resources, the use to which people put these works need not have mirrored the reason why they were written. The fact that popular authors such as Saikaku, Ikku, and Bakin all wrote about whales using information that appeared in more scholarly works shows that their contents could be interesting to a wide audience. Complex and overlapping realms of interest and social networks all contributed to the ways that people thought about the world around them, including the marine environment. A general fascination with whales thus could bring together a scholar like Ōtsuki Gentaku trained in Dutch studies (wanting to understand foreign natural history books and medical texts) and his Confucian philosopher cousin Heisen who was far more concerned about political stability. Because most illustrations of whales have no indication of either the copyist, the artist, or the reason they were created, similar connections between different interests and levels of society are harder to see for those sources. But it is likely, given the variation in quality of artwork alone, that whale images fascinated many different kinds of people, who created and circulated such scrolls for reasons beyond wanting to understand the place of whales in the natural order.

One of the important results of the melding of different viewpoints in peoples' imagination of and curiosity about whales was the way that this information traveled. The different interpretations of whales described in this chapter all serve to show how the marine environment was a part of the general consciousness of the people of early modern Japan, no matter how far they lived from the shore. The natural world in which they lived did not stop at the shoreline, even if they never saw the ocean. Following their images and descriptions on scrolls and in books and manuscripts, we can trace the way that intangible ideas about whales made their way inshore and helped make Tokugawa Japan truly archipelagic. The descriptions of whales in this chapter are examples of ways to bring a representation of the physical reality of whales into places where the actual whale could not survive. Entire whales were not always physically confined to the coastal areas where they were hunted, as their infrequent appearance as *misemono* shows. But even if they had been physically present only in the ocean near shore, written descriptions and images of whales had the capability of traveling much farther. The many text and illustrated versions of whales, at all levels of accuracy or realism, made marine space part of the lives of people all over Japan. Particularly talented authors even adapted these ideas of whales to fit their human understanding of the world, telling stories about very human-like whales traveling with other anthropomorphic animals to perform tasks that made sense within the social order of the day: if all the domainal lords had to travel to Edo at one point within the alternate attendance system, bringing their tax money with them, why would whales also not travel to Edo and distribute gold and silver when they arrived?

The thriving print culture of the period and increasing travel combined to popularize texts that described strange and distant places, including the curious animals, plants, and other things that might be found there.[72] Illustrations helped make these descriptions of things a reader had never seen become more real. For example, in an 1851 preface to Andō Hiroshige's "Fifty-Three Stations of the Tōkaidō" woodblock print series, Ryūkatei Tanekazu exclaimed, "Looking at these pictures is even greater pleasure than travel itself! Those who have never traveled will find instruction [in these pages] while those who have visited these places will be vividly reminded of them and their associations."[73] Sometimes personal experience could be obtained when specimens appeared in shows in the major cities, in scholarly exhibits of natural history specimens or in *misemono* for the truly bizarre sideshow monsters (although such rarities could also be part of an exhibit of a natural history scholar's collection). In the same way that new interest in places in the far north arose with works like Suzuki Bokushi's *Snow Country Tales* (Hokuetsu seppu), which introduced people to the ways of life in an environment very different from the major cities of Japan, the coastal waters and their strange inhabitants were generally easier to visit in texts than they were in person.[74] Thus, with these kinds of descriptions and images of fascinating creatures, like the exotically large whales and other strange fish that tended to be included on picture scrolls with them, the marine world was reachable for everyday people. Just as the whaling groups all along the coasts of southern Japan were part of an interconnected network of expertise, information about whales was part of an interconnected set of scrolls, manuscripts, and books whose contents were copied and recopied in different areas, influencing popular stories as well as descriptions of how strange creatures like whales fit into the natural order.

Tokugawa-period understanding of the world included oceanic denizens like whales in specific roles that they no longer hold within the modern view of the world, which has replaced *honzōgaku* with biology and the literary conventions of Bakin and Ikku with other types of stories, not to mention an entirely different system for accessing and spreading information. The construction of natural history and natural philosophy was based on the notion that understanding the world meant understanding these creatures so that humans could best make use of them, showing one of the ways that the marine environment was integral to more than just the coastal residents of fishing villages. Furthermore, the conceptualization of whales in scholarly sources shows how people were beginning to understand the natural world through observation and personal experience. Some of those representations paralleled the ways that people were starting to look in new ways at the usually invisible interior of human bodies.

While it is still unclear why whale anatomical illustrations are the only ones to appear with human anatomy drawings during this period, these illustrations may well have been prompted by more than just the experience of whaling groups dismembering whales into component parts. Perhaps they come in part from the liminality of whales as they crossed familiar categorical lines: animals that appeared in coastal waters like other migratory fish but had to surface to breathe and were far larger than anything else in those waters. Interactions between land-based people out in boats and ocean-based whales they were hoping to haul up on the beach do seem to have contributed to a consciousness of whales fitting close to humans in the natural order, as the anatomical diagrams show. While this closeness seems quite peculiar from a modern perspective, such interpretations of the ways that whales relate to people and their place in the world were essential to a culture that was beginning to integrate a variety of specialized fisheries into its economy and interpreting new roles for the products of such fisheries. It should also be remembered that Tokugawa-period attitudes toward whales must always be interpreted within the commercial framework of organized whaling: popular understandings of whales' place in the natural order were inextricably tied to the industry that killed them and turned them into products for human use.

FIVE

MEMORIALIZING WHALES

Religious and Spiritual Responses to Whale Death

THE BRIDGE MADE WITH WHALE BONES THAT CAN STILL BE FOUND
on the grounds of the Zen temple Zuikōji in Osaka is a unique example
of early modern whale memorials (figure 5.1). In 1756, the fourth head
priest of this temple, Tanjū Chinin, stayed in the whaling village of Taiji
during a pilgrimage to the Kumano area (map 3). While he was there,
the village head Kakuemon and his relative Jiemon petitioned Chinin
to pray for the village. They said they were suffering from a recent lack
of whales. But the priest rejected their request, explaining that there
were commandments against killing in Buddhism. Kakuemon and
Jiemon argued that without his help, the people of the village would
die. At that point, Chinin agreed that the lesser evil of killing whales
would be acceptable for the greater good of keeping the villagers alive.
He prayed for them, and a few weeks later the villagers caught some
whales. In thanks for their renewed success, the Taiji whalers brought
thirty ryō of gold and eighteen whale bones to Zuikōji, and Chinin used
the bones to construct the bridge as a prayer for the whales' happiness
in the next world.[1]

This story illustrates the complex relationship between religious
views of humanity's proper interaction with living things and the practices and beliefs of whalers. As Chinin explained, Buddhism's strictures against killing and its emphasis on compassion should have
caused most priests and devout Buddhists to disapprove of the practice
of whaling. The fact that this was a thriving industry involving

FIGURE 5.1. The bridge made of whale bones at Zuikōji, Osaka. The original bridge has been rebuilt five times, most recently with fin whale bones in 1975. Photograph by the author.

thousands of people might lead one to suspect that Buddhist values simply were not that influential in early modern Japan, at least in whaling areas. But if that were the case, then why would Taiji whalers want to ask for a priest's help to increase their catch?

In reality, Buddhism did have a broad impact on Japanese society during this period, including on whalers and those who profited from whale deaths. In the early seventeenth century, the shogunate passed a law requiring every household to belong to a state-approved Buddhist temple.[2] In return, this temple would perform registrants' funerals and memorial services. The ruling government further supported Buddhism during the mid-eighteenth-century tenure of the shogun Tokugawa Tsunayoshi, who instituted the Laws of Compassion, Buddhist-inspired laws regulating people's behavior toward other living things. In general, people in the Tokugawa period focused on this-worldly rather than other-worldly concerns, but even outside of these two government mandates, somewhere between a third and a half of all books published in the period were on Buddhist topics.³ Therefore, people like whalers who made a living from the deaths of other beings were forced to confront at least some disapproval of this practice. In the process, they balanced spirituality and practical behavior, incidentally drawing the boundaries between human and nonhuman in ways that put whales metaphysically closer to people than perhaps any other animal, even domesticated ones.

The deaths of whales, out of all possible animal deaths, were commemorated in the most human fashion, with posthumous Buddhist names recorded in a death register (*kakochō*). These records allowed for the proper regular interval of prayers that helped send a soul on to the heavenly realms rather than force it to reincarnate and continue suffering. Some fetal whales even were given their own graves, with other whale deaths marked with memorial stones. Domestic animals, even though they lived more closely with people, generally did not get this same treatment, and the few early memorials for horses, dogs, or cats did not appear until nearly a century after the construction of the first whale memorial. Just like the curious parallel anatomies of humans and whales discussed in the previous chapter, the religious response to whale deaths shows that people in early modern Japan felt that human and whale spirits were more similar than the spirits of humans and domestic animals.

Buddhists consider all living beings, not just humans or whales or even solely animals, to be part of the same cycle of reincarnation, but there are two different scriptural perspectives on the positions of humans in this cycle. One important Mahayana Buddhist sutra focuses on the interconnectedness of all living beings, due to the relationships formed through perpetual reincarnation. In another, the Golden Light Sutra, cycles of reincarnation and rebirth occur within a hierarchy where humans hold a higher position than other animals but a lesser one than Buddhas, bodhisattvas, and *kami*.⁴ Human karmic punishment in this interpretation comes in the form of rebirth as a beast instead of a human, or as a stint in one of many hells.⁵ This second sutra's idea of different levels of hell awaiting humans depending on their behavior and adherence to Buddhist doctrine in life became a major feature in lay people's religion in Tokugawa Japan. During this period, Buddhism spread to nonelite sectors of the population through temple registration's connection to funeral duties, and popular teachings focused on the salvation of individual spirits of the dead from the types of punishment listed in the Golden Light Sutra. Philosophies about reincarnation tying all living beings together became less influential with the rise of this funeral-focused Buddhist practice, and the general public assumed that the role of Buddhist prayer was to free the dead from the bonds of human existence and the perpetual cycle of reincarnation.[6]

Giving whale spirits funerals or memorial rites that were very similar to human ones made them peculiarly close to humans on this karmic hierarchy, and did not fit into the usual expectations of the place of animal spirits in the cycle of reincarnation or the afterlife. Usually, religious teachings emphasized the difference between humans and other animals, rather than treating animals like people. Sinners who mistreated or killed animals are sometimes shown in hell suffering the same things they had inflicted, as a warning against cruelty to animals. The souls that ended up in the animal realm, next to hell, were generally consigned there as punishment for being too attached to their children, for blurring the line between more bodily and more spiritual (detached) emotions. Buddhist doctrine states that you must release all attachments to the world in order to be free of its suffering, so humans reborn in the lower beastly realm were being punished for showing animalistic attachment to this world instead of the next.[7]

The Japanese framework for understanding death thus included ideas that other living beings intersected with human lives and afterlives, but usually placed beasts solidly below humans in the karmic hierarchy.[8] The Zenkōji priest's concern for the life of a whale could eventually be eclipsed by concern for all of Taiji village's human inhabitants, not just because there were more of them, but also because humans were more worthy souls. Animals had to suffer because their souls had done something that deserved it, such as being a farmer in a past life who abused the creatures working for him. However, the interesting thing about whales in Tokugawa Japan was that they were not merely living beings bound to suffer, or beings whose deaths should be measured against the lives of others who might starve without the body of a whale to support them. The uneasy balance between religious expectations and actual practice dealing with whale spirits thus provides an unusual perspective on spiritual interactions with the natural world in Tokugawa Japan.

The spiritual boundaries of people living in early modern Japan included beings from the marine environment, and even prioritized them over some of the creatures to which humans were physically closer. The practices surrounding whale deaths discussed in this chapter show that the marine environment was indivisible from the terrestrial world, at least in the spiritual sense. Whales lived and died in spiritual spaces surprisingly congruent with those that humans lived and died in, and it is possible that the changeable, liminal nature of coastal waters made it easier for people to see that interconnection with whales than with animals with whom they shared purely terrestrial spaces. But this sense of closeness arose out of the practice of hunting whales, and it did not necessarily reflect a greater respect for the lives of whales than for other organisms. As the whale bridge at Zuikōji shows, religious practices surrounding whale death did not prevent people from killing whales, nor did they necessarily show a particular respect for the natural world for its own sake. Whale souls existed within a human framework, rather than being dealt with on their own terms, but their deaths show that this framework was influenced by some awareness of the nonhuman world, and furthermore was not a purely terrestrial space.

NAMING WHALES: DEATH REGISTERS FOR ANIMALS

If the most important aspect of Buddhism in the Tokugawa period was helping souls to find salvation after death, one of the most important tools for achieving that end was a posthumous Buddhist name for the soul, recorded in a death register (*kakochō*). This was a name addressed in regular prayers timed to usher the soul along its path through the afterlife. In the death register held by the temple of Kōganji in Kayoi Village (part of modern Nagato City, Yamaguchi Prefecture; map 2), there are 243 posthumous Buddhist names listed, such as Kanyo Myōhaku, an individual who died in March of 1807.[9] Priests commonly gave the second character of this name (*yo*) to people who had come to the temple for a five-day Buddhist training, even if they were not highly devout. But this name, along with approximately one thousand others recorded in this death register, belongs to a whale. Why were these whales treated so much like humans after their deaths? Western, Christian-influenced philosophy usually strictly divides human and nonhuman, with humans holding a position as the favored beings of God and the only ones with souls. But from a Buddhist perspective, all beings have souls, albeit on a hierarchy that generally places animals lower than humans. If this practice of providing posthumous names was merely an indication of Buddhist concern for the souls of all beings, there should be other animals included in the register, but all the names belong to whales. So this register specifically demonstrates that the whaling group's regular work required a unique response from the local Buddhist temple in comparison to hunters or other people who made a living off of the death of animals that never were recorded in death registers. But the posthumous names were not the only way that people even in this one whaling village reconciled Buddhism with their work as whale killers.

Temple death registers are tied to the performance of memorial services, brought out and read at regular intervals after death to help the soul continue its journey toward becoming a Buddha. While some death registers exist from the medieval period, they were not in widespread use for recording commoners' names, alongside those of monks, nuns, and high-ranking members of the temple, until somewhere between 1700 and 1720. To have a posthumous Buddhist name entered into the register, the deceased's family would have to pay the temple. Higher-ranking Buddhas came from higher payments for favored posthumous names.[10] The practice of recording the death of individual whales with posthumous Buddhist names in temple death registers is thus quite strange: the whales' families were not contributing a donation to the temple. It is likely some part of the whaling group contributed to the temple to record the whales' posthumous names, since each record also includes the name of the harpooner who dealt the death blow, the whale's species, size, sex, and when and where it was caught.[11] This would mean spending some of the profit from the whale's death on its memorial services, so there had to have been a counterbalancing benefit to the loss of money.

The initial impetus for the Kayoi whale death register can be traced back to the fifth head priest of Kōganji, Sanyo Shōnin, who instigated the regular memorial services attached to the death register honoring whales.[12] Upon his retirement to the temple's hermitage in 1679, he began conducting memorial services for whales killed by the Kayoi whaling group, who had just begun net whaling in 1673. He continued preaching the need for commemoration of whale deaths, and by 1692, he had gained whalers' cooperation in erecting a whale grave for fetal whales (discussed in more detail in the following section), as the whaling group captains and the Kayoi village headman's names are listed on the gravestone as sponsors.[13] Perhaps the priests of Kōganji also convinced them and their successors to pay for the posthumous names of the adult whales they killed as a way of atoning for the killing without having to give up the practice entirely. The death register continued to add names after Shōnin's death in 1734, so his perspective on the need to provide a way for whale spirits to become Buddha in the afterlife was maintained by his successors through the decline and local collapse of net whaling in the 1840s. The temple still practices an annual memorial service for the names in the register today.

Unique as it is, the Kayoi whale death register was not merely the project of a single eccentric monk who happened to think that whale spirits deserved extra consideration. Even though only Kayoi's temple seems to have kept an entire death register that recorded solely whale names, other temples' registers have a few whale names mixed in with people's names (recognizable through the extra information in the entry talking about the context of the death and providing details about the individual). This latter type of register even more clearly equates the whale spirits with human dead by including them in the same book. Examples of occasional posthumous whale names in human death registers generally come from areas where organized whaling did not take place, especially along the Bungo Strait that passes between Shikoku and Kyushu and links the Pacific with the western end of the Inland Sea (map 2). This strait opens onto whale migration routes but was not part of them, so the only time people were likely to see whales there would be when individual whales or small groups would become stranded or trapped. These whales would have wandered off usual migration routes, perhaps after escaping whalers further up the coast. The singular nature of rare encounters with whales in these areas may have contributed to the desire to treat a whale's death with a higher level of respect, and in a similar fashion to individual human deaths.

I have only found three examples of other animals in death registers, all of which are domesticated animals. They of course arose from a very different context than the kind of interaction people would have had with wild whales passing coastal villages. It would be much more difficult to form a personal attachment to an individual whale than to a domestic animal; whales' lives are mostly invisible to people seeing them for a brief section of their migrations, and it takes long hours of observation to begin to recognize individual whales. Even though whaling groups clearly had close interactions with whales, they were not at all similar to the kinds of closeness that develops between humans and individual domestic animals working and living with them. Thus, it is surprising that there are so few domestic animal examples of posthumous names in comparison to whale ones.

First, in the traditionally horse-breeding area of Iwate Prefecture, horses were important enough to the family to share living space. Stables were connected to the interior of the house, so that people sitting around the fire in the living room could watch the horses in the stable under the same roof. The Pure Land temple at a post station town in Tōno, Iwate Prefecture, recorded names for forty horses in their death register between 1704 and 1783. The horse names stand out because they all use the character for livestock (*chiku*) in their names. The records also note the year and town where they died, their owner's name, and then "horse" (*uma*) to finish the entry.[14] Presumably, working side-by-side with horses at a busy post town along a major road filled with people needing pack horses encouraged local people to feel their horses were individuals deserving of just as much consideration in the afterlife as they did. Even with this desire to respect deceased horses, the animals' names are recognizably horse-specific rather than similar to humans.

The even fewer cases of cats and dogs recorded in death registers arose from a closeness to an individual animal, much like the love that people in the modern era have for pets that leads them to bury them in pet cemeteries (in Japan and elsewhere).[15] A death register from Shibaku in the city of Edo (modern Minatoku, Tokyo) contains two cats, from 1761 and 1785, presumably belonging to someone connected to the temple. Both records begin with the same four-character name or phrase, *sokutenchikujo*, rather than a unique or humanlike posthumous name. A dog's posthumous record in a Shizuoka Prefecture temple is similar to these cat examples in showing a personal attachment driving their presence in the death register. An old monk from this temple remembers that in the early Meiji period (1868–1912), there used to be a childless couple who loved their dog like a child, and convinced the head of the temple to perform memorial services, erect a stone memorial, and also to record the posthumous name of Shōtenkenji in the temple's death register. However, the next head of the temple did not approve of this practice and the name was erased from the register.[16] His reaction shows how unusual it was to memorialize pets before the modern era.

The practice of recording posthumous names for whales differs from these other animal examples in more than just focusing on a wild instead of domestic animal. The Kōganji register alone contains far more names than were recorded in total for all other nonhuman animals in the Tokugawa period. This is surprising because one might expect that closeness to domestic animals in people's daily lives would have led to more references to their souls than for whales. While whalers did meet the whales they killed in a very up close and personal fashion, they certainly did not live with them over extended periods of time or come to know their personalities. Nor did whalers have the opportunity to feel like whales were members of the same household. While one might expect some blurring of boundaries between humans and domestic animals living closely with people, the rationale behind whales occupying a liminal space between humans and other animals is less clear.

Certainly, the memorialization of animals as commodities is a common thread during this period, and it is interesting that animals existed simultaneously as resources for human use and as spiritual beings within the same system of reincarnation as humans. But the question still remains, why did people feel the need to provide whales with human-style posthumous names upon their deaths? How did people balance whales' use as resources with the recognition of their spiritual existence? The multiplicity of responses to whale death show that there was no easy solution to the moral problem of profiting off of the suffering of other beings.

BEYOND DEATH REGISTERS: KUYŌ MEMORIALS FOR NONHUMANS

Death registers were only one way whalers recognized the spirits of whales that they had killed, even as they processed the body into products to consume and sell. There were also whale graves and memorial (*kuyō*) towers erected for the dead; the stone markers for each are similar, but graves contain bodily remains while memorials simply commemorate a death. While most whale memorials are not graves, Kayoi village also contains one of today's best-known whale graves (figure 5.2). This grave holds the remains of seventy-five fetal whales, honoring the calves taken from inside pregnant whales. Because it is difficult to see when a whale is pregnant, whalers captured some gravid whales without knowing they were killing two whales instead of one. As the inscription on the grave notes, the fetuses would not be able to live even if released back into the water. Thus, the whalers hoped that the spirits of unborn whales whose lives were cut short could become Buddhas, by giving them respectful burial and holding yearly prayer services for them, rather than rendering them down like adult whales.[17] It would not make sense for all whales killed by whalers to be buried in this grave: even if the inscription did not make it clear that the grave focused on calves, whalers in Kayoi caught far more than the seventy-five whales whose remains are buried there. Of course, if they buried all of the whales they caught it would negate the purpose of hunting them in the first place. For the whaling group to function, the grave could not provide any and all whales killed by someone from Kayoi a respectful burial. Rather, something about the accidental death of a baby whale that never had a chance to be born was particularly affecting, and perhaps could serve as a surrogate for all the other whales whose bodies were broken down and sold rather than buried.

For whale memorials, Kayoi again is an extreme but not unique example: while it was rare to bury dead whales, plenty of other places erected a stone memorial for dead whales, which looks much like a gravestone without the bodily remains. One memorial erected in Yobuko (in modern Saga Prefecture), a prosperous whaling center in the Saikai area (map 2), has an inscription noting that it was erected in 1748 by Nakagawa Yoshibei Shigetsugu, a member of one of the four families involved

FIGURE 5.2. The fetal whale grave at Seianji in Kayoi, Nagato City, Yamaguchi Prefecture. Photograph by the author.

in Yobuko whaling. On the back it notes "ten thousand whales' souls become Buddhas."[18] This is likely a reference to all souls of whales killed by whalers, rather than limiting the memorial to unintentionally killed fetuses or perhaps even to the whales killed by this particular group. The number is one usually used to indicate countless or multitudes, rather than referencing a specific total of whales—in other words, this memorial hopes for all whales to be able to leave the cycle of suffering and become Buddhas. At least fifty other whale memorials or graves of different forms can be found throughout the country, and no whaling area seems to have failed to mark whale deaths in some fashion.[19]

In cases where it is not clear that "grave" is a proper term to use, there being no body or body parts buried under the marker, the stone towers raised to mark deaths are often referred to as *kuyō* (memorial) towers. The term *kuyō* is a general one, and can be applied to remembrance for humans, whales, or even birds, insects, or plants.[20] Trends in human grave markers influenced the construction of these memorial towers for dead whales, so even though they do not contain bodily remains, whale *kuyō* towers essentially look like graves: the practice of constructing human graves with stone markers began sometime around the 1650s, and the earliest known whale grave marker followed not long after, in 1671.[21] Despite the resemblance to graves, *kuyō* towers are not always focused on the death of whatever they memorialize. They also can serve as generic remembrances for the past lives of animals that have served humans.[22]

Service or usefulness (particularly economic benefits) for humans seems to have been a frequent element in the decision to build nonhuman graves or *kuyō* towers in the Tokugawa period. Many memorials were for animals that could be hunted or harvested, such as the herring whose capture was a major industry in Ezo (Hokkaido) and for which there was a memorial tower built in 1757. There were even memorial towers built for wild-harvested plants: the earliest known example (labeled *sōmoku kuyō tō* or plant memorial tower) was built in 1780 in what is now Yamagata Prefecture by people whose livelihood derived from logging. Even today nearly 70 percent of these plant monuments are located in Yamagata.[23] The profits associated with the exploitation of these different natural resources meant that some extra money would be available to spend on memorial towers. Visible sponsorship of memorials for the organism that provided one's wealth may have been as much about showing off that wealth in a socially acceptable manner as it was about concern for the afterlives of the harvested being. Given how much some whaling groups could make, whale *kuyō* towers should definitely be included in this category. Thus, whale graves appear to have been an early expression of an increasing tendency to include the spirits of economically important nonhuman animals and plants in the same kinds of Buddhist death ceremonies and memorial markers that were developing for humans during the Tokugawa period. Even though they share the same form as human graves, they might not reflect the same emotional response to the deaths they commemorate as human-focused markers.

Death memorials eventually came to include inanimate objects that, never having been alive, could not technically die. The major example of this is the practice of *hari kuyō* or memorializing needles, which first appeared in the Tokugawa period. As with the case of economically-driven memorials for animals, *kuyō* for inanimate household objects arose from a feeling of connection, obligation, and gratitude toward the objects used closely by the people carrying out the rite. These rituals show how religious rites reflected anthropocentric concerns, and help to explain why whales' spirits after death might come to be treated like human ones. With many more instances of *kuyō* for inanimate objects than for plants, which are living organisms at least, the degree of human investment appears to have been a major motivation for *kuyō*. Instead of these Buddhist rituals reflecting an awareness of the interconnectedness of all things, "it is perhaps not the buddha-nature of plants, but the human-nature of the objects that inspires the performance of kuyo rites."[24] Perhaps the value that whales could provide as commodities, the investment that a whaling group made in hunting them and performing the heavy labor of processing their bodies, added to the sense that people should recognize whales' contributions to human lives by memorializing their sacrifice.

This anthropocentric perspective would help explain why in the Tokugawa period people in areas that relied on the harvest (and thus death) of whales, herring, or trees performed *kuyō* for them. It also may explain why it took longer to develop *kuyō* for household pets, which people could be close to but did not necessarily rely on in the same way. People may also have had a greater fear of retribution from the spirits of animals and objects that were exploited rather than cherished as part of the family. Indeed, one scholar has noted that the motivations behind *hari kuyō* might have hearkened back to early needles made of fish bones, where their disposal may have involved the desire for placating vengeful animal spirits.[25] Whether performed out of a sense of guilt for discarding a formerly useful object to which someone had become attached, or fear of vengeful spirits paying back poor treatment, these memorials reflect a very practical sense of nature as a resource for human use, and a recognition that humans benefit from and thus should be grateful for the sacrifice or consumption of these resources.

MOTIVATIONS FOR MEMORIALS: THE LAWS OF COMPASSION AND BUDDHIST MORAL IMPERATIVES

Before assuming that memorials were specifically driven by the wealth of whaling groups and their gratitude for that success, we should consider the possibility that an increased focus on compassion for living things led to remorse for their deaths. The text on existing memorials is sparse and not usually helpful in determining the motivations behind their construction. However, the timing of their construction provides some clues: the number of monuments erected for whales peaked during both the Genroku era (1688–1703) and again during the latter half of the nineteenth century. The peak in the nineteenth century is likely related to the massive decline in Pacific whale stocks and thus much more variable success of whaling at that time, but the earlier peak is more complicated. Although general trends in the institution of kuyō over time may have had some influence on the desire to build whale memorials, the increase in monument construction in the Genroku period came with the spread of the more efficient net whaling methods. This period was also a time of great wealth and cultural development, so an increase in monuments could have come less from the changing practices of whalers, and more from the greater availability of cash and desire to show it off by spending it on publicly visible projects such as monument construction.[26] It is perhaps not a coincidence, however, that Tokugawa Tsunayoshi was shogun during the Genroku period. While he was shogun, he instituted the Laws of Compassion toward Living Things (Shōrui Awaremi no Rei), generally referred to simply as the Laws of Compassion. These laws prohibited various forms of cruelty toward people and animals, based on the Buddhist ideal of compassion.

If people were treating dead whales' souls much the same way they did human ones, as the granting of posthumous Buddhist names seems to indicate, we would expect that people might be more likely to feel compassion toward their deaths than gratitude for what those deaths provided humans. An increase in memorials for whales in the same period that saw the institution of the Laws of Compassion would seem to support this interpretation. Whale memorials in the form of statues of the bodhisattva Jizō add to the emotional parallels between human and whale experiences of death, since Jizō offered mercy and compassion to the suffering, and in particular watched over the human spirits of unborn dead and those who died young. The graveyard in Kayoi, apart from the fetal whale grave, also has a stone Jizō that marks prayers for whales and fish (figure 5.3). This Jizō statute was erected in 1863 by

FIGURE 5.3. Jizō statue marking a grave at Kōganji, Kayoi, Yamaguchi Prefecture. It was erected in 1863 during the decline of whale populations in the Pacific and commemorates dead whales and fish. Photograph by the author.

the head of one of the major local whaling groups, the Hayakawa, when the decline in Pacific right whale populations led to no right whales taken after 1860.[27] The other well-known Jizō whale grave is from Kyushu's Ogawajima (in modern Saga Prefecture), built in the same year for a fetal whale.[28] These are not the only memorials of this type, however: an extensive list of whale graves and monuments collected by Araki Kimitoshi includes a whale grave in a Jizō temple in Kanagawa Prefecture from 1835, a grave from 1809 in Ikata, Ehime Prefecture, which, while now destroyed, seems to have been one of six Jizō statues there, and at least two other whale memorials associated with Jizō of unknown dates.[29]

Whale memorials to Jizō are interesting because of Jizō's strong ties specifically to stillborn or aborted human children. A child-centered cult of Jizō had developed during the medieval period, tied to concerns about abortion and infanticide. In this context, Jizō became the savior of lost children (whether lost through intentional death or otherwise) and provided an avenue through which the retribution or revenge of the dead upon the living could be averted. Because suffering led the dead to desire vengeance, prayers to Jizō could turn away this vengeance by helping dead children and fetuses to cross the river to the spiritual realm where they could be reborn. For simple stillbirths and death from childhood illness, parents could still feel guilt about not being able to help their child onto a better rebirth, but the guilt and possible vengeance would be much worse if they had a hand in sending the child or fetus there through infanticide or abortion.[30] The use of Jizō statues for the memorials of dead whale fetuses seems to indicate a parallel feeling of a need for mercy and compassion toward unborn whales, who were on similar paths to rebirth as the human children that Jizō usually watched over.

Interestingly, popular miracle tales in the Tokugawa period showing Jizō as a protector of dead children did not characterize these dead as vengeful spirits, and rarely specifically referred to aborted fetuses. In fact, funeral rites and memorials rarely were the same for fetuses and adult humans. Fetuses were called *mizuko* (literally "water-child") to indicate their state of fluidity, since they were not quite in the world and thus could be sent back to the cycle of rebirth more easily than a fully realized older child or adult could. In contrast to the funeral rites given to adults, the idea for *mizuko* was to send them back without burdens and let them try again to be born.[31] Practices such as posthumous Buddhist names and marked graves were for people who were going on to become Buddhas, not for those who were supposed to be reborn into human lives. The grave for whale fetuses in Kayoi includes an engraving indicating the sponsors' desire for the whales to become Buddhas, but the priests at Kōganji do not appear to have given the fetuses posthumous names in the death register for adult whales. Thus, whale fetuses were similar to human *mizuko*, but not entirely in the same category. What whale fetuses' link to Jizō shows is that people were concerned about showing compassion toward and protection of dead whales in a similar way to that shown for human children.

This brings us back to the Laws of Compassion, which seem like the best source for a rise in concern for animal welfare, or at least a sense of value in their deaths deserving of a memorial. However, a closer look at these laws shows them to be more political than religious in their motivation, or at least in their implementation. The first was promulgated in 1685, but they were revoked after shogun Tokugawa Tsunayoshi's death in 1709. Furthermore, they were never universal: they only applied within shogunal territory. While the shogunate was the major governmental institution of the period, and the shogun controlled large land holdings directly, he was not directly in charge of the domains themselves. These were under the relatively independent management of their daimyo, who owed some level of loyalty to the shogun but did not have to follow his laws within their own lands. Some daimyo may have individually decided to follow along with a shogun's policy, but they were not legally obliged to do so. These revoked laws also did not set the tone for views of animals throughout the Edo period, even if one assumes that they successfully mandated compassionate behavior while they were in effect. The continuation of whaling practices during and after the introduction of the Laws of Compassion is thus not particularly surprising. But given the large number of memorials erected when they were in effect, they could have had some impact on people's understanding of whale deaths and how they should respond to them.

Tsunayoshi became known unflatteringly as "the Dog Shogun" because of the protections for dogs he included in the Laws of Compassion, but dogs were not the only animals protected by these laws.[32] The

Laws of Compassion also included prohibitions meant to protect hawks, horses, oxen, various food animals from birds to shellfish and fish, and humans needing care (particularly infants and the elderly). From this list, it would seem that whales, as food animals, ought to have been among the living things whose deaths should be prohibited. But there were exceptions for "essential" practices: Tsunayoshi recognized the abalone and sea cucumbers in the shogun's kitchens as necessary for entertaining the court, and the targets for mountain hunters and other major fisheries like whaling as necessary for these professional livelihoods.

These specific exceptions to the targets of the Laws of Compassion indicate a focus on the regulation of social roles within shogunate-controlled territory, rather than on spreading moral behavior to everyone in Japan. If Tsunayoshi had intended for the Laws of Compassion to focus on improving the behavior of all people, then he would not have included exceptions for hunters or fishermen whose work revolved around killing. The cessation of hawking mandated by these laws did remove work from falconers when they were made to release their tamed hawks back into the wild, so why not other animal-based professions? The laws forbidding fishing applied only to townsfolk fishing in one of the many rivers in Edo, making an exception for professional fishermen. Likewise, while the laws made it illegal for farmers to hunt or kill wild animals, professional hunters could still get licenses to carry guns and kill animals.[33] The difference between the newly unemployed falconers and the professional hunters or fishermen who could still make a living under the Laws of Compassion may have simply been a lack of alternative employment. The shogunate reemployed their falconers as keepers of the dog pounds built in Edo to provide for the dogs people were no longer allowed to kill. The change in allowable hawking practices thus helped reduce personnel and maintenance costs for the shogunate, although it may also have arisen from a personal distaste for hawking. However much Tsunayoshi did not wish to continue the practice of falconry, he did still continue to participate in hawking for the emperor until 1706.[34] Such political considerations show that the process of imposing a desire for a certain moral outlook on the populace was not a simple or straightforward one.

If the Laws of Compassion did not apply to professional fishermen such as whalers, the introduction of compassion into human behavior toward dead whales may have come more from the recognition of whales' capability for compassion themselves. It was well-known that adult whales (especially mothers) would protect calves, to the extent that they would remain near an entangled calf trying to free it rather than fleeing, even when it meant whalers could capture them too. Perhaps this direct expression of compassion toward the very young helped people to see whales as more humanlike and led to human-style memorials. If one of the virtues of proper Buddhists is compassion, then whales showed with their compassionate behavior that they too were virtuous and close to humans on the hierarchy of beings. Even though the brief era of government-mandated compassion under Tsunayoshi did not extend to prioritizing whales' lives over the need for whalers to make a living, whalers' exemption from the Laws of Compassion did not prevent the idea of compassion from being an important part of religious conceptions of how people should think about whales—particularly the fetal whales that whalers were not intentionally targeting.

PLACATING ANGRY SPIRITS: WHALE DREAMS AND PRAYERS

One spiritual but not necessarily Buddhist perspective on whales, in stories of whales appearing in dreams, offers further evidence for motivations behind memorials and other prayers for whale spirits. These stories also show some of the variation in attitudes toward whales in different areas of Japan, particularly between whaling and nonwhaling villages. In central Honshu on the Japan Sea coast, the locals referred to whales as "lords of the open sea" (*oki no tonosama*) and held them in awe or dread, with some people praying to escape from harm when they saw whales. In contrast, people living in areas where whales tended to strand on the beach and thus bring in a windfall of food often thought of whales as an incarnation of Ebisu, the god of fishing, and honored them.[35] We should not lose sight of the fact that whaling brought whales and ideas about whales to people unevenly throughout Japan, and that this unevenness likely led to complex motivations for people's memorialization of whales.

The moral of dreams with whales in them depended on whether or not the warning in the dream was heeded. Stories about whale dreams usually include a whale appearing to tell the dreamer not to kill them. These dreams could come to members of the whaling group, or to others unaffiliated with the group such as local priests. Whoever had the dream, if their warning was ignored and someone killed a whale after hearing about the dream, the dead whale could curse the village. Usually a mother whale with her offspring or a pregnant whale was the one who appeared in someone's dream, so whalers who avoided killing female whales after such a dream would be more likely to avoid the curse. However, it is very difficult to sex a whale from a quick glimpse of their upper back as they breathe, so whalers would only discover what they had captured (male or female, pregnant or not) after hauling the dead whale ashore for processing. To further complicate the interpretation of these warnings, dream-whales did not always warn people entirely away from killing: one example from Kayoi tells how a wealthy member of the whaling group's management dreamt of a whale during a period when they had not been able to catch any. While the mother bringing along her calf in the dream begged for forbearance as they swam through the open sea near Kayoi, in return for safety on the first pass, she promised to swim into their nets on her way back, presumably after her calf had grown enough to be left on its own.[36] The moral of stories about whales appearing in dreams was thus not simply that killing whales inevitably made them into vengeful spirits. Instead, they show a justification for adjusting the timing of hunts and for stopping to think about when it was appropriate to kill a whale.

Legends about dream-commands to not capture whales often frame the whale's movement as a pilgrimage (to Ise Shrine, for example, the center of emperor worship in Japan and a major pilgrimage destination in the Tokugawa period). Perhaps because whales have regular migration routes along both the Japan Sea and Pacific coasts of Japan, dream stories justify the prohibition on taking the whale as it passed by the first time by saying that people must allow the whale to complete a pilgrimage before killing it.[37] One example of a dream-legend with this rationale has the mother whale explain that she had a difficult delivery and was going to visit a nearby temple, and thus she asked to be captured on her way back rather than before she completed her pilgrimage.[38] Local historian Yamamoto Tōru explains that Ōjiro Shrine, which is currently located up a mountain in Mie Prefecture (within the Kumano coast whaling area, map 3), was moved from its original location on the beach after angry whales sent a fierce storm that caused it to float away. These two whales (he describes them as "married," so presumably they were thought of as a male and female) were headed for Ise Shrine on pilgrimage, and told the priest at the shrine that they wished to pass safely. The local fishermen failed to listen to the priest and chased the whales, who were injured but escaped. After the retaliatory storm, the villagers rebuilt their shrine out of the angry whales' reach up on the mountain.[39]

Such legends generally claim that an accidental death or similar sort of misfortune fell upon the families that ignored warnings or promises made to whale spirits in dreams. Sometimes the anger of unheeded whales would manifest directly, as whales that overturned or destroyed whalers' boats.[40] The storm that washed away Ōjiro Shrine is a slightly more indirect version of a whale attack. At other times the curse would appear as a disease in the village or a famine. The disaster might be mitigated by placating the whale's anger through memorial services (kuyō).[41] This is the reason given for construction of the monument at Jōrinji, a temple near the Ōjiro shrine. A spirit appeared to the head priest of Jōrinji in 1758 and told him that "a large whale with a child inside its belly is passing through the open sea, but until she safely gives birth to a child I wish you to remain quiet."[42] Another version of this story says that the beautiful woman who appeared to the priest in the dream said she was inside a pregnant whale and that was why they should hold their hunt after the whale had delivered, promising the whalers that they could catch the whale upon its return without her inside.[43] Unfortunately, although the priest rushed down to the beach, the whalers had already killed the pregnant whale from his dream. That same day there was no catch in the village and a sickness appeared that they thought was a manifestation of the whale's curse; in Nakamura's account, the curse also included a haunted house. So in order to pacify the angry whale spirit, villagers constructed a memorial tower over the whale's bones, along with creating a mortuary tablet that still remains in the temple, where memorial services continue to be performed on the whale's death anniversary. Further monuments appear to have been erected there for pregnant whales captured in the following two hundred years as well.[44]

This need to placate angry spirits of the dead is of course not limited to whales, or to the aborted or stillborn human fetuses discussed earlier. At the end of a successful hunt, hunters performed two ceremonies, one with the idea of honoring the animals that gave their lives to benefit the hunters (or at least the *kami* that helped bring the animals to them), and another meant to placate the dead who might be angry with the hunters.[45] Traces of such practices are visible in the inscription on the Kayoi whale grave, where, after invoking the name of Buddha, there is a prayer from the *Suwa engi no koto* (Story of the origin of the Suwa deity). The Kayoi grave's prayer expresses the desire for the buried spirit to become a Buddha in the same way that humans can.[46] However, despite the invocation of Buddha, the form of this prayer originates from the Shinto tradition honoring Suwa Myōjin, the god who protected hunters. The *Story of the origin of the Suwa deity* "proposes to transform a sinful practice into an act of spiritual realization" by saying that this god accepts animal sacrifices in order to enable those animals to achieve spiritual salvation, something which they as non-humans could not achieve otherwise.[47] The assimilation of Shinto practice into Buddhist form through this kind of prayer shows one way in which whaling could be justified, even in traditions that condemned killing, by finding practices within existing religious belief that mitigated the impact of the death of whales in the hunt.

The inclusion of a prayer from a hunters' tradition on the Kayoi grave marker shows how little distance there was between people living in this whaling village and the whales that passed by their shores. Both hunters in the mountains and whalers living on the shore felt the need to placate the potentially angry spirits of the animals they killed, at least in part because they were living in spaces occupied by those animals. Or rather, they saw the animals as occupying the same spaces as humans, with whales going on pilgrimages just like people. Stories about whale spirits do not contain any sense that simply being on land would keep humans safe or apart from creatures of the sea. If whales could appear in one's dreams, then they could also exact revenge on people who did not comply with their requests. None of the stories about warning dreams suggest that there was somewhere people could go to get far enough away from whales to avoid their anger. In other words, the coastal marine environment was part of the space in which coastal villagers lived in the Tokugawa period. Inhabitants of the water could live or at least appear in the spaces humans inhabited, acting just like people on their pilgrimages and search for safe childbirth—in spiritual form if not in material form. Therefore, histories of this period must consider the marine environment as part of the everyday human world even though no one built homes out on the water. Responses to whale death show that their open-water spaces had an impact on humans' more terrestrial lives.

WHALE DEATHS IN NONWHALING AREAS

Even in areas without active, organized whaling, people felt the need to mark the deaths of whales as something special. The shores of modern-day Ehime and Oita prefectures are a good place to consider the reactions of nonwhaling people to whale death. These coasts bracketing the Bungo Strait were not along the regular migration routes of whales (maps 1 and 2). However, as whaling efforts intensified along other areas of the coast, the whales that entered this strait tended to be injured and dying individuals that had been hit by whalers elsewhere (in Tosa Bay or even as far off as the Kumano area) before veering off their regular migration route. They may have been easy prey for an opportunistic fishing expedition, or might simply strand on the shore and die there without human interference. While there is no record of organized whaling groups in Ehime or Oita, people there had enough exposure to whales to give them death register entries, talk about their appearances in dreams, and build whale graves or memorials.

One temple in Usuki, on the Kyushu side of the Bungo Strait (Oita Prefecture), records in its death register a mass for the dead with a service for the benefit of the suffering spirits of stranded whales that died in the inlet in 1870.[48] A whale grave erected in 1809 in Mitsukue, on the Shikoku side of the Bungo Strait (modern Ehime Prefecture) memorializes a whale that followed a large school of sardines into Mitsukue Bay and became trapped there, unable to exit, even with the help of local fishermen. When their attempt at assistance failed, they decided to kill it and erect a memorial in its honor.[49] These kinds of whale graves and *kuyō* towers show a concern for the whales' spirits that could not have arisen from an organized practice of killing whales, because there were no whaling groups in either of these areas. The unusual appearance of such whales likely increased the desire of local people to mark the occasion somehow, as with the notation on the Mitsukue grave of a "strange/mysterious whale."[50] Such monuments tend to be for individual whales rather than a collection of whales killed over time as with the fetal grave in Kayoi. Even if the majority of whale graves and memorials are found in whaling areas, these people of villages without whaling groups or any tradition of organized whale hunting also saw the merit in respectful burial or memorials for dead whales.[51]

While they shared some commemorative practices with whaling villages, one of the essential differences in attitude between professional whaling areas and these areas of more opportunistic hunting appears in their versions of the stories about whale spirits in dreams. In whaling areas, the person who had the dream usually cannot stop others from killing the whale, while in Ehime the dreamer successfully stops the kill. The moral of nonwhalers' dream stories is not one of placating the angry whales who were killed despite appearing in dreams; instead, they show that prosperity can come from listening to the whale and keeping the promise not to hunt them until the agreed-upon time. In places where whaling was not a major livelihood, people only killed whales that seemed to offer themselves for sacrifice by becoming trapped in an inlet or otherwise appearing in unusual circumstances. The message of holding back may well have been easier to accept in these places than it was where residents depended on a steady catch of whales. There is thus a difference in the kind of gratitude implied by the construction of a memorial for whales killed by a whaling group, and the gratitude shown by constructing a memorial for a whale found already dying from injuries sustained elsewhere.[52]

In nonwhaling areas, many of the whale graves seem to mark the place where a whale stranded, for example in the scattering of sites off the Ehime coast, some of them on uninhabited islands. People who did not plan to continue to bring back more whales that needed memorializing simply set up one for each individual and extraordinary whale death. In whaling areas, in contrast, there are at least three graves for multiple whales: in Kayoi, Yamaguchi Prefecture, in Mie Prefecture, and in Yobuko, Saga Prefecture.[53] However, this does not mean that opportunistic stranding and single-whale graves/memorials were restricted to nonwhaling areas. Some of the memorials in Mie Prefecture along the Kumano coast were also erected for specific stranded whales rather than as monuments for a whaling group.[54] Rather than placating an angry spirit, such individual monuments in nonwhaling areas are far more likely to celebrate the benefits gifted to the village by the injured or stranded whale they found. Thus, their stories of whale dreams show that adhering to a whale promise brings a reward, in place of the curses brought to those who broke their promise in the stories from Kayoi and Kumano. A whale that was already dying, or at least far weaker than usual, would be the only target tempting enough for people unpracticed in whaling. Even then, they would probably only pursue such whales in extraordinary circumstances, where the meat or money would be particularly useful. This is certainly the motivation behind, for example, the 1892 memorial at Mankichiji in Ehime Prefecture, commemorating a whale injured by killer whales and found on or near the beach. Villagers took the body and sold it, and with the proceeds bought back the land that they had been forced to sell off in more desperate times, leading them to erect a memorial to thank the whale for this bounty.[55]

BEYOND WHALE GRAVES: WHALERS' SPIRITUALITY

The construction of whale graves and memorials was sometimes driven by people not directly participating in whaling, such as the local priest Sanyo Shōin in Kayoi, but whalers themselves also had particular religious responses to whales' deaths. Some of their rituals fit into the same sort of practice as hunters' expressions of thanks for their prey having given up its life, and are thus not unique to whaling. Donations of *ema* (votive pictures) or other indications of thanks given to a local shrine for the prosperity brought to a village by whales, especially in places where whaling was an organized practice rather than an opportunistic one, were a regular seasonal practice. This is equivalent to the practices for other forms of fishing or farming, which had a tendency to vary in their bounty from season to season or year to year. Tokugawa period sources describing whaling also sometimes mention the harpooners' dance (*hazashi odori*), a yearly practice that is the root of some of the whaling dances still performed today in places like the town of Taiji. The section on this dance in one whaling scroll explains that it was customarily the first dance in the first month of the year, in a parade beginning in front of the shrine and ending at the processing sheds. The gongs used as part of the accompaniment of the dance "have the meaning of a whale *kuyō*" or, in other words, were used because they were meant to memorialize the whale spirits taken by the dancing harpooners.[56] Consciousness of whale spirits also seems to have been present in the hunt itself, as in some places there was a ceremonial sake cup passed around above the whale carcass as it was being towed between two boats on the way to the beach.[57]

Two old histories of whaling not written by whalers themselves but written by people in close contact with whalers in Hizen (in Kyushu, map 2) provide further insights into the beliefs of whalers. The first, *Saikai geigeiki* (Chronicle of Western Ocean whales), is the oldest remaining whaling history, from 1720. In this text's description of the hunt, the author explains that before the whale died, as its last breath gurgled in its throat, the crew and the harpooner would in one voice chant the *nembutsu* (Namu Amida Butsu) three times.[58] This chant for Pure Land Buddhists was supposed to bring rebirth for one's soul in the Pure Land and out of the cycle of suffering. Practices such as these provide a glimpse into the pervasiveness of the religious responses to whale death; it was not just the duty of the local priest to care for the spirits of whales killed by whalers, but rather something that the harpooners and other crew directly involved in the hunt paid at least ritual attention to.

The description in "Ogawajima geigei kassen" (Ogawajima whale battles), written in 1847 about the so-called whale battles in northern Kyushu's Ogawajima, confirms that this Buddhist-inspired relation to whales continued through the following century.[59] While the description in *Chronicle of Western Ocean whales* is in the form of a relatively matter-of-fact history, the later Ogawajima story has a much more dramatic frame. The battles in the title were not conflicts between human whaling groups, but rather references to the ways in which the practice of whaling centered on one of the last remaining warlike endeavors in the peaceful Tokugawa period. This is clear from the beginning of the text, where the author explains: "In this world of universal peace, where bows are left in their cases, and swords are closed in their boxes, there are none who have seen war, and the condition of battlefields has unfortunately become old stories. In this kind of world, I would like to show in detail before your eyes the conditions of the battle to catch whales."[60]

The description of the whale's death is where the spirituality of whalers specifically comes to the fore. The warlike process of hunting whales included a prayer said before going out to battle, and other non-whaling-specific prayers sung to bring success in the hunt. But then, the author explains the strong ties between the mother whale and her young, and brings up the idea not just of the whale's affection for her young (using the same word for human children, *ko*) but also the corresponding compassion that should be felt by the harpooners as they remorsefully kill such impressively affectionate and caring creatures. This leads naturally to the question of how moral people feeling Buddhist compassion could reasonably make a livelihood based on the suffering and death of whales. The answer given to that dilemma, which may or may not be what the whalers themselves provided to the author of the text, is that "even for humans there is life and death, the ten thousand things [i.e., everything] are all thus."[61] Therefore, death was simply unavoidable. Given the inevitability of death, and also the many whaling groups operating from the Kumano coast to the Saikai area of Kyushu, "if one is not able to take [whales] in this place, they will be killed in another."[62] Whaling was like any other use of once-living creatures for human benefit, where the happiness and aid that the whale's body could give to many hundreds or thousands of people outweighed the misfortune and suffering of one whale. Such a practical cost-benefit analysis does not preclude an acknowledgement of the whale's side of things, because at the end of every whaling season the monks at Ryūshōzenji in the village of Yobuko (on the mainland near Ogawajima) conducted memorial *kuyō* for the whales caught that year, recording their death days and posthumous names and sending offerings out to sea to show the people's thanks for the benefits that the death of the whales provided to them. The harpooners, as the people most directly related to the death of the whale, chanted the *nembutsu* in hopes that the whale would become a Buddha, and brought the spirits of the whales into the regular spiritual practices surrounding death for the people of the area.

Buddhism was most often used to deal with death, but other religious practices also included an acknowledgement of whale deaths.[63] In the context of a society with many local festivals based on experiences in everyday lives, there were of course also festivals that included whales in areas with whaling groups. Some of these festival practices linger even today, long after the villages in question have ceased whaling. For example, a whale float spouts water during the Kunchi Festival's parade in Nagasaki, and a reconstruction of a whale hunt using parade-floats appears in Yokkaichi, which is in the upper end of Ise Bay. While only a few such examples remain today, this does not mean that festivals relating to whaling were rare during the early modern period. The fact that the remaining practices are not all the same suggests how closely tied to individual locations earlier ones may have been. Similarities between forms of whale grave or *kuyō* or shrine practices are on a broad scale, indicating common forms of Buddhist or other religious philosophies, but the differences in specific festival practices show how these ideas were interpreted through local lenses of experience and lifestyle. This is clearer in the case of Shinto practices, because the Buddhist influences on whalers were more standardized philosophical ideas. Thus, it is important to remember that any given evidence of a specific religious practice such as whale graves or the festival floats in the Nagasaki Kunchi Festival does not stand in for a common practice throughout all whaling areas, even while the distribution of these practices indicates that there generally was some kind of religious component to the interactions between whalers and whales throughout Japan.

In the case of shrine donations and ceremonies, the emphasis was on having the local *kami* bring good fortune to the hunt. Such rituals did not focus on an awareness of bringing death to individual whales so much as on an awareness of how to gain the benevolent attention of a *kami* that would be willing to provide whales as resources to whalers during the hunt. While acknowledging the importance of whale deaths, without which the whalers could not make a living, these practices were intended to celebrate the hoped-for success of the next whaling season.

For example, at the Asuka Shrine in Taiji, Wakayama Prefecture, on the thirteenth day of January, whalers participated in an archery cere-mony (*oyumi no shinji*) where an arrow was fired at a target with three carved wooden whales attached. *Oyumi no shinji* in general are ceremo-nies performed at a shrine in order to predict, using the number of arrows that hit the target, the weather and success of the harvest in the coming year. The whale-shaped pieces added to the target in Taiji are said to help bring in a good catch for the following year of whaling.[64] There are also some *ema* and other donations to local shrines still in existence, which show the image of a hunt whose success they com-memorate or hope for. This is a different expression of respect for whales and what they might bring to local fishing villages than that shown by Buddhist whale graves, focusing on the ways in which whales were much like any other natural resource rather than on their close spiritual relationship to humans.

CONCLUSION: THE SPIRITUAL PLACE
OF WHALES, HUMANS, AND OTHERS

Supporters of the idea of the modern importance of Japan's whaling culture often interpret expressions of thanks to whales who have given up their lives for the benefit of humans as an indication of the Japanese people's strong ties to the natural world and respect for its inhabitants. Despite repeated counterarguments, both Japanese and foreigners often assume, based on the Shinto tradition of investing the natural world with divine spirits and Japan's long aesthetic tradition that makes heavy use of natural elements, that Japan's culture is particularly close to nature.[65] In this framework, the tendency of Tokugawa period Japanese to treat whales in very human ways looks like another piece of evidence for respect for nature and better ecological understanding than is usu-ally found in Western cultures. However, I argue that the similarities between humans and early modern Japanese descriptions of whales are evidence of a desire to remake nature on human terms. By framing whales as human-like beings that went on pilgrimages, felt concern for their young, and deserved posthumous Buddhist names, people in Tokugawa Japan were not necessarily showing a strong respect for liv-ing in harmony with nature. While whale graves do show a particular consciousness of the spiritual connection between humans and whales, this connection made whales more like humans rather than giving humans any kind of special insight into a nature distinct from human experience.

Even if based in the complex combination of Shinto animism and Buddhist philosophies of the interconnectedness of all living things in the Tokugawa period, a spiritual understanding of the natural world in Japan does not preclude manipulation or exploitation of that world for human ends. Religious rituals can be just as much tools for manipulating the natural world as the physical tools that harvest resources and reshape landscapes. Memorial towers or other forms of *kuyō* did not necessarily show signs of respect for other living beings, or at least not respect strong enough to stop people from harvesting whales. Whalers could sponsor such rites in order to placate angry whale spirits, so the whalers could go on to kill more of their brethren, or in order to assuage whalers' guilt and bad karma accrued from killing so that they need not worry about killing again in the future. The modern trend in animal memorials in Japan shows how increasing commercialization and use of animals as commodities has led to "animal memorial rituals that acknowledge their status as sentient beings but turn them into willing martyrs."[66] In other words, even if some people sincerely desired for whales to become Buddhas and be saved from the world of suffering, such spiritual understandings of the place of whales in the human world were not merely insufficient to stop whalers from killing whales. Instead, they could have been more likely to validate and facilitate whaling as a commercial enterprise.

Because of the essentially commercial nature of early modern whaling, one also must be cautious about how much sincerity of feeling might have been behind sponsorship of *kuyō*. For example, one recent survey of Japanese elementary and middle school students focused on a moral tale that was supposed to educate them in the need for reverence and thankfulness for the plants and animals that gave their lives to become food. The survey found that over 70 percent of the students always spoke the word that serves the same function as saying grace in Christian culture (*itadakimasu*) before eating, but 60 percent of students had barely thought about the meaning at all, simply speaking it by rote.[67] Thus, the presence of practices expressing thanks for the bounty of nature does not guarantee that the practitioners feel thankfulness. Like the children offering "thanks" for their food, people might instead perform a ritual because they have been taught that it is appropriate to do so at that particular moment, not because they attach any particular emotional resonance to the action. Whalers might have felt it was important to be seen by human society giving thanks for their bounty, perhaps because that would increase their status in the community, but that kind of ritual thanksgiving for the sacrifice made by a whale would look the same as a memorial service intended to sincerely thank the whale's spirit.

With very few sources remaining from the Tokugawa period that provide any information about people's feelings toward rituals associated with whale deaths, some of the interpretation of early modern rituals comes from the few ongoing yearly memorial services that have been performed continuously for over a hundred years, particularly because those ongoing rituals have helped preserve some of the evidence. Kayoi's death register only has one original volume left, and the two others that remain are copies that likely would not have been made if priests were not still performing yearly rites for the whales in the register. It is tempting to assume that today's explanations about whale deaths have continued in an unbroken line, but even with the best intentions information is often imperfectly passed down from generation to generation. Ideas attached to ongoing rituals are thus likely to have changed with cultural shifts and different priorities over decades and centuries. Outside of Ogawajima, where we have much less detailed information about memorials, it is much harder to strip away present-day perspectives to determine what people at the time thought their memorials signified.

Today, the prowhaling faction in Japan presents whale memorialization as evidence for a special place for whales in Japanese culture, making whaling more than just simply a commercial industry, even though modern whaling companies were among the sponsors of such memorials.[68] During the period when commercial whaling was still legal in the mid-twentieth century, some whalers did continue to sponsor memorials for whale spirits. For example, a Tōyō Whaling Company captain who had also been a harpoon gunner erected a memorial in 1957 (when he was eighty-three years old) out of shame for the over two thousand whales he killed from 1907 onward—a reasoning which highlights the desire to expiate his karmic debt rather than concern for whales specifically.[69] Since the 1986 moratorium on commercial whaling, the relationship between corporations and whaling has once again shifted, so even these more modern practices are not necessarily a reflection of the place of whales in Japanese culture of either the Tokugawa period or the twenty-first century. It is worth noting that the author of *Ogawajima geigei kassen* was already acknowledging in the mid-nineteenth century that, even though people should pity the whales being killed, "a dead whale is worth a huge amount of money."[70] The balance between regret over death and desire for profit has always been a part of memorializing whale death in Japan, but the discourse around that balance is necessarily different in such divergent temporal and cultural contexts.

The struggle to preserve a distinctive culture for towns and areas that are facing population loss, as is the case today in villages such as Taiji, Kayoi, Arikawa, and Ikitsukishima, which were all formerly centers of whaling, can sometimes lead residents to overstate the historical continuity of cultural practices, including religious ritual or memorials. One description of the whale-jaw shrine gateway (*torii*) in the village of Taiji says that it was "reconstructed" in the modern era based on there being a mention of such a gate in a satire written by famous Tokugawa-period writer Ihara Saikaku in his *The Japanese Family Storehouse* (Nippon eitaigura).[71] There is, however, no other evidence that the shrine had such a gate in the past, and this detail may well have been something that Saikaku added to his story to show the exaggerated wealth and ostentatious behavior of the character who earned much of his money from whaling.[72] So it may be more apt to say that it was first constructed in the modern era rather than reconstructed. Thus, current explanations of attitudes toward memorials should be carefully compared with the earlier context in which they were created to make sure that the ongoing nature of the tradition does not obscure changes in the underlying rationale since their inception. Whatever the motivations behind memorial practices, the continuation of whale *kuyō* year after year in just the same fashion as ones performed for the human dead does show a strong consciousness of the presence of whales not just in the physical world, but also in the spiritual world.

While a perceived similarity to humans did not save whales from being killed, dismembered, and having their parts sold for a profit, religious practices were an important part of ameliorating the damage of those whales' deaths. Buddhism provided a framework for understanding spirits on a continuum (for most lay people in the Tokugawa period, a hierarchical one with humans beneath only divine beings). Shintō added to this a way of interpreting the sense of awe people felt when confronted with particular aspects of the natural world. That feeling indicated one was in the presence of *kami*, for example in one of the gigantic trees marked out as sacred space in shrines across the country. Whales were by far the largest animal that anyone in Japan could encounter, so someone facing the immense body of a hunted whale likely felt the same sense of divinity that was interpreted as *kami* in vast mountains or towering trees or other natural features that fill viewers with a sense of awe. As Tokugawa-period scholar Motoori Norinaga explained, *kami* were the deities that appeared in origin stories, the founders of the Japanese imperial line, but were also "anything whatsoever which was outside the ordinary, which possessed superior power, or which was awe-inspiring."[73] Therefore, the emotional reaction of someone in the presence of a huge whale helped to mark whales as closer to the divine. Such beliefs, combined with signs of human-like behavior such as compassion for their young, could have led to an interpretation of whales' place in a Buddhist- and Shinto-influenced spiritual realm as higher up the karmic hierarchy than other animals. Thus, while death rituals did serve to justify the exploitation of whales as commodities, their underlying philosophies may also have created a sense that whales existed somewhere in the liminal space between humans and the divine, as well as between humans and animals.

Whales also existed, or rather died, in a liminal space on the shore, tying together the maritime and terrestrial realms. Whatever the reasons behind the desire to treat them as quite similar to human spirits, people memorialized whales to a much greater extent and beginning earlier in history than the domestic animals they lived in closer physical proximity to. Therefore, our interpretation of the importance of the marine environment must include its metaphysical spaces, and how humans tried to make sense of them as part of their world. In Tokugawa

Japan, spiritual understandings of nature may not have made humans more likely to live in balanced harmony with the natural world, but a closer look at the specific example of whale spirits shows that people brought whale spirits into very similar if not the same spaces as human spirits. If whales existed within human metaphysical space, then the spiritual boundaries of early modern Japan, like the physical boundaries, did not stop at the shore.

CONCLUSION

Japan and Its Maritime Space

EVEN THOUGH TRAVEL OUT TO SEA WAS CONSTRAINED BY TOKUGAWA government policy, whales and other migratory animals linked people to a wider Pacific they did not directly visit. The Japanese people may have been focused on coastal waters for transportation and natural resources, but human boundaries meant little or nothing to the inhabitants of those waters. Furthermore, shogunal control of coastal waters also did not apply to non-Japanese people, and foreign incursions increasingly drew Tokugawa Japan into the Pacific World in the nineteenth century. The particular role of whales in Japan changed along with the shifting dynamics of the Japanese interactions with maritime space in the modern era. The details of Tokugawa whaling groups and the place of whales in early modern Japan discussed in this book are thus relevant in two different areas: in relation to contemporary Japanese whaling, and in relation to marine environmental history of both Japan and the Pacific more broadly. First, I will discuss how the industry changed with the modernization of Japan and what that means for contemporary references to Japan's whaling tradition. Then I will turn to the insights that tracing the path of whales from sea to shore in Japan can bring to our historical understanding of Japan, in particular how they have dealt with natural resources and the question of sustainability. In both cases, it is clear that Japan was deeply entangled with the Pacific even during the Tokugawa "closed-country" era, with both the natural resources of the Pacific Ocean and with the other peoples who chased those same organisms for their own benefit.

BEYOND THE EARLY MODERN ARCHIPELAGO

The expansion of British and then American whaling in the Pacific in the nineteenth century were integral to imperial expansion and the push to open Asian ports to trade with European and American markets. The steady encroachment of foreign ships on the waters that were part of the archipelago, starting with Russians in 1792 in the north and quickly including British, French, and American ships as the nineteenth century progressed, made it increasingly difficult for the Tokugawa shogunate to enforce an open-ocean boundary for Japan. Japanese whaling groups of the period, constrained by the need to tow the whale carcasses back to a beach for processing, were not able to push further out into the Pacific. But foreign whalers, who processed their whales aboard large sailing vessels, made up a large portion of the new ships sailing ever closer to Japan as they headed for less-exploited whaling grounds between Hawaii and Japan, including in and around the Okhotsk Sea.

Rethinking the history of this period within a marine environmental framework that highlights ties to oceanic space thus brings Japan back into the political side of Pacific history.[1] As American whalers decimated Pacific whale populations in the mid-nineteenth century, Japanese coastal whalers depending on those populations (although catching them in different areas) had to adapt as well. Their connection with the rest of the Pacific became more explicit as foreign whalers and other foreign ships appeared off of Japan, but it was not completely divorced from earlier changes that whaling groups made in techniques and equipment following the smaller-scale impact of harpoon groups on the availability of migratory right whales. The adaptation that whaling groups had to make before foreign powers began harvesting migratory Pacific whale populations was less dramatic, but the shift from harpoon groups to net whaling groups was just as much a response to changing whale availability as the transition to foreign, modern whaling techniques was. The latter transition, since it had to deal with a much greater decline in whale numbers, and also a dramatic shift within Japanese society with the Meiji Restoration of 1868 and the modernization projects that followed, involved a greater break with the past than the harpoon to net whaling transition demanded, as Japanese coastal whaling groups collapsed and new pelagic whaling companies formed to chase whales much farther from the shores of the archipelago.

Whaling groups did not start trying to change their techniques and technology to more closely match foreign, open-ocean whalers until the collapse of whale populations started to become apparent in the 1850s, and the complete transition to pelagic whaling took until the turn of the century. However, the importance of whalers' harvest of marine resources in the many ways discussed in this book made them harbingers of the political changes in the Pacific even before the mid-nineteenth-century whale population collapse. As more foreign ships appeared in the waters nearer and nearer Japan, many of them whalers, the shogunate had to grapple with their ability to set boundaries and claim control over access to the resources in coastal waters even as these incursions highlighted the impossibility of maintaining control over the fluidity of that space. Japanese whalers were some of the first to feel the effects of competition with whalers from other nations, but competition over access to fisheries became an increasingly important part of modern Japanese government policy and international politics.[2] They, along with other fishermen, also were on the front lines of foreign incursions, given the coastal boundaries of most of early modern Japan.[3]

Even before the earliest encroachment of foreign ships, officials concerned with defense recognized whalers as a good potential source of naval power and expertise relevant to fighting something other than whales on the ocean. Tokugawa Yoshimune used his experience as former lord of the Kii domain to defend Edo (Tokyo) Bay when he was shogun (1716–45) with ships based on the design of Taiji whaleboats.[4] Then, when Russian imperial expansion began in and around Ezo (now Hokkaido), Japanese whalers were part of the attempt to control this territory for Japanese interests instead. Two harpooners from Hirado were sent in 1800 to survey Ezo and try to find a site for a whaling group. After a twenty-five-day survey, they gave up on the idea, because they saw no right whales, only the less-profitable humpback whales, and they did not find a good site to set the deep nets used in the coastal whaling technique they were most familiar with. In their report, they estimated that it would cost the government around twenty thousand ryō to establish a whaling group in such an inconvenient site, so the plan was never implemented.[5] It was not until the first attempts to shift away from coastal whaling to the style of open-ocean whaling practiced by American whalers in the 1860s that the northern waters around Ezo again became a possibility for Japanese whaling.[6]

Because whales themselves migrated throughout the Pacific and came in contact with people from many different countries looking to exploit marine resources, Japan was drawn into global imperial competition for resources even before Japan's political ambitions took the form of imperial ambitions. People who wanted access to whales after the mid-nineteenth century crash had to consider larger boundaries for Japanese territory (or at least for Japanese whaling territory) than just coastal waters. As whalers turned farther afield, the Meiji government promoted successful, maximally efficient fisheries in order to improve their global economic position and feed their growing population. But this promotion also served the government's desire to lay claim to the resources of newly adjacent territories, and whalers were an early part of that slow colonial expansion.[7] Because the new, open ocean environment and the deep-sea whales like sperm whales, fin whales, and blue whales that inhabited it were so different from the coastal waters and migratory populations of baleen whales that had been the focus of early modern Japanese whaling, modern Japanese whaling has a very different character to it than its predecessor—despite modern whaling supporters' emphasis on continuity. The shift to modern whaling required more than just reconstructing the whaling industry to match new techniques and equipment being used by other nations. More importantly, it required shifting the boundaries of Japan to encompass a whole new pelagic environment and the species within it.

This transformation of Japanese whaling techniques from coastal groups to pelagic ship-based processing occurred patchily, with a great deal of trial and error, from the 1860s through the early twentieth century.[8] But eventually, new Japanese whaling companies arose, using the same engine-driven ships out in the open ocean, with bow-mounted harpoon guns, that other whaling nations like Norway and Britain were using. The modernization of whaling brought Japanese techniques and targets in line with other global whaling efforts, all of which were generally conducted far from the home ports of the whaling ships in part because closer populations had been fished out already. The Meiji period (1868–1912) saw a parallel expansion of Japanese territory out beyond the bounds of the Tokugawa archipelago, and a massive cultural and social transformation within those boundaries. The Tokugawa shogunate cemented territorial claims in Ezo in the 1850s as a buffer against Russian claims. By 1872, the southern Ryūkyū islands had been annexed, becoming the Okinawa Prefecture seven years later. Imperial claims to territory continued to radiate outward from the central Japanese islands to nearby areas. This led first to the acquisition of Taiwan and a concession on China's Liaodong Peninsula after the Sino-Japanese war over Korea (1894–95), then to another war between Japan and Russia over Korea and areas of Manchuria (1904–5). Although the first two expansions of territory resulted in prefectures that did not include areas of successful whaling, the later acquisitions did include offshore whaling areas exploited from factory ships, some acquired directly from Russia after the Russo-Japanese War.

One important result of this modernization was the fact that whalers were no longer bringing whales ashore quite as literally as they had in the era of coastal whaling groups. While modern whalers brought back and sold whale products in Japanese markets, the processing happened at first on new shores far from earlier whaling communities (both in the north of Japan and as far as Korea) or after 1920 on board a factory ship, separate from the rest of Japanese society.[9] The lives of early modern Japanese took place in a space that melded marine and terrestrial aspects, but this space shifted into a new configuration in the modern era, and the cultural place of whaling likewise changed. In the process, the close and complex ties that the people of Tokugawa Japan had to the ocean were forgotten.

The disjuncture between the premodern past and the modern present was particularly strong in Japan, where the late nineteenth-century Meiji industrialization and modernization project worked hard to cut away memories of aspects of Japanese culture that might hold the country back from political and cultural parity within the global modern. This deliberate forgetfulness paved the way for an ahistorical view of the past that rested on broad generalizations rather than specific detailed knowledge of earlier eras. It highlighted only the mainstream view, which ignored coastal occupations in favor of the impact of rice-based agriculture, or focused on urbanization, protoindustrialization, and other precursors to the modern. This same distancing process also helps explain why a rather nonspecific "traditional" Japanese whaling, rather than a detailed account of historical whaling and how it transformed into modern industrial whaling, is promoted by contemporary supporters of modern Japanese whaling.[10]

In a modern Japanese culture that seems to have forgotten most of their personal ties to the ocean environment, an argument for an unbroken cultural heritage of whaling operates on superficial assumptions of continuity, assumptions that regular school histories barely mentioning the ocean can do little to counteract. The lack of direct contact with coastal waters in favor of consumption of products of globally distant, industrial fisheries is another part of this changing relationship that removes the personal experiences of the early modern period into a modern urban forgetfulness about the physical realities and importance of the ocean. For example, the Japanese people currently consume the majority of the world's tuna harvest, but because that harvest happens so far from their everyday lives, it is too easy for people eating prime cuts of sushi to think about the ocean as a machine for producing fish rather than an ecosystem into which the Japanese archipelago is integrated. The more complex intersections of many relationships to ocean products discussed here have for the most part given way to a simplified supply chain that does not require multifaceted engagement with the ocean as a complete environment.

The impression of continuity in the whaling industry comes from glossing over the earlier complexity of Tokugawa whaling in order to frame it in terms that fit better into current practices. For example, some prowhaling histories will summarize the various stages of whaling technology's development from harpoon groups to net whaling groups, but this is presented as part of a steady trajectory of technological improvement moving toward factory-ship whaling out in the open ocean. Instead of considering near-shore Tokugawa whaling as a practice with distinctive ties to the society and culture of the period in the same way that open-ocean modern Japanese whaling is a practice with very different ties to modern society and culture, these accounts present a matter-of-fact progression of whaling equipment and techniques toward its current form.[11] The richness of the earlier practices vanishes in simple descriptions of whaling tools and their uses through time.

By downplaying the disruption and change brought by modernization, arguments for historical continuity have the additional effect of diminishing the past role of the ocean in Japanese society to the same relatively low level that it has today. While seafood is still quite important in the Japanese diet, the fishing industry operates much farther from shore and with a much smaller percentage of the Japanese population working with it than in the past. The urbanization and industrialization of Japan pulled many people away from working on and with the ocean and coastal spaces of the archipelago. One result of the modern diminished awareness of the marine environment in Japan is that whaling supporters can convince many people today that a whaling industry employing a few hundred people and supplying meat to a diminishing number of connoisseurs in Japan has reasonable continuity with Tokugawa whaling.

The ahistorical nature of current arguments for whaling elides some of the connections between whaling and particular historical contexts, especially in the explanations for why coastal whaling groups vanished in favor of modern pelagic whaling corporations. The problems and changes that whaling groups faced with the crash of Pacific whale populations cannot be divorced from the territorial expansion of imperial powers in the Pacific and the opening of Japan to trade.[12] In fact, this context helps explain some of the emotional force behind current arguments, even though they do not focus on the process of transition between "traditional" and modern whaling. The emotional tie to preservation of a Japanese cultural whaling tradition draws some of its strength from parallels with the unequal treaties forced upon Japan in the nineteenth century. Beginning with the Harris Treaty in 1858, the shogunate was forced under threat from Commodore Perry's gunships to sign agreements with the major Western powers opening Japan to trade and giving foreigners extraterritoriality. The campaign for revision of the humiliating treaties was a major influence in the politics of the modernization of Japan.[13] Such treaties were thought to prove that Japan was the focus of racist attempts to reshape their nation as a colony or tribute state rather than a major world power, and the rhetoric around contemporary whaling echoes this concern with a dismissal of the opposition as racist rather than logical.[14]

But the argument for continuity of whaling traditions also has power because, without detailed information readily available about the historical role of the ocean in Japan, there is little to counteract relatively shallow arguments about the tradition. The most direct modern descendants of earlier coastal whaling groups now operate with a different relationship between people and whales than existed historically, as after the numbers of whales plummeted beginning in the mid-nineteenth century, coastal whalers were forced to turn to species not hunted in the Tokugawa period. Even if modern coastal whalers still hunted right whales, gray whales, or humpback whales instead of dolphins and pilot whales, the cultural and social context of that whaling in postwar Japan would be vastly different, since the country has changed in so many ways. Pelagic whaling, adopted from other nations' practices, is even more divergent from earlier versions of Japanese whaling.

Of course, there are some continuities between Tokugawa and modern Japanese whaling, but for the most part they are exaggerated. Yes, some of the families who were involved in whaling groups moved to work for whaling corporations, but many others moved on to entirely different kinds of work. Yes, some of the memorial services for whale spirits continue to be held regularly, for example in Kayoi. However, these are carried out now as part of the village's identity as a historical whaling town, not as a place that still hunts whales. With whaling taking place far offshore, almost all of the local dimensions of interaction with dead whales have vanished. The blurring of ocean/land boundaries that was echoed by the blurring of human/whale boundaries in religious and scholarly conceptualizations of whales was a characteristic particular to the way that whaling was practiced in early modern Japan. Stories about whales appearing in dreams to direct the behavior of people living in places that whales migrated by have far less resonance in a Japan where corporations, and now the government-backed "scientific" replacement for those corporations, rather than village-based whaling groups, are the ones killing whales. The particular connections between local residents and the migratory patterns of whales that led to the religious understanding of the role of whale spirits in Japan can no longer exist without the regular contact of people and migrating whales.[15] Whales are no longer exceptional in being treated as human-like spirits after death, because they are not seen frequently enough for people to remark upon their behavior as part of their daily lives. The focus on honoring dead animals has shifted to center today on household pets, which were rarely honored with commemorative ceremonies in the Tokugawa period, and which people interact with far more often than they can with the diminished whale population today.[16]

Finally, while a strong connection between the marine environment and the terrestrial human one may also be found in other forms of pre-industrial and aboriginal whaling, Japan's case offers a unique perspective because even in the first stages of organized whaling, this was more than just a subsistence activity. The major draw for someone to want to start whaling in the Tokugawa period, the most common popular perception of the goal of whaling groups, was the potential for whalers to become rich.[17] Because the international moratorium instituted in 1986 is for commercial whaling, the focus today in Japan on traditional whaling, and on whaling-related culture such as the consumption of whale meat, is meant to emphasize noneconomic values in order to argue that their whaling is not commercial and therefore should not be banned. But it should not be forgotten that the coastal whaling they evoke with these calls to tradition was a big business in Tokugawa Japan—it was never just about subsistence.

Whether from a whale caught near shore by Tokugawa whalers or one targeted far away in Antarctic waters by modern whalers, the most profitable products sold to make money from whale resources came from the two major categories of oil and meat. Whale oil has been replaced by synthetic chemical pesticides in modern agriculture and by cheaper vegetable oils in cooking. Electricity has replaced oil lamps. Whale meat's availability also shifted with new preservation methods. However, the ability to keep unspoiled meat for longer periods did not produce a steady or clear continuity with earlier whaling groups or replace the profits lost when replacement products reduced the demand for whale oil.[18] Because whaling proponents present whale meat as an important part of Japan's cultural heritage, the discontinuity between the impact of early modern and modern whaling is actually most apparent in changes in whale meat consumption. The Tokugawa period had very local markets for fresh whale meat and only slightly less local markets for salted whale meat. It was not until the end of the nineteenth century and the early twentieth century that whale meat consumption began to spread to the rest of Japan.

Watanabe Hiroyuki explains how the needs of military supply and the marketing efforts of whaling corporations combined to make canned whale meat available and increasingly popular in the twentieth century. Its popularity had less to do with any particular attachment to the taste of whale and more to do with the fact that it was a very inexpensive meat available during the depression that followed World War I, particularly for use in military provisions in the 1930s and '40s.[19] One reason why it was so inexpensive was because, for Antarctic whaling, meat was a byproduct of the collection of whale oil sold to European buyers to earn foreign currency.[20] The American Occupation of Japan finalized the spread of Antarctic whale meat as a cheap protein source throughout the country, unlinking awareness of or contact with the source of the meat.[21] So much effort has been expended in proving the centrality of whale meat to Japanese food culture that the possible uses of other products are rarely noted today, in contrast to the wide diversity of whale products circulating in the Tokugawa period. The focus on the one remaining major product is less about whether it is commercially viable and more about its role in modern Japanese culture. Whaling is not commercially viable in Japan's current conditions. The Institute for Cetacean Research is heavily subsidized by the Japanese government, despite paying some of its bills through the sale of whale meat. These subsidies are not due to a lack of meat, as stockpiles have continued to grow since 1997.[22] Furthermore, the Institute for Cetacean Research tried to auction off frozen whale meat stockpiles four times in 2011 and 2012 and failed to sell 908.8 tons, or three-quarters of the meat offered.[23] This is hardly a good argument for a strong cultural attachment to the consumption of whale meat.

SUSTAINABILITY AND THE JAPANESE ARCHIPELAGO

The drama of the nineteenth-century crash of whale populations caused by foreign whalers, as well as foreign whalers' push further and further into spaces that could be or were claimed by Japan as part of their archipelagic territory, tends to overshadow the earlier impact of Japanese whalers. Arguments for some kind of cultural attachment to whales and whaling, which try to present Japanese whaling culture as more similar to aboriginal subsistence whaling than to modern commercial whaling, also promote an assumption of sustainability in traditional Tokugawa whaling practices. However, a closer look at the role of whales as a natural resource in early modern Japan complicates this assumption. The reliance of the people of the Tokugawa period on marine resources like whales to supplement other terrestrial resources that were increasingly scarce in the face of a booming population and economy proves that Japan at this time was not a sustainable closed system, because its marine resources were unbounded rather than closed.

Whales may have been an exceptional example of interaction with the marine environment simply because of their great size and thus versatility as products, but they were far from the only marine species whose harvest shaped life in the archipelago. The new specialized fisheries for other organisms like herring, tuna, sardines, abalone, octopus, and even kelp each had their own impacts, both on human society and on the harvested populations. It is simply harder to measure impacts on marine species than on terrestrial ones because the locally visible coastal portion of the population may be continually and invisibly replenished by a much larger oceanic population. Even if some of these harvests were at a sustainable level for the target populations (a difficult thing to calculate even today when we have much more sophisticated ways of tracking and measuring marine populations), that is likely by accident rather than by design.

The form of whaling that developed in unique coastal conditions, bounded by the Kuroshio and Tsushima currents and the shallow waters of a relatively narrow continental shelf, tied together coastal and inland society from the 1600s through the 1800s in Japan. By bringing whales ashore, the people of Tokugawa Japan became invested in a part of their world beyond the inland plains where rice cultivation had traditionally been placed at the center of society. Focusing on this intertwined sea and shore space in the Japanese archipelago shows how Japan in this period was far more a part of the Pacific basin as a whole, even before the nineteenth century, than the restricted movements of Japanese people would seem to indicate. Without the resources pulled from the shallow waters of the archipelago, Tokugawa society would have lacked important sources of protein, fat, fertilizer, pesticide, and oil. These contributions to the consumption habits of a population that grew rapidly after the instigation of the Tokugawa peace came out of the ecosystem of the Pacific Ocean basin, not just from the waters close to Japan. Whales fed in the nutrient-rich North Pacific waters and then brought those nutrients south on their migrations to calving grounds, where some of them were intercepted to add their nutrient stores to terrestrial Japan. As noted earlier, they also brought other people closer to Japan, as foreign whalers chased them to and through the Japan Grounds and forced the Japanese to deal with more international politics. In the early stages of their period of imperial expansion around the turn of the twentieth century, Japan was characterized as a small, resource-poor nation that needed to expand colonial possessions to make up for the lack of native resources. However, many of those resources were things like rubber and oil, which had not been necessary before the modern industrial era. Tokugawa Japan also dealt with the problem of a limited land area and therefore constrained terrestrial resources by expanding outward, in what seems like the more limited area of ocean within sight of land, but in fact was the whole expanse of the Pacific through which swam all the whales and other marine organisms they harvested.

The fluidity of the boundaries of an archipelagic system, marked not by the shoreline but by the variable positions of major ocean currents and the limits of regular wind patterns, negates the possibility of a closed system in the limited space of the islands. If Tokugawa Japan was not a closed system, then the lack of human population collapse after a period of high growth cannot reflect an equilibrium of sustainable living within limited means. The newly increased population of peacetime Japan was maintained with continually increasing inputs from the ocean. Meiji Japan did suddenly need new resources as they imported new technologies that required different inputs of iron, steel, and eventually petroleum, but the dynamics of their ever-expanding empire were not as dramatically different from Tokugawa resource use as it might appear to someone thinking that Tokugawa resources were limited to the terrestrial spaces of the islands. Neither state was sustainable without some kind of expansion. The Meiji expansion merely crossed more political boundaries. It was also effected through the movement of people rather than taking advantage of the resources' ability to swim to them. In both cases, the partially maritime nature of the Japanese archipelago was critical.

It is clear from the dynamic nature of whaling practices, the constant beginning and collapse of different groups moving to different places along the coast and adapting new techniques to follow new species, that most of the organized whaling in Japan was not likely to have been sustainable over the long term even without the impact of American whalers. These adaptations and constant movement into less heavily exploited whaling grounds show that close interconnections and relationships with the marine environment in the Tokugawa period are not incompatible with unsustainable harvests from the ocean—the biggest difference between the kind of whaling that led to frequent collapses of whaling groups in the Tokugawa and the overharvesting that led to near-extinction of many whale species today is the length of time over which the different types of whaling could be sustained, not the fact that one was sustainable and the other was not. As baleen whale populations plummeted to a tiny fraction of what they were in the Tokugawa period, most of the coastal whalers stopped whaling not because they could no longer make money selling whale products, but because there were no longer enough whales to sell. However, individual whaling groups collapsed due to lack of whales even before the middle of the nineteenth century. While whaling in a broad sense has continued from the early modern to the modern eras, the texture of the interactions between humans and whales has been altered to include new areas of the ocean, species that were not previously hunted, and more global and international pressures than existed in the past.

The actual harvest of whales was not the only dynamic aspect of the whaling system in early modern Japan. Following highly mobile whales across the ocean/land boundary, the mobility of Tokugawa society as a whole becomes more visible. Whalers and their products, scholars and curiosity-seekers all circulated along with knowledge and stories about whales, tying the migratory species and currents of the Pacific to the terrestrial spaces of Japan. Even the human construction of spiritual space made room for whales to live right alongside people, no matter how difficult that would be in the physical realm. The complex network of relationships visible between whales and people may contain more vectors of connection than those for other marine organisms, but it is otherwise representative of the nature of Tokugawa Japan as an archipelagic and Pacific-linked society blending terrestrial and marine space.

NOTES

INTRODUCTION

1   For example, Jiji, "Endangered Gray Whale Spotted in Aichi Bay."
2   International Court of Justice, "Whaling in the Antarctic."
3   Given changing attitudes toward whaling internationally since the imple-
     mentation of the moratorium, it is unlikely that a review will lead to it being
     lifted at this point. For more on the contemporary politics of whaling that
     led to the moratorium, see Dorsey, Whales and Nations.
4   Summit of Japanese Traditional Whaling Communities and Nihon Kujirarui
     Kenkyūjo, Report and Proceedings, 5.
5   Ibid., 7. This is a message Komatsu repeats in many of his publications about
     Japanese whaling.
6   Hobsbawm and Ranger, The Invention of Tradition. For more detailed discus-
     sion of the relevance of this concept of invented tradition in modern Japan,
     see Vlastos, Mirror of Modernity. For the whaling controversy in particular,
     see Arch, "Whale Meat in Early Postwar Japan."
7   Two Japanese sociologists have written texts now available in translation
     counteracting the prowhaling argument that focus mostly on the modern
     whaling industry: Morikawa, Whaling in Japan, and Watanabe, Japan's Whal-
     ing. Apart from these books, most of the English-language scholarship with
     any detail of Tokugawa period whaling is by anthropologist and whaling
     supporter Arne Kalland: Kalland and Moeran, Japanese Whaling: End of an
     Era?; Kalland, Fishing Villages in Tokugawa Japan. The issue of historical whal-
     ing also comes up in Jessamyn Abel, "The Ambivalence of Whaling," and
     Nicol, Taiji—Winds of Change. Frank Hawley attempted to write a compre-
     hensive history of Japanese whaling based on his experience with modern
     whalers in Japan, but never completed more than the first volume: Hawley,
     Whales and Whaling in Japan.
8   Kalland and Moeran, Japanese Whaling; Abel, "The Ambivalence of Whal-
     ing"; Nicol, Taiji—Winds of Change. Hawley, Whales and Whaling in Japan.
9   Some examples of his publications include Komatsu, Kujira sono rekishi to
     bunka; Yoku wakaru kujira ronsō; Kujira to Nihonjin; Rekishi to bunka tanbō. His

Kujira to sanpo, 102–8 even has six pages listing places where one can buy whale meat today. See also Normile, "Japan's Scientific Whaling."

10 For example, in both Komatsu, *Kujira sono rekishi to bunka* and *Yoku wakaru kujira ronsō*, he begins with evidence that the people of the Jōmon period hunted whales in some fashion, even though this was at least two thousand years before the appearance of organized whaling groups in Japan and there is no evidence of a continuous whaling practice in the intervening time. See also Takahashi, *Kujira no Nihon bunkashi*.

11 Yamase, *Geishi*.

12 In comparison, American whaling ships from the nineteenth century had crews of about thirty-five men each and usually operated as independent units. Numbers are hard to find for factory ship whaling, but one report noted a crew of three hundred men on a single factory ship—it is unclear whether that included the twelve- to sixteen-person crew on each of the half-dozen or so catcher or killer boats that accompanied the factory ships. Walsh and Capelotti, *Whaling Expedition of the Ulysses*.

13 Ibid., 14.

14 For example, the series of books by former chief of the Japanese Fisheries Agency Komatsu Masayuki. Examples include *Yoku wakaru kujira ronsō*; *Kujira sono rekishi to bunka*; *Rekishi to bunka tanbō*.

15 Morikawa, *Whaling in Japan*, 20.

16 Nishiwaki, "Failure of Past Regulations and the Future of Whaling," 45. This comment was repeated in a much more recent work, so it has a lingering negative influence on our image of Tokugawa whaling; Abel, "The Ambivalence of Whaling," 323.

17 Taiji whalers caught ninety-five whales in 1681. Kondō, *Nihon engan hogei no kōbō*, 33. Arikawa whalers caught eighty in 1695. Sueta, "Kinsei Nihon ni okeru hogei," 439. They were far from the only groups operating in either the Kumano area or the Saikai area of Kyushu at the time.

18 While we have no census of whale populations before this point, the population clearly had to be larger than the total taken in this decade, especially since whales only give birth to one offspring every two years on average. Reilly et al., "*Eubalaena japonica*."

19 Ellis, *Men and Whales*.

20 Arch, "From Meat to Machine Oil."

21 Watanabe, *Japan's Whaling*.

22 Statistics Bureau of Japan, "Chapter 5: Agriculture, Forestry, and Fisheries;" Statistics Bureau of Japan, "Chapter 7: Agriculture, Forestry, and Fisheries," under "39 Households, Household Members and Persons Engaged in Marine Fisheries (1953–2003)."

23 Nippon Suisan Kaisha, "A History of Hundred Years of Nippon Suisan Kaisha, Ltd.," www.nissui.co.jp/english/corporate/100yearsbook/pdf/100years book.pdf. 20.

24 The Institute for Cetacean Research (ICR) had "over fifty employees" in 2004. Morikawa, *Whaling in Japan*, 41. The 170 crew members who operate the ships and kill whales under IWC "scientific" whaling permits come from Kyōdō Senpaku, which also employs twenty-eight people on shore. This company is the privately held remains of the last commercial whaling companies in Japan, and performs whaling operations under charter to the government subsidized nonprofit ICR: Kaisha gaiyō, www.kyodo-senpaku. co.jp/corporate.html#link_02. The International Court of Justice ruled in 2014 that the supposedly scientific permits that Japan issued to allow the ICR with the cooperation of Kyōdō Senpaku to hunt whales in Antarctica were not actually for the purposes of scientific research, and thus should not fall under the scientific exemption allowed by the International Whaling Commission to their 1986 commercial moratorium on whaling. For details on the court decision, see International Court of Justice, "Whaling in the Antarctic" and the summary of the judgment at www.icj-cij.org/docket /files/148/18160.pdf.

25 There are still a few coastal whaling groups operating, but they generally focus on smaller species like dolphins, with the exception of the few beaked whales still caught on the Bōsō Peninsula.

26 In 1993 Amino discussed increasing interest in considering the ocean's relationship to Japan. Clear examples of how Amino viewed Japanese history from a marine as well as terrestrial perspective can be seen in Amino, *Umi to rettō no chūsei* and *Umi kara mita Nihon shizō*. For one of the major exceptions to the marginalization of the oceans in premodern Japanese history, see Shapinsky, "Predators, Protectors, and Purveyors" and "From Sea Bandits to Sea Lords."

27 For example, one recent summary of Japan's geography notes that after rice cultivation began, the plains were the focus of activity in contrast to the prehistoric reliance on mountains and seashore. She goes on to discuss dry fields, rice paddies, and forests but neglects to mention coastal activity in any period after the prehistoric. Barnes, "Japan's Natural Setting," 5.

28 Amino, *Nihon shakai saikō*, 181–82.

29 Morris and Howland, *Yachting in America*.

30 For a discussion of beaches as sites of recreation in European and American context, see Lenček and Bosker, *The Beach*.

31 Discussions of contemporary Japanese beach-going customs can be found at www.bbc.com/news/magazine-29429742 and www.planettokyo.com/blog /japanese-culture/japans-swimming-season.

32 For a recent example of the way this discredited idea still shapes our understanding of Tokugawa Japan, see Ravina, "Tokugawa, Romanov, and Khmer."

33 See Cullen, "Statistics of Tokugawa Coastal Trade," for details of coastal trade. He also points out the importance of fisheries (which are not counted in the trade statistics) in Cullen, *A History of Japan 1582–1941*, 84.

34   For more on how whales illuminate the Pacific World's interconnections, see Jones, "Running into Whales."

35   For more on the concept of modern Japan as a pelagic empire, see Tsutsui, "The Pelagic Empire."

36   Totman, *Early Modern Japan*, 4–5; Barnes, "Japan's Natural Setting."

37   For an overview of Japanese demographics during the Tokugawa period, see Akira, *The Historical Demography of Pre-Modern Japan*.

38   See, for example, Osamu, "The Frequency of Famines as Demographic Correctives in the Japanese Past"; Jannetta, "Famine Mortality in Nineteenth-Century Japan."

39   Totman, *Early Modern Japan*, 272–74.

40   Diamond, *Collapse*.

41   Richards, *The Unending Frontier*.

42   Ibid., 192.

43   Walker, *The Conquest of Ainu Lands*. Walker has also worked to illuminate atmospheric connections to famines that, similar to the Pacific Ocean, worked to draw Japan into a more global network in this period. See Walker, "Commercial Growth and Environmental Change in Early Modern Japan" and *A Concise History of Japan*.

44   Igler, *The Great Ocean*, is a good example of the kind of new Pacific history that is currently being written, focused on more than just one particular cultural region or people. Armitage and Bashford, eds., *Pacific Histories* and Matsuda, *Pacific Worlds*, also call for new perspectives on the Pacific as a whole.

45   Matsuda, *Pacific Worlds*.

46   Ibid., 5.

47   Rozwadowski, "Oceans: Fusing the History of Science and Technology with Environmental History," 44.

48   For more details on this example, see the discussion of "mountain whale" meat and the use of whale oil pesticides on rice crops in chapter 3.

CHAPTER ONE: SEEING FROM THE SEA

1   For example, Alter et al., "DNA Evidence for Historic Population Size and Past Ecosystem Impacts of Gray Whales."

2   The History of Marine Animal Populations project undertaken by the Census of Marine Life has made an effort to reconstruct the historical ecologies of the ocean, but for whale populations most of the historical data comes from American whalers' records. Starkey et al., *Oceans Past*. Observations of whale behavior were rarely recorded by anyone but whalers, so it is impossible to compare, for example, prewhaling and postwhaling behavior.

3   Scientists have recently tracked a few individuals from the western gray whale population swimming all the way across the Pacific to join the larger eastern gray whale population, so the degree of isolation of current

subpopulations is uncertain. It is unknown whether these individuals would have made such a long journey if there were more than a few hundred gray whales remaining in the western Pacific. NOAA Fisheries, "Globe Trotting Gray Whales Slowly Reveal their Secrets."

4   Bolster, "Opportunities in Marine Environmental History," discusses this problem in the context of marine environmental history and how this concept is relevant for historians, as well as making use of the concept for framing his argument in *The Mortal Sea*. See also the History of Marine Animal Populations (HMAP) project, www.hmapcoml.org.

5   Japanese names for whales are the same from the early modern period as they are today, although they are now written in katakana (one of the Japanese phonetic alphabets) rather than with kanji (the characters borrowed from Chinese). The historical species categories in Japanese are also similar to modern scientific designations, except without distinctions such as North Pacific right whale versus North Atlantic right whale, since Japanese at the time did not know about related populations or subpopulations of the whale species in their coastal waters.

6   They may also have caught Bryde's whales (*Balaenoptera brydei*), a species very similar to sei whales, which in turn are very like smaller fin whales. They likely also caught the newly recognized distinct species of Omura's whale (*Balaenoptera omurai*), which until 2003 was considered a type of Bryde's whale. They may also have considered minke whales (*Balaenoptera acutorostrata*) to be very small fin whales. All of these rorquals are much faster swimmers than right, gray, and humpback whales and therefore were not preferred targets of whaling efforts, so their exact identification is less important to a consideration of the historical coastal whale populations most heavily targeted.

7   Both humpback and gray whales have been observed feeding while migrating. Right whales' migratory behavior has been observed less closely, but it is possible they also took advantage of the convenient food source within these currents during their migrations. Geijer et al., "Mysticete Migration Revisited." For more on the Kuroshio as a transport system, see Belkin et al., "X-23 Kuroshio Current."

8   Hain et al., "Swim Speed, Behavior, and Movement of North Atlantic Right Whales." This study focused on the behavior of Atlantic right whales in and around Florida, which may not be completely accurate for North Pacific right whales' swimming speeds. However, whaling records show they were easier to catch than the slightly faster humpback and gray whales in Japan, so I assume there was not a large difference in swimming behavior in the Pacific population.

9   Noad and Cato, "Swimming Speeds of Singing and Non-Singing Humpback Whales during Migration;" Perryman et al., "Diel Variation in Migration Rates of Eastern Pacific Gray Whales."

10 Parsons et al., *An Introduction to Marine Mammal Biology and Conservation*, 130.

11 Baleen whales show a wide variety of migratory behaviors within species, and likely adapt their movements to factors such as the availability of food and physical conditions of the ecosystem. Geijer et al., "Mysticete Migration Revisited." There is no reason why they would not also adjust their movements under whaling pressure.

12 Nash, "Ship Prudent of Stonington Bound on a Whaling Voyage," entry for March 27, 1849.

13 Qiu, "Kuroshio and Oyashio Currents."

14 I will discuss some of these stranded whales in more detail in chapter 5.

15 Sullivan et al., "Observations of Gray Whales (*Eschrichtius robustus*) along Northern California."

16 Reilly et al., "*Eschrichtius robustus* (western subpopulation)."

17 Omura, "History of Gray Whales in Japan."

18 NOAA Fisheries, "Globe Trotting Gray Whales Slowly Reveal their Secrets."

19 Reilly et al., "*Megaptera novaeangliae*."

20 For example, Anonymous, "Kujira no zu."

21 Alter et al., "DNA Evidence for Historic Population Size and Past Ecosystem Impacts of Gray Whales"; International Whaling Commission, "Whale Population Estimates," https://iwc.int/estimate.

22 Omura, "History of Gray Whales in Japan;" International Whaling Commission, "Whale Population Estimates."

23 Bettridge et al., "Status Review of the Humpback Whale (*Megaptera novaeangliae*)."

24 Reilly et al., "*Eubalaena japonica*."

25 Shoemaker, "Whale Meat in American History," 275.

26 Ibid., 276–82.

27 Dolin, *Leviathan*, 94–108.

28 Anonymous, "Kii no kuni Kumanokai geizu"; Beiga, "Rokugei no zu."

29 Ellis, *Men and Whales*; Dolin, *Leviathan*.

30 See Dorsey, *Whales and Nations*.

31 The two anonymous manuscripts both titled "Kii no kuni Kumanokai geizu" are probably copies. It is unknown whether they are both copies of another original source or if one is a copy of the other.

32 Hyaku and Kanda, "Geishō seizu."

33 For example, Anonymous, "Kujira oyobi iruka kakushu no zu," third scroll.

34 Oyamada, *Isanatori ekotoba*, vol. 3.

35 Culik, "*Berardius bairdii*, Baird's Beaked Whale."

36 Kawaoka, *Umi no tani*, 241–42.

37 Wilson and Wilson, *The Complete Whale-Watching Handbook*, 66–67.

38 NOAA Fisheries Office of Protected Resources, "Melon-headed whale (*Peponocephala electra*)."

39 In the definitions provided for *kujira* and *iruka* by the *Nihon kokugo daijiten* dictionary, there is no clear distinction between whales and dolphins. The dictionary then gives a definition for whales starting around five meters in length. Dolphins are considered to be cetaceans reaching less than five meters. Accessed through the Japan Knowledge database, https://japan knowledge.com/contents/nikkoku/index.html. The character for *kujira* (鯨) combines those for "fish" (魚) and "capital" (京, which can also indicate a very large number, either way pointing at great size). The characters for *iruka* (海豚) are literally "ocean-pig."

40 For a discussion of the problems of classifying whales as fish or mammals in early nineteenth-century America, see Burnett, *Trying Leviathan*.

41 Terajima, *Wakan sansai zue*, 198–258.

42 Ibid., 198–99.

43 Ibid., 201.

44 Yamase, *Geishi*.

45 In comparison, the American whaling fleet at its peak in 1846 was 736 ships. Dolin, *Leviathan*, 206. With an average crew of around thirty, that works out to around twenty-two thousand whalers.

46 Totman, *Early Modern Japan*, 272–74; Howell, *Capitalism from Within*.

47 Cullen, "Statistics of Tokugawa Coastal Trade," 185.

48 Ibid.

49 Vaporis, *Breaking Barriers*, 32–38. The importance of coastal routes can also be seen in the maps of Japan discussed by Yonemoto, *Mapping Early Modern Japan*, which usually include the sea routes as well as major roads.

50 Local resident of Shingu and descendant of the Taiji whaling family Taiji Akira notes that people tended to travel between villages by boat far more frequently than over land along the Kumano coast even into the twentieth century (personal communication). A good illustration of the sea-based ties between these three villages is the anonymous six-panel screen painting *Kumanoura hogei zu byōbu* held in the Wakayama Prefectural Museum, with an interactive version available at http://taiji.town/byobu.

51 Flershem and Flershem, "Migratory Fishermen on the Japan Sea Coast."

52 See especially Constantine Vaporis's work on alternate attendance and travel: "To Edo and Back," *Breaking Barriers*, and *Tour of Duty* for discussions of the intersection between political concerns, the alternate attendance system, and roadways.

53 Yonemoto, "Maps and Metaphors of the 'Small Eastern Sea.'"

CHAPTER TWO: BRINGING WHALES ASHORE, WHALERS OFFSHORE

1 Hōshūtei Riyū, "Ogawajima geigei kassen," 284.

2 Tetsuo, "Catching Dolphins at the Mawaki Site, Central Japan."

3 Japanese whaleboat dimensions provided in the display text at the Shima no

Yataka museum, Ikitsukishima, Hirado. American whaleboat dimensions from Ansel, *The Whaleboat*.

4   The number of boats would vary both by whaling group and also by what type of whaling: the later net whaling technique required more boats of different types than the single whaleboat type used in early stages of Japanese whaling. See Anonymous, *Kumanoura hogei zu byōbu*, with an interactive version available at http://taiji.town/byobu, showing multiple whaling groups in action on the water at once.

5   There are few sources in English dealing with the history of Tokugawa whaling. Kalland, *Fishing Villages in Tokugawa Japan*, and Kalland and Moeran, *Japanese Whaling*, are the most detailed. Japanese sources with summaries of Tokugawa whaling techniques include: Fukumoto, *Nihon hogei shiwa*; Kondō, *Nihon engan hogei*; Torisu, *Saikai hogei no shiteki kenkyū*; Morita, *Kujira to hogei no bunkashi*; Nakazono, *Kujira tori no keifu*; Nakazono and Yasunaga, *Kujiratori emonogatari*; Ōsumi, *Kujira to Nihonjin*; and Yamashita, *Hogei*. They generally agree about the basics of the historical development of whaling.

6   There is a small possibility that Japanese whalers borrowed the design of harpoons from Dutch sailors with whaling experience trading in Japan. But the harpoon is a relatively simple design, and since the earliest record of Japanese organized whaling comes from Ise and Mikawa bays, far from any of the Dutch trading ports in Kyushu, this is unlikely.

7   American harpooners also gained more prestige and a larger share of the profits from the whales they dispatched, but they did so from within the whaleboat.

8   The circulation of other goods in the growing commercial economy of the period also promoted movement and networking between nonwhaling villages. The ability of whales to bring people together was therefore representative of the trends of the period rather than an exceptional case. For more on the tension between interconnections and the self-contained nature of village organization, see Satō, "Tokugawa Villages and Agriculture," and Nakane, "Tokugawa Society."

9   Totman, *Early Modern Japan*, 234.

10 Ibid., 273–74.

11 The chronicle is the encyclopedic history of whales and whaling, Ōtsuki Heisen's "Geishikō" (Whale history manuscript), an unpublished but widely circulated manuscript. Wada, "Kinsei hogeigyo no keiei ni tsuite," 33–34.

12 Wada, "Kinsei hogeigyo no keiei ni tsuite," 33, cites these instances from the Harutoyoki without further reference to specifics of this source.

13 Although most baleen whales are migratory, there have been populations or subgroups of whale species that do not migrate, such as the humpback whale population in the northern Indian Ocean near the Arabian Peninsula:

Rosenbaum et al., "Population Structure of Humpback Whales." Thus, a nonmigratory population in these bays is a possibility, although the probability of it happening is unknown.

14 Wada, "Kinsei hogeigyo no keiei ni tsuite," 34, from information in the Kenbun ketsugishū.

15 Mie-ken Owase shiyakusho, *Owase-shi shi*, 627–28. Unfortunately, this city history does not provide a reference to the source of this information, which was likely found in local records belonging to the city.

16 Kondō, *Nihon engan hogei no kōbō*, 29.

17 These figures are from Mie-ken Owase shiyakusho, *Owase-shi shi*, 628, with an unknown original source.

18 Ibid., 629.

19 Miyamoto, *Umi no tani*, 149–52.

20 Takigawa, *Kumano Taiji no denshō*.

21 Ibid., 107.

22 For a detailed family history, see Taiji Akira, *Taiji Kakuemon to kujirakata*. For more on the role of village elites and their ties to samurai society, see for example Ooms, *Tokugawa Village Practice*, 76. The rural elites or entrepreneurs discussed in Pratt, *Japan's Protoindustrial Elite*, did not appear until the mid-eighteenth century, but they evolved from the earlier major landholders like village founders and rusticated samurai, and the whaling group leaders held similar positions in whaling villages that the gōnō Pratt examines did in their villages.

23 Muroto-shi shi henshu iinkai, *Muroto-shi shi*, 89.

24 Ibid., 89–91.

25 Dohi, "Saikai oyobi Ikishima ni okeru kujiragumi."

26 Hirado-shi kyōiku iinkai, *Saikai geigeiki*; Dohi, "Saikai oyobi Ikishima ni okeru kujiragumi." The range in dates for Han'emon's presence comes from a tendency to note historical events by era name during this period, so the source said it was in the Kan'ei era rather than providing an exact date.

27 Dohi, "Saikai oyobi Ikishima ni okeru kujiragumi."

28 As indicated by the description in Hirado-shi kyōiku iinkai, *Saikai geigeiki*, also Morita, *Kujira to hogei no bunkashi*, 144–45.

29 Wakayama kenshi hensan iinkai, *Wakayama kenshi. Kinsei shiryō*, vol. 5, source 4.1.

30 Source 3.1.1 Kushimoto chōshi hen-san iinkai, *Kozachō shiryō*, 499.

31 Wakayama kenshi hensan iinkai, *Wakayama kenshi. Kin-gendai*.

32 Kondō, *Nihon engan hogei no kōbō*, 32.

33 It is possible that there was some work developing a net-entangling technique in Taiji before 1675. This is simply the first year that documented evidence of specialized net boats appear in the tax records for Taiji. Ibid., 33.

34 Nakazono and Yasunaga, *Kujiratori emonogatari*, 34.

35 Kawaoka, *Umi no tani*, 20–23.

36 Kondō, *Nihon engan hogei no kōbō*, 33.

37 Morita, *Kujira to hogei no bunkashi*, 144–45.

38 For example, the people of one fishing village near Owase repaid a debt to Taiji from 1751 onward by sending whaling crew to Taiji, with as many as nineteen men being sent to work by 1781. Mie-ken Owase shiyakusho, *Owase-shi shi*, 627.

39 Miyamoto, *Umi no tani*, 153–64.

40 See graph 3 in Sueta, "Kinsei Nihon ni okeru hogei gyojō," 439.

41 Kukiura whaling is described in two places in Kuramoto, *Kumanonada (Owase chihō) gyoson shiryō shū*; the description on page 28 mistakenly notes the end of the whaling effort begun in 1754 as Meiji 6 (1873) despite also noting it lasted only sixteen years. Because the later reference on page 142 correctly notes this as Meiwa 6 (1769), the first instance is clearly a typographical error.

42 Source 3.3.2, Kushimoto chōshi hen-san iinkai, *Kozachō shiryō*, 503–4. The other village referenced in this source is Kukiura.

43 Source 3.3.2, Kushimoto chōshi hen-san iinkai, *Kozachō shiryō*, 503–5: the equipment is referred to as odōgu 御道具, not just dōgu.

44 Muroto-shi shi henshu iinkai, *Muroto-shi shi*, 90–91.

45 Anonymous, "Tosa no kuni hogeisetsu," section 1: Hogei raiyu no koto. There are no page numbers given in the text, but the reference is on the third page of this section.

46 This petition was noted in a timeline of Taiji whaling events published in the research report, Anonymous, "Wakayama-ken Higashimuro-gun Taiji-chō chōsa hōkoku," 99–100. There appears to have been a similar fight which brought in shogunal government oversight during the Genroku period in the Gotō Islands. Sueta, "Kinsei Nihon ni okeru hogei gyojō."

47 Sueta, "Kinsei Nihon ni okeru hogei gyojō," calculated from data in "Geishikō" with nineteen for all areas outside Kyushu, seventy-one inside Kyushu.

48 Torisu, *Saikai hogeigyōshi no kenkyū*, 81.

49 See, for example, maps on pages 106, 109, 113, 120, etc. showing work around Ejima in Sueta, *Hansai hogeigyō no tenkai*.

50 Ibid., 49, citing the sixth scroll of *Ōmura gōsonki*, 307.

51 Ibid., 46–55.

52 It is difficult to do monetary conversions over such a long period, so I have left this as a plain total which includes some shifts in what a ryō was worth. An average farmer or craftsman would be unlikely to see thirty ryō a year. Hanley, "A High Standard of Living."

53 Ōtsuki, "Geishikō"; Oyamada, *Isanatori ekotoba*.

54 Mori and Miyazaki, "Bunka 5, Ōtsuki Seijun 'Geishikō' seiritsu no seijiteki haikei."

55 Before the North Pacific population of right whales became a target in the mid-nineteenth century, it contained at least ten thousand whales. The exact number remaining today is unknown, but a rough estimate for the entire Pacific Ocean is around nine hundred whales, with likely less than a few hundred in the western Pacific. For a good summary of the status of the North Pacific right whale, see National Marine Fisheries Service, "Endangered and Threatened Species: Proposed Endangered Status for North Pacific Right Whale"; catch data from Scarff, "Historic distribution and abundance of the right whale (*Eubalaena glacialis*)," 489.

56 Wage-equivalency based on Hanley, "A High Standard of Living."

57 Wakayama kenshi hensan iinkai, *Wakayama kenshi. Kinsei*, 4:713.

58 Kushimoto chōshi hen-san iinkai, *Kozachō shiryō*, 602.

59 Takigawa, *Kumano Taiji no denshō*.

60 Sources 1.1 and 1.2, Kushimoto chōshi hen-san iinkai, *Kozachō shiryō*, 1–3.

61 Ibid., sources 1 and 2.

62 Ibid., source 2, p. 2.

63 Ibid., source 2.

64 See graph in Torisu, *Saikai hogei no shiteki kenkyū*, 92.

65 See graph in ibid., 191.

66 For 1797 the source is number 37, for 1803 it is number 46, and there are at least nine lack of whale notes (75, 83, 133, 134, 136, 142, 152, 157, 158) and five with his name and an actual year. Fukuoka daigaku sōgō kenkyūsho, *Kinsei saikai hogeigyō shiryō*. There is a large enough gap between the two that they might be two people with the same name, rather than a continuous management by one person.

67 Nakazono, *Kujira tori no keifu*, 107.

68 Nagaoka Moriyoshi, first preface to Fujikawa, *Hogei zushiki*, 5b.

69 Hamanaka, *Taiji chōshi*, 442–43.

70 See Watanabe, *Japan's Whaling*; Kondō, *Nihon engan hogei no kōbō*, 182–83.

71 His invention was part of the inspiration for Svend Foyn's construction of the Norwegian ship-mounted harpoon cannon system. Ellis, *Men and Whales*.

72 Fukumoto, *Nihon hogei shiwa*, 220 onward; Kondō, *Nihon engan hogei no kōbō*, 206.

73 For a discussion of the difficulty traditional whalers could have in shifting their targets and techniques, see Arch, "From Meat to Machine Oil."

74 The argument for sustainability comes from both supporters, for example, Nishiwaki, "Failure of Past Regulations," 45, and those who do not support contemporary Japanese whaling: Morikawa, *Whaling in Japan*, 20.

75 Nakazono and Yasunaga, *Kujiratori emonogatari*, 34.

76 For more information about these whales, see chap. 5.

77 Howell, *Capitalism from Within*.

78 Anthropologist Arne Kalland provides a brief introduction to some of the other important fisheries in Fukuoka such as sardines, sea bream, squid, and tuna in *Fishing Villages in Tokugawa Japan*, but as yet there are few studies of other early modern fisheries in English.

CHAPTER THREE: MOVING WHALES FROM COASTS TO MOUNTAINS

1 Toboke, "Kujira bōsatsu hyakuhiro kōryū." This source will be discussed in more detail in chap. 4.

2 While the idea of framing the growing commercial/mercantile economy of Tokugawa Japan as protoindustrial or protocapitalist began with Smith, *The Agrarian Origins of Modern Japan*, the case of whaling groups is more easily compared to similar developments in other capital-intensive businesses like the silk-reeling industry in Nagano (Wigen, *The Making of a Japanese Periphery*), or the herring fisheries of Hokkaido (Howell, *Capitalism from Within*).

3 Nakazono and Yasunaga, *Kujiratori emonogatari*, 145–46.

4 The emphasis on whaling tradition by modern prowhaling supporters is in part an attempt to place Japan's whaling within an exception to the moratorium on commercial whaling. The International Whaling Commission ceased allowing commercial whaling in 1986, with an exception for aboriginal subsistence whalers and for necessary scientific research. Arguments for a long unbroken tradition of whaling and the existence of a whaling culture in Japan are meant to equate Japanese whaling with aboriginal subsistence whaling even though they were not recognized as one of the groups in that category. For more on the strategies related to the moratorium, see Morikawa, *Whaling in Japan*.

5 Totman, *Early Modern Japan*, 273–74.

6 Cushman, *Guano and the Opening of the Pacific World*, is a good example of a resource-focused Pacific story that centers on the effects of industrialization rather than the period before the nineteenth century. See also Pomeranz, ed., *The Pacific in the Age of Early Industrialization*.

7 This idea arises particularly from Conrad Totman's studies of forestry in Tokugawa Japan, which admittedly is limited to terrestrial spaces. See, for example, Richards, *The Unending Frontier*, chap. 5, which drew heavily on Totman's work. For another example of the assumption of Tokugawa Japan as an example of sustainable prosperity within the fixed environmental limits of an island nation, see Diamond, *Collapse*, 295–306.

8 Richards, *The Unending Frontier*, 149.

9 Howell, *Capitalism from Within*; Walker, *Conquest of Ainu Lands*.

10 Pomeranz, *The Great Divergence*, particularly pages 243–47 for a discussion of ghost acres and their significance.

11 Vaporis, "To Edo and Back."

12 Howell, "Urbanization, Trade, and Merchants."

13 Walthall, "Peace Dividend"; Totman, *Early Modern Japan.*
14 Barnes, "Japan's Natural Setting," 5.
15 Walthall, "Peace Dividend"; Walker, "Commercial Growth and Environmental Change in Early Modern Japan."
16 Higuchi, "Japan as an Organic Empire."
17 The Basques, who began whaling sometime around the year 1000 CE, did sell meat and blubber in Western Europe, but Ellis notes that "the meat was fed to the poor and to the ships' crews," which would indicate it was not a preferred food by those who had access to better options, except perhaps during meatless calendar days designated by the Catholic church. Ellis, *Men and Whales,* 44.
18 Shoemaker, "Whale Meat in American History."
19 Zallen, "American Lucifers"; Dolin, *Leviathan*; Ellis, *Men and Whales*; Davis et al., *In Pursuit of Leviathan,* 342–68.
20 Nakazono and Yasunaga, *Kujiratori emonogatari,* 146; from the *Honchō shokkan,* which commented that whale oil was better than fish oil, but not used when people could get flaxseed oil instead.
21 Ibid.
22 Segawa, *Hisagime,* 111–14.
23 Ihara, *The Japanese Family Storehouse,* 49–52.
24 Koga, "Saikai hogeigyō ni okeru geiniku ryūtsū."
25 Hanley, "A High Standard of Living."
26 As there was no income tax or other system based on a calculation of profits, the percentage of the Masutomi's money that went to these taxes is unclear.
27 Ikitsuki Island Museum, Shima no yakata, Nagasaki Prefecture.
28 Koga, "Saikai hogeigyō ni okeru geiniku ryūtsū," 89.
29 Hanley, "A High Standard of Living," 185.
30 Koga, "Saikai hogeigyō ni okeru chūshō kujiragumi no keiei to soshiki."
31 The official conversion standard varied greatly over the course of the Tokugawa period, so I have kept the monetary amounts in the units provided within the sources.
32 Koga, "Saikai hogeigyō ni okeru geiniku ryūtsū."
33 Kasahara, *Kinsei gyoson no shiteki kenkyū,* 216–17.
34 Nakajima, *Mono ni naru dōbutsu no karada,* 70–72.
35 Fujimoto, "Geiyū no ryūtsū to chihō shiba no keisei," 126–28.
36 Fujimoto, "Geiyū no ryūtsū to chihō shiba no keisei," 131–32. The units for pricing are mostly left out of the original source, but there is one part which mentions *to* (斗), a barrel of approximately eighteen liters, so prices are probably set per *to.*
37 This series of letters, "Taiji kujirakata kako kengōryū," is reprinted as source 6 in section 4 of Wakayama kenshi hensan iinkai, *Wakayama kenshi. Kinsei shiryō,* 4:726–32. While they give no evidence for the price increase, Kasahara's data supports their claim, indicating that expenses for the Koza

whaling group more than doubled between 1824 and 1867. Kasahara, *Kinsei gyoson no shiteki kenkyū.*

38 Monetary conversion depends on the highly variable market conditions for specific times and areas, but based on the official conversion standard of 1 ryō = 50 monme or approximately 187.5 grams of silver, this amount of money is equivalent to approximately 32.8 ryō.

39 Wakayama kenshi hensan iinkai, *Wakayama kenshi. Kinsei,* 4:714.

40 Yamashita, *Hogei I,* 250.

41 Hamanaka, *Taiji chōshi.*

42 This practice was reflected in delicacies offered by Ise Bay whalers to the court in the early history of organized whaling. Referenced in the diary by Kajūji, "Seihōki."

43 Harada, *Edo no ryōrishi,* 24–27.

44 Nagayama, *Tabemono Edo shi,* 39.

45 Harada, *Edo no ryōrishi.*

46 Examples of references to mountain whale meat include woodblock prints showing restaurant signboards advertising *yamakujira,* such as Utagawa, *Bikuni Bridge in Snow.*

47 Toboke, "Kujira bōsatsu hyakuhiro kōryū," sixteenth story.

48 For a discussion of the problems of classifying whales as fish or mammals in early nineteenth-century America, see Burnett, *Trying Leviathan.*

49 de Ganon, "The Animal Economy," discusses this problem particularly in chap. 2, 6–31.

50 Jaffe, "The Debate over Meat Eating in Japanese Buddhism," 259, points out that two-thirds of the Japanese Buddhists in the Tokugawa period belonged to Jōdō Shinshū.

51 Harada, *Rekishi no naka no kome to niku,* 257.

52 Harada, *Edo no shokuseikatsu,* 39.

53 de Ganon, "The Animal Economy," 7–9.

54 de Ganon, "The Animal Economy," 13–14. See also Harada, *Rekishi no naka no kome to niku,* 106–8.

55 Katsushika, "Hokusai manga," volume 14, has an illustration of a boar swimming through the waves like a whale, which shows how strongly the tie between ideas of boar and whale were in Nagata, *Kachōga,* 115. See also the discussion of Bakin's *kibyōshi* in chap. 4.

56 Kuboi, *Zusetsu shokuniku,* 119.

57 Takatori, *Shintō no seiritsu,* 261.

58 Koga, "Saikai hogeigyō ni okeru geiniku ryūtsū."

59 The word I have translated as "packets," 苞, generally refers to leaves, which in this case appear to have been wrapped around pieces of whale meat, based on the following sentence.

60 Kikuchi Motoshū of Kii, *Sanzan kiryaku,* likely written sometime around 1802. Original text reprinted in Taiji, "Kumano Taijiura hogei no hanashi," 74–75.

61 Anonymous, "Tenpō nendai monourishū," depicts a man carrying *uwami kujira* or whale meat from the upper body among 219 various wandering vendors selling fish, meat, and other products in the Wakayama castle town (*jōkamachi*).

62 Koga, "Saikai hogeigyō ni okeru geiniku ryūtsū," 48.

63 There are two major versions of this type of image, with many copies made in different scrolls. One version is from the scroll "Shōni no rōgei ikken no maki." The other version appears with the scene generally titled, "Kashiura nayaba ni te geibaki no zu." Nakazono and Yasunaga, *Kujiratori emonogatari*, chap. 4.

64 As cited in Nakazono and Yasunaga, *Kujiratori emonogatari*, 133.

65 Ibid., 134.

66 Koga, "Saikai hogeigyō ni okeru geiniku ryūtsū," 54. He notes that they had regular trips to Shimonoseki, Hakata, and Karatsu which took two to three days, and also to Togitsu and Sonogi near Nagasaki which took five to nine days.

67 Ibid., 61.

68 de Bary et al., *Sources of Japanese Tradition*, 2:602.

69 Satō, *Baiyō hiroku*.

70 While other ground-up bones such as horse or cow could serve this purpose, Nobuhiro said that whale bones were best for this kind of nutrient renewal. Satō, *Baiyō hiroku*.

71 Sources describing fertilizer with whale-based instructions include ones from: Kaga-shi (Ishikawa Prefecture), another location on the Noto Peninsula (Ishikawa Prefecture), Higo in Kumamoto Prefecture, Aichi Prefecture, Fukushima Prefecture, Yamanashi Prefecture, one which is not specified more closely than Kyushu, and another not localized but with an author from Fukuoka. Yamada et al., *Nihon nōsho zenshū*.

72 Nakajima, *Mono ni naru dōbutsu no karada*, 70–72.

73 Ibid., 71.

74 McWilliams, *American Pests*, 47, provides a good chronicle of the war between humans and insects in American agriculture. Although chrysanthemums were also quite popular in China and Japan, pyrethrum was developed from Caucasian chrysanthemums and was not used in Japan until the late nineteenth century. Hiroki, "Historical Development of Pesticides in Japan," 25.

75 Ota, "Historical Development of Pesticides in Japan," 19–20, notes that the first record in Japan of pesticide treatments (a combination of plant derivatives and minerals) was written in 1600, Matsuda Naiki's *Kaden satchū san* (Family traditions on the killing of insects). The use of whale oil was the next major development. Histories of whaling often reference this use briefly without much analysis of what impact it might have had. Walker, *Toxic Archipelago*, also includes some discussion of whale oil insecticide, although not in the context of the whaling industry.

76 Rehmeyer, "A Whale's Tale."

77 There is very little reference to marine oil in Needham's extensive work on the history of science in China. Needham, *Mathematics and the Sciences of the Heavens and the Earth*, 657, contains a reference to oil that had been extracted in large kettles from "dragon blubber." In the sixteenth century a treatise by Ma I-Long called *Nung shuo* describes a treatment for planthoppers using tung oil sprinkled on rice; Needham, *Biology and Biological Technology*, 506. If they read this reference, it might have inspired farmers in Kyushu to try the same thing with the oil they had most available to them, which was whale oil, but there is no evidence one way or the other to indicate how much influence this work may have had on the practice.

78 Matsubara, *Nihon nōgakushi nenpyō*, 23 lists at least three distinct instances for Hizen in 1670, 1720, and 1732, and unrelated use in the neighboring Fukuoka domain in 1670. "Gaichū kujo hakkensha chō [Investigation of harmful insect extermination discovers]," as cited in Nakazono and Yasunaga, *Kujiratori emonogatari*, 147, provides more details on the Fukuoka use.

79 For a more detailed discussion of the use of whale oil as an insecticide, see Arch, "Whale Oil Pesticide." Walker, *Toxic Archipelago*, also discusses this practice.

80 For example, Yamase, *Geishi*.

81 Matsubara, *Nihon nōgakushi nenpyō*, 23–24. See also Nakazono and Yasunaga, *Kujiratori emonogatari*, 148, for details of whale oil stores in Kyushu.

82 To Hirado, Fukuoka, and Higo domains in northern Kyushu. Ikitsuki Island Museum Shima no yakata, Nagasaki Prefecture.

83 Some of this water was in rivers, particularly for lumber coming from deep in the mountains, but even that was transported in coastal cargo ships as well. Totman, *The Lumber Industry in Early Modern Japan*.

84 Higuchi, "Japan as an Organic Empire."

85 Westerners mostly used whale oil for illumination, and sometimes in noncosmetic soaps. They do not appear to have known about its insecticidal properties, although that may partly be due to the differences in staple crops grown in the West and Japan.

86 de Ganon, "The Animal Economy," 83–108.

87 Marcon, "Inventorying Nature."

88 Yasuda Ken, *Edo kōki shokoku sanbutsuchō shūsei*, vol. 12.

89 Marcon, "Satō Nobuhiro and the Political Economy of Natural History."

90 For a discussion of the issue of protoindustrialization in Japan, see Pratt, *Japan's Protoindustrial Elite*, 5–7. Howell, *Capitalism from Within*, and Wigen, *Making of a Japanese Periphery*, are good examples of other case studies on this topic.

CHAPTER FOUR: SEEDING STORIES

1 Isono, "Edo jidai kujirarui zusetsu kō (Old Illustrations of Whales)"; his original name is Niwa Teiki.

2   Toboke, "Kujira bōsatsu hyakuhiro kōryū."
3   For a comprehensive look at the developments in natural history (honzōgaku),
     see Marcon, The Knowledge of Nature.
4   Imahashi, Edo no dōbutsuga.
5   For details on the influence of Western methods of representation on Japa-
     nese ones during this period, see Screech, The Lens Within the Heart, and
     Fukuoka, The Premise of Fidelity.
6   Collins, A Systeme of Anatomy.
7   For a discussion of how exotic species can drive shifts in natural history or
     scientific understanding of the natural world, see Ritvo, The Platypus and the
     Mermaid.
8   Beiga, "Rokugei no zu."
9   Ibid.
10   The scrolls Hanii, "Hogei no zu," in the National Institute of Japanese Literature
     and Anonymous, "Hogei no zu," in the Barthelmess Whaling Collection have
     similar images to "Rokugei no zu," but these are both later copies. There are
     also the two "Kozaura hogei emaki" reproduced in Kushimoto chōshi hen-san
     iinkai, Kozachō shiryō, which at least are labeled clearly as originating from Koza.
11   Kuriyama, The Expressiveness of the Body.
12   A copy is held in the University of Tokyo library: www.lib.u-tokyo.ac.jp
     /tenjikai/tenjikai2004/tenji/case14.html#26.
13   Kulmus, Kaitai shinsho, trans. Sugita Genpaku et al. The Dutch text was itself
     a translation of the German Anatomische Tabellen. For background informa-
     tion on Dutch studies and the people involved, along with portions of the
     original texts, see the online exhibition by the National Diet Library, "Japan-
     Netherlands Exchange in the Edo Period," www.ndl.go.jp/nichiran/e/index
     .html, 2009.
14   Kuriyama, The Expressiveness of the Body particularly chap. 3, 111–51, discusses
     the problem of anatomical sight and why it is intertwined with Western
     medical practices and not Asian ones. Screech, The Lens Within the Heart,
     88–89, also discusses briefly the Kaitai shinsho's publication and what it
     meant for ways of seeing in Japan.
15   Ogawa, "Nihon kaibōgaku shi," 85.
16   While these people had been hereditary butchers, tanners, and leatherwork-
     ers from long before the Tokugawa period, their status as outcaste was codi-
     fied in the late fifteenth and sixteenth centuries and the solidifying of the
     status system in the Tokugawa period cemented their difference from main-
     stream society. Totman, A History of Japan, 276.
17   Although some fishing groups, particularly migratory ones, were discrimi-
     nated against as outcastes, they were not eta and the basis of discrimination
     was therefore not about ritual pollution, but instead about other differences
     from mainstream society. Flershem and Flershem, "Migratory Fishermen on
     the Japan Sea Coast."

18 Ueno, *Nihon dōbutsugakushi*, 246–47.

19 Kushimoto chōshi hen-san iinkai, *Kozachō shiryō*, 630.

20 The version of Johnston's book that was available in Japan was a Dutch translation from the original Latin, entitled *Naeukeurige beschryving van de Natuur der vier-voetige dieren, vissen en bloedlooze water-dieren, vogelen, kronkel-dieren, slangen en drunken* (Accurate description of the nature of four-footed animals, fish, and bloodless fish, birds, insects, snakes and dragons), published in Amsterdam in 1660; Marcon, "The Names of Nature," 220. For more on Dodonaeus in Japan, see Vande Walle and Kasaya, *Dodonaeus in Japan*.

21 Ueno, *Nihon dōbutsugakushi*, 246.

22 Wakayama shiritsu hakubutsukan, *Edo jidai no dōshokubutsu zukan*, 61.

23 Ueno, *Nihon dōbutsugakushi*, 247.

24 For example, the whale species and some short description such as the length and amount of oil taken from them are given for the whales in Yamauji, "Kujira emaki," but no whale parts are labeled.

25 For example, Anonymous, "Kujira emaki: Kishū Kumano shogei no zu," has recognizable depictions of an ocean sunfish, hammerhead shark, and other sharks and rays along with the whales illustrated.

26 There are multiple scrolls with this title. The one referred to here is currently held by the National Institute of Japanese Literature.

27 Kushimoto chōshi hen-san iinkai, *Kozachō shiryō*, 41–51. Included species: right whale (side view, and with mouth open), humpback whale, gray whale, sperm whale, fin whale, some kind of dolphin, what might be a pilot whale, Baird's beaked whale, killer whale, and sei whale.

28 Kushimoto chōshi hen-san iinkai, *Kozachō shiryō*, 51.

29 For a comprehensive view of the history of traditional Chinese medicine, see Unschuld, *Medicine in China*.

30 Ueno, "The Western Influence on Natural History in Japan." For a discussion of *Bencao gangmu*, its contents and its place in the development of natural history in early modern China, see Nappi, *The Monkey and the Inkpot*.

31 For a more detailed discussion of the ties between natural resource development and natural history, see Arch, "Whale Oil Pesticide," and Marcon, *The Knowledge of Nature*.

32 Morita, *Kujira to hogei no bunkashi*, discusses the links between *honzōgaku* and whales and whaling in chap. 4.7, "Honzōgaku to kujira," 210–16.

33 Marcon, "Inventorying Nature."

34 Entries for whales appear in at least seven different domains, including Etchū, Owari, Kii, Nagato, Tsushima, Chikuzen, and Mikawa. The whale entries in the surveys for each of these areas are found, in order, in Yasuda, *Edo kōki shokoku sanbutsuchō shūsei*, 1:269, 328, 420; 2:44; 4:553, 877–78; 6:116, 190; 8:354; 10:95, 313, 380; 11:289, 410; 12:308; 14:312.

35 Marcon, "The Names of Nature," chap. 4.

36 Marcon, "Inventorying Nature," 202.

37 Imahashi, *Edo no dōbutsuga*, 12–30.

38 Also, two copies from the Edo period have survived the intervening centuries to become part of National Diet Library's collection today, showing that it was more than a privately held and uncirculated manuscript.

39 For more on the practice of Dutch studies and the networks of scholars involved, see Jackson, *Network of Knowledge*.

40 Ōtsuki, "Geishikō," vol. 3, p. 50 of digitized version (original version has no page numbers).

41 For a thorough discussion of *Isanatori ekotoba*, see Nakazono and Yasunaga, *Kujiratori emonogatari*; Mori and Miyazaki, "Tenpō sannen 'Isanatori ekotoba' hankō no haikei."

42 For information on Gentaku's scholarship and reproductions of the text, see part 2.2 of the National Diet Library's online exhibit of Japan-Netherlands Exchange in the Edo Period, "Activities of Dutch Studies," www.ndl.go.jp /nichiran/e/s2/s2_2.html.

43 Mori and Miyazaki, "Bunka 5, Ōtsuki Seijun 'Geishikō' seiritsu no seijiteki haikei."

44 Mori and Miyazaki, "Tenpō sannen 'Isanatori ekotoba' hankō no haikei," 12.

45 Ibid., 5–7.

46 For comparison, Hanley, "A High Standard of Living" estimates an average farmer's yield from one year's cash crop to be approximately twelve ryō. Thus, the taxes paid during this period were the equivalent of the total average cash crop yield of one hundred farmers per year every year for six years. The cost of the book, with a detailed account of production expenses, is given in Mori and Miyazaki, "Tenpō sannen 'Isanatori ekotoba' hankō no haikei," 4–5.

47 Anonymous, "Illustrated Scroll of Whaling (*Geigeiki mokuroku*)."

48 Markus, "The Carnival of Edo," 499.

49 *Bukō nenpyō* (Chronicles of Edo), cited in Markus, "The Carnival of Edo," 509.

50 Ibid., 518.

51 Ibid., 512, 27.

52 Kalland, *Fishing Villages in Tokugawa Japan*, 183–84; Morita, *Kujira to hogei no bunkashi*, 157–60.

53 Asakura, *Misemono kenkyū*.

54 Anonymous, "Ōkujira no ezu."

55 Toboke, "Kujira bōsatsu hyakuhiro kōryū," preface.

56 Ibid., section 1.

57 Ibid., section 2.

58 This is a play on words with *kanejaku*, a carpenter's measure, and *kujirajaku*, a cloth measure. If you trimmed the difference in length between these (the two-*sun* pieces) off of a whale (*kujira-*), you would end up with the shorter carpenter's version (*kane-*), the same word for money. Ibid., section 3.

59 Ibid., section 4, is a joke about the whale not wanting to eat local noodles because their name *morisoba* sounds like "harpoon noodles"; section 5 also

puns on *mori* with the names of various places and the Shinagawa prostitutes known as *meshimori*. Section 6 has a pun with a brand of tea called Ichimori that supposedly paralyzed the whale upon drinking it due to the harpoon in the name, as well as a reference to Ōmori (place) being dangerous due to the strength of the whale in section 8.

60 Ibid., section 7. The whale, while wanting to live, because it was being struck and being robbed of its oil, said, "Please allow my body's light (innocence) to shine"—i.e., "I am innocent, please let me show proof (instead of beating me like a criminal)." The phrasing for innocence is shining is a pun on the fact that whale oil was used for lamps. Section 16 has the reference to meat.

61 Ibid., section 13.

62 Jippensha, *Taigei hōnen no mitsugi*; Takizawa, *Kujirazashi shinagawa baori*.

63 Jippensha, *Taigei hōnen no mitsugi*, 4 (reverse), 5.

64 Ibid.

65 *Kambun* is the Japanese way of writing in literary Chinese. Much like Latin in Europe, classical Chinese was a lingua franca for Japanese scholars, but they read the meanings of the characters rather than the pronunciation of them, leading to convoluted ways of marking the different order sentences should be read in if the reader interpreted it in Japanese. Takizawa, *Kujirazashi shinagawa baori*, 1, is the advertisement, then the reverse of page 1 has the *kambun* prologue.

66 Ibid., 2.

67 Ibid., 2 (reverse).

68 Ibid., 3.

69 Ibid., 3 (reverse).

70 Foucault, *The Order of Things*, 125–65.

71 Ritvo, *The Platypus and the Mermaid*.

72 See Bolitho, "Travelers' Tales" for a description of the importance of travel and the kinds of publications that arose from it during the early modern period.

73 Translation of the preface to vol. 1 of the "Fifty-Three Stations of the Tōkaidō" prints is provided by Strange, *Hiroshige's Woodblock Prints*, 52–53.

74 Suzuki, *Snow Country Tales*.

CHAPTER FIVE: MEMORIALIZING WHALES

1 Zuikōji, "Yakuyoke kaiun anzan fukutai Zuikōji."

2 The shogunate instituted this requirement as a way of assuring that Christianity had been completely eradicated from Japan: they feared missionaries had been leading converts to hold a greater loyalty to foreign powers like the Pope than toward the Japanese state. The Shimabara rebellion in Kyushu (1637–38) was the final straw in an ongoing concern about the political influence of Christianity. While the uprising was led by masterless samurai and

starving, overtaxed peasants, the fact that it happened in a heavily Christian area reinforced fears of the independence of Christians from shogunal rule, and provided an excuse for the extermination of Christianity in Japan. Ambros, "Religion in Early Modern Japan," 378–79.

3   LaFleur, *Liquid Life*, 71.

4   Early modern Japanese religion was highly syncretic, and Buddhists reinterpreted the Indian *devas* as the native Japanese *kami*. A strong division between Shinto beings (*kami*) and Buddhist ones (Buddhas and bodhisattvas) did not appear until after the end of the Tokugawa period with the development of State Shinto. Ambros, "Religion in Early Modern Japan."

5   The Sutra of Brahma's Net, Brahmajāla Sūtra in Sanskrit or Bonmōkyō in Japanese, is related to the Indra's net metaphor of interconnected souls. The emphasis is on connection rather than ranking, such that all living beings can be seen as one's parents at some point in the reincarnation cycle, so killing any living being is the same as killing one's parents and thus the source of your self. The Golden Light Sutra, Suvarṇaprabhāsa Sūtra or Konkōmyōkyō in Japanese, contains a story about fish who had listened to an incarnation of Buddha preaching and therefore were able to escape their bestial existence after death and instead were reincarnated at a higher level. Long, "Grateful Animal or Spiritual Being?" 30–32, 46.

6   See Bitō, "Thought and religion, 1550–1700"; Hur, *Death and Social Order in Tokugawa Japan*.

7   In contrast, animals can be reborn in a higher realm as humans or heavenly beings by hearing about the Buddhist Law, so a soul had a chance of becoming human again or even moving further up the karmic ladder after a lifetime as a beast. Kimbrough, "Preaching the Animal Realm in Late Medieval Japan."

8   This Buddhist karmic hierarchy is not unlike the European notion of the Great Chain of Being, which put man in the center of a chain linking lower nonhuman animals and the higher celestial realms on the way to God. Lovejoy, *The Great Chain of Being*, 183–207.

9   寒誉妙白. There is no pronunciation recorded in this *kakochō* for the names given, so I have chosen one of the possible combinations of *on* readings, but it could also be pronounced Sayo/Sanyo Myōshiro/Myōbyaku. The three remaining registers cover from 1719–1842, but the earliest volume reaching back to the start of memorial services in 1679 has been lost. Kato, "Prayers for the Whales," 296; Nakamura, *Nihonjin no shūkyō to dōbutsukan*, 69.

10 Tamamuro, "Local Society and the Temple-Parishoner Relationship."

11 Kato, "Prayers for the Whales," 296.

12 Kato, "Prayers for the Whales," gives the name as Shoyo, but the official Nagato City website article on Kayoi's whale prayers (www.city.nagato.yamaguchi.jp/sys/photo/detail.php?detailID=1027) glosses the name as Sanyo, which fits with the usual pronunciation of the first character in 讃誉.

13 Yamamoto, "Kumano no kujira meguri"; Tokumi, *Chōshū hogei kō.*

14 Kirita, *Kakochō,* 137–39.

15 For a detailed examination of the modern practice of pet cemeteries in Japan, see Ambros, *Bones of Contention.*

16 Kirita, *Kakochō,* 140.

17 A discussion of the meaning of the inscription can be found in Nakamura, *Nihonjin no shūkyō to dōbutsukan,* 69.

18 There are many possible pronunciations for this man's given names; without a gloss on the inscription, I have made my best guess. This monument and its inscriptions are described in Nishiura, "Genkainada de kiita kujira honekiri uta," 5–6.

19 Nakamura, *Nihonjin no shūkyō to dōbutsukan,* 72, cites Yoshiwara's survey as including 130 graves, but Kato, "Prayers for the Whales" counts only fifty-four, including nine constructed in the twentieth century. With such a large discrepancy in count, I have chosen to provide the minimum number here.

20 As discussed in Matsuzaki, *Gendai kuyō ronkō,* with a summary of different kinds of kuyō on pp. 103–4.

21 For trends in human graves, see Hur, *Death and Social Order in Tokugawa Japan,* 197–98. Kiyomizu, "Kujira no haka," 40, has a table showing whale graves.

22 One example of this type is the *kuyō* tower raised to commemorate all of the insects collected as pets over the course of the Tokugawa period in Chōsei (in modern Chiba prefecture). This memorial was raised in the 1920s in response to the rise of radio and concurrent decline in the practice of keeping singing insects in cages. Tanikawa, "A Monument of Scarified Insects in Chosei Village."

23 Matsuzaki, *Gendai kuyō ronkō,* 103–4; Nakamura, *Saishi to kugi,* 236; monument numbers from Kato, "Prayers for the Whales," 289.

24 Kretschmer, "Mortuary Rites for Inanimate Objects," 384.

25 Ibid., 402.

26 Trends in memorial construction are discussed, for example, by Miyawaki and Hosokawa, *Kujirazuka kara mietekuru Nihonjin no kokoro,* 123–35; Nakazono and Yasunaga, *Kujiratori emonogatari,* 160–63.

27 Kato, "Prayers for the Whales," 299.

28 Daimaru, "Dōbutsu no ohaka." This Jizō statue is also mentioned in Nishiura, "Genkainada de kiita kujira honekiri uta," 21, where it is described as a memorial for a whale fetus specifically.

29 Araki, "Kujira bunka."

30 LaFleur, *Liquid Life,* 51.

31 Hardacre, *Marketing the Menacing Fetus,* 30–45.

32 See Bodart-Bailey, *The Dog Shogun.*

33 Nakazawa, ed., *Rekishi no naka no dōbutsutachi,* talks about this distinction in

general. For a slightly more detailed description of the situation for hunters, see Tsukamoto, *Shōrui o meguru seiji*, 69–70.

34 Nakazawa, *Rekishi no naka no dōbutsutachi*; Tsukamoto, *Shōrui o meguru seiji*.

35 Akimichi, *Kujira wa dare no mono ka*, 111.

36 Ibid., 112.

37 Matsuzaki, *Gendai kuyō ronkō*, 94.

38 Akimichi, *Kujira wa dare no mono ka*, 112.

39 Tōru, "Kumano no kujira meguri."

40 Akimichi, *Kujira wa dare no mono ka*, 112.

41 One example of this is in Shiroura in 1758 where the head priest of Jōrinji dreamt of a pregnant whale, after which the villagers caught a very large pregnant right whale and were punished by disease. Akimichi, *Kujira wa dare no mono ka*, 112. The same story is given in Tōru, "Kumano no kujira meguri."

42 Tōru, "Kumano no kujira meguri," 6.

43 Nakamura, *Nihonjin no shūkyō to dōbutsukan*, 89.

44 Tōru, "Kumano no kujira meguri"; Nakamura, *Nihonjin no shūkyō to dōbutsukan*, 89.

45 Matsuzaki, *Gendai kuyō ronkō*, 95.

46 The text of the inscription is 業尽有情, 雖放不生, 故宿人天, 同証仏果. Nakamura, *Nihonjin no shūkyō to dōbutsukan*, 69–71, discusses this prayer in relation to the *Suwa engi*.

47 Marra, *Representations of Power*, 128.

48 Nakamura, *Nihonjin no shūkyō to dōbutsukan*, 78.

49 Information about this memorial is available from the Ehime Learning Center website, section 9: Ehime Prefectural Lifelong Learning Center, "Uwakai to seikatsu bunka (Heisei 4 nendo)."

50 The inscription is not completely legible, but the reference to a *myōkujira* (妙鯨), implies a whale that is either unusual or excellent. Ehime Prefectural Lifelong Learning Center, "Uwakai to seikatsu bunka."

51 Nakamura, *Nihonjin no shūkyō to dōbutsukan*, 74.

52 Miyawaki and Hosokawa, *Kujirazuka kara mietekuru Nihonjin no kokoro*, 40, 68.

53 Ibid., 123–24.

54 Matsuzaki, *Gendai kuyō ronkō*.

55 Miyawaki and Hosokawa, *Kujirazuka kara mietekuru Nihonjin no kokoro*, 68.

56 As described in *Hazashi odori* section of the whaling scroll collected in *Hizen no kuni sanbustu zukō 4*, reprinted in Saga kenritsu hakubutsukan, *Genkai no kujira tori*, 137.

57 This appears, for example, in one of the illustrations in one of the illustrations of the anonymous eighteenth-century scroll, "Illustrated Scroll of Whaling (*Geigeiki mokuroku*)."

58 Hirado-shi kyōiku iinkai, *Saikai geigeiki*, 32.

59 Ambros, *Bones of Contention*, also discusses this text in relation to animal memorial rites balancing the recognition of animals as spiritual beings with the potential for enlightenment with the problem of their role as commodities for human use.

60 Hōshūtei, "Ogawajima geigei kassen," 288–89.

61 Ibid., 361.

62 Ibid., 362.

63 For a discussion of the role of Buddhism in dealing with death during this period and how it came to be the practice most concerned with the problem of death, see Hur, *Death and Social Order in Tokugawa Japan.*

64 Fukuoka-shi hakubutsukan, "Fukuoka-shi hakubutsukan tokubetsu kikakuten: Nihon to kujira," 192. The definition of *oyumi no shinji* comes from the online *Daijirin* dictionary available at www.weblio.jp/cat/dictionary/ssdjj.

65 Kalland and Asquith, "Japanese Perceptions of Nature," argued against this idealized view of Japanese culture in 1997, but Ambros, *Bones of Contention*, was still pushing back against the idea of Japanese closeness to nature in 2012. For further discussion of the problem of Japanese perceptions of nature, see Thomas, *Reconfiguring Modernity.*

66 Ambros, *Bones of Contention*, 50.

67 Ōtsuka, "Iyo no kujirazuka kara Saikaiiki no kujirazuka e," 164.

68 Mostly this argument focuses on ongoing rites like the ones at Kayoi, where whaling is no longer practiced. Watanabe, *Japan's Whaling*, particularly in chap. 6, notes that there are some indications that rituals are performed by contemporary whalers or at least by whaling corporations on their behalf, but generally without specifics that would allow for reasonable comparison to Tokugawa practices.

69 Yoshihara, *Kujira no haka*, 421.

70 Hōshūtei, "Ogawajima geigei kassen," 362.

71 Anonymous, "Wakayama-ken Higashimuro-gun Taiji-chō chōsa hōkoku."

72 Local historian Taiji Akira believes that this archway was a modern construction based on Saikaku's reference rather than being a reconstruction of a whalebone gate that actually existed in the past. Personal communication.

73 Motoori Norinaga, *Kojikiden*, cited in de Bary et al., *Sources of Japanese Tradition*, 1:18.

CONCLUSION: JAPAN AND ITS MARITIME SPACE

1 As noted earlier, scholars of Japan have long since moved beyond the closed country idea, and even nonspecialists complicate the narrative of total isolation; for example, Diamond, *Collapse*. However, that recognition does not mean that Tokugawa Japan actually appears as a major part of the Pacific World in histories of this period.

2 See, for example, Muscolino, "The Yellow Croaker War."

3   The interaction between Japanese and Ainu in the southern portion of Ezo (now Hokkaido) meant that Tokugawa Japan did not draw all its boundaries solely in the water, but most imperial powers arrived by sea. For more on the frontier space of Ezo/Hokkaido, see Walker, *The Conquest of Ainu Lands*, and Howell, *Capitalism from Within*. For more on the interaction of other fishermen with foreigners, see Howell, "Foreign Encounters."

4   Hashiura, "Whaling at Taijiura, a Series of Scrolls," 2.

5   Mori and Miyazaki, "Bunka 5, Ōtsuki Seijun 'Geishikō' seiritsu no seijiteki haikei," 71–73.

6   Iwasaki and Nomoto, "Nihon ni okeru kita no kai no hogei," 174–79.

7   See also Tsutsui, "The Pelagic Empire."

8   For one case study, see Arch, "From Meat to Machine Oil."

9   For more details on the modern whaling industry, see Watanabe, *Japan's Whaling*.

10 Komatsu Masayuki is the most prolific writer in support of this idea. See, for example Komatsu, *Yoku wakaru kujira ronsō*; *Kujira sono rekishi to bunka*; and *Rekishi to bunka tanbō*.

11 Komatsu, *Kujira to Nihonjin*.

12 In fact, Commodore Perry included the needs of American whalers for resupply of food and water as part of his rationale for forcing Tokugawa Japan to open trade ports. The importance of whaling to this diplomatic process is discussed in Abel, "The Ambivalence of Whaling."

13 Perez, "Revision of the Unequal Treaties."

14 Tanno and Hamazaki, "Is American Opposition to Whaling Anti-Japanese?"

15 Although Kato, "Prayers for the Whales," argues that the continuation of these ceremonies shows a particular, sustainable connection to nature in Kayoi, this cannot be said to apply broadly to Japanese culture as a whole.

16 Ambros, *Bones of Contention*.

17 As the caricature of whalers in literature shows, for example Ihara, *The Japanese Family Storehouse*.

18 Adachi, *Backstage at Bunraku*.

19 Watanabe, *Japan's Whaling*, 98, in reference to Maeda and Teraoka, *Hogei* [Whaling], 170–73.

20 Watanabe, *Japan's Whaling*, 98 and chap. 1, particularly 45–46.

21 For more on this process, see Arch, "Whale Meat in Early Postwar Japan."

22 International Fund for Animal Welfare, "The Economics of Japanese Whaling," 7–8 (based on Japanese Fisheries Agency statistics).

23 Sakuma, "Whale Meat Doesn't Sell."

BIBLIOGRAPHY

HISTORICAL MANUSCRIPTS, SCROLLS, AND IMAGES

Anonymous. "Hogei no zu." Barthelmess Whaling Collection. Cologne, Germany.

Anonymous. "Illustrated Scroll of Whaling (*Geigeiki mokuroku*)." Eighteenth century. 1985.647. Bequest of the Hofer Collection of the Arts of Asia, Harvard Art Museums/Arthur M. Sackler Musem.

Anonymous. "Kii no kuni Kumanokai geizu." National Diet Library, Japan. doi:10.11501/2543152.

Anonymous. "Kujira emaki: Kishū Kumano shogei no zu." 1723. National Institute of Japanese Literature.

Anonymous. "Kujira no zu." National Diet Library, Japan. doi:10.11501/2543151.

Anonymous. "Kujira oyobi iruka kakushu no zu." National Diet Library, Japan. doi:10.11501/2573223.

Anonymous. *Kumanoura hogeizu byōbu.* Catalog no. 122, Wakayama Prefectural Museum.

Anonymous. "Ōkujira no ezu (misemono banduke) Dōtonburi Hōzenji nigatsu." 1823. Osaka Museum of History.

Anonymous. "Tenpō nendai monourishū." 1830–44. Wakayama Prefectural Library.

Anonymous. "Tosa no kuni hogeisetsu." 1836–81. In *Tosa no kuni gunsho ruijū*, edited by Yoshimura Harumine. Held in the National Archives of Japan.

Anonymous. "Wakayama-ken Higashimuro-gun Taiji-chō chōsa hōkoku (2004/10/23–25)." *Rikkyō daigaku nihongaku kenkyūjo nenpō* 5 (2006): 97–100.

Beiga. "Rokugei no zu." 1847. National Diet Library, Japan. doi:10.11501/2543153.

Collins, Samuel. *A Systeme of Anatomy, Treating of the Body of Man, Beasts, Birds, Fish, Insects, and Plants Illustrated with Many Schemes, Consisting of Variety of Elegant Figures, Drawn from the Life, and Engraven in Seventy Four Folio Copper-Plates. And after Every Part of Man's Body Hath Been Anatomically Described, Its Diseases, Cases, and Cures Are Concisely Exhibited. The First Volume Containing the Parts of the Lowest Apartments of the Body of Man and Other Animals, Etc.* In the Savoy [London]: Thomas Newcomb, 1685.

Fujikawa Sankei. *Hogei zushiki.* Kobe: Inoue Shinkōdō, 1888.

Hanii. "Hogei no zu." 1882. National Institute of Japanese Literature.

Hōshūtei Riyū. "Ogawajima geigei kassen." 1840. In *Nihon nōsho zenshū*, edited by Nōsan gyoson bunka kyōkai, 58:281–406. Tokyo: Nōsan Gyoson Bunka Kyōkai, 1995.

Hyaku Shōgen and Kanda Gensen. "Geishō seizu." 1729. National Diet Library of Japan. doi:10.11501/2543155.

Ihara Saikaku. *The Japanese Family Storehouse, or the Millionaires' Gospel Modernized (Nippon eitai-gura or Daifuku shin chōja kyō)*. 1688. Translated by G. W. Sargent. Cambridge: Cambridge University Press, 1959.

Jippensha Ikku. *Taigei hōnen no mitsugi*. Edo: Enomotoya Kichibei, 1799.

Kulmus. *Kaitai shinsho*. Translated by Sugita Genpaku, Maeno Ryōtaku, Nakagawa Jun'an, and Katsuragawa Hoshū. Wa-490.9–15 in the National Diet Library, Japan. Tobu: Suharaya Ichibei, 1774.

Nash, Ellery. "Ship Prudent of Stonington Bound on a Whaling Voyage." 1849. Mystic Seaport.

Ōtsuki Heisen. "Geishikō." 1808. National Diet Library, Japan. http://dl.ndl .go.jp/info:ndljp/pid/2610476.

Oyamada Tomokiyo. *Isanatori ekotoba*. Edo, 1832. National Diet Library, Japan. http://dl.ndl.go.jp/info:ndljp/pid/2609233.

Takizawa Bakin. *Kujirazashi shinagawa baori*. Edo: Tsuruya Kiemon, 1799.

Terajima Ryōan. *Wakan sansai zue*. 1712. Reprinted as Tōyō bunko, vol. 471, edited by Shimada Isao, Takeshima Atsuo, and Higuchi Motomi. Tokyo: Heibonsha, 1987.

Toboke. "Kujira bōsatsu hyakuhiro kōryū." 1798. doi:10.11501/2533906.

Utagawa Hiroshige. "Bikuni Bridge in Snow, 114 of One Hundred Famous Views of Edo." 1858.

Yamase Harumasa. *Geishi*. Osaka: Kashimoto Kanbē (reprint), 1794.

Yamauji Tokishige. "Kujira emaki." 1778. National Institute of Japanese Literature.

OTHER SOURCES

Abel, Jessamyn. "The Ambivalence of Whaling: Conflicting Cultures in Identity Formation." In *JAPANimals: History and Culture in Japan's Animal Life*, edited by Gregory M. Pflugfelder and Brett L. Walker, 315–40. Ann Arbor: Center for Japanese Studies, University of Michigan, 2005.

Adachi, Barbara C. *Backstage at Bunraku: A Behind-the-Scenes Look at Japan's Traditional Puppet Theatre*. New York: Weatherhill, 1985.

Akimichi Tomoya. *Kujira wa dare no mono ka*. Chikuma shinsho 760. Tokyo: Chikuma Shobō, 2009.

Alter, S. Elizabeth, Eric Rynes, and Stephen R. Palumbi. "DNA Evidence for Historic Population Size and Past Ecosystem Impacts of Gray Whales."

Proceedings of the National Academy of Sciences of the United States of America 104, no. 38 (September 18, 2007): 15162–67.

Ambros, Barbara R. *Bones of Contention: Animals and Religion in Contemporary Japan*. Honolulu: University of Hawai'i Press, 2012.

———. "Religion in Early Modern Japan." In *Japan Emerging: Premodern History to 1850*, edited by Karl F. Friday, 378–90. Boulder: Westview Press, 2012.

Amino Yoshihiko. *Nihon shakai saikō: Kaimin to rettō bunka*. Tokyo: Shōgakkan, 1994.

———. *Umi kara mita Nihon shizō: Oku-Noto chiiki to jikokka o chūshin to shite*. Kawai bukuretto 25. Nagoya-shi: Kawai Bunka Kyōiku Kenkyūjo (Kawai Shuppan), 1994.

———. *Umi to rettō no chūsei*. Tokyo: Nihon Editaaskuuru Shuppansha, 1992.

Ansel, Willits D. *The Whaleboat: A Study of Design, Construction and Use from 1850–1970*. Mystic, CT: Mystic Seaport Museum, 1978.

Araki Kimitoshi. "Kujira bunka: Kujira o tomuratta kujirahaka, kujirazuka nado." 2012. www.geocities.jp/tibakuzira98/kujirahaka.html.

Arch, Jakobina. "From Meat to Machine Oil: The Nineteenth-Century Development of Whaling in Wakayama." In *Japan at Nature's Edge: The Environmental Context of a Global Power*, edited by Ian Jared Miller, Julia Adeney Thomas, and Brett L. Walker, 39–55. Honolulu: University of Hawai'i Press, 2013.

———. "Whale Meat in Early Postwar Japan: Natural Resources and Food Culture." *Environmental History* 21, no. 3 (2016): 467–87.

———. "Whale Oil Pesticide: Natural History, Animal Resources, and Agriculture in Early Modern Japan." In *New Perspectives on the History of Life Sciences and Agriculture*, edited by Denise Phillips and Sharon Kingsland, 93–111. Cham, Switzerland: Springer International Publishing, 2015.

Armitage, David, and Alison Bashford, eds. *Pacific Histories: Ocean, Land, People*. New York: Palgrave Macmillan, 2014.

Asakura Kamezō. *Misemono kenkyū*. Tokyo: Shun'yōdō, 1928.

Barnes, Gina L. "Japan's Natural Setting." In *Japan Emerging: Postmodern History to 1850*, edited by Karl F. Friday, 3–15. Boulder: Westview Press, 2012.

Belkin, I., M. C. Aquarone, and S. Adams. "X-23 Kuroshio Current: LME No. 49." *LME Briefs, Large Marine Ecosystems of the World*. 2017. http://lme.edc .uri.edu/index.php?option=com_content&view=article&id=23:kuroshio -current-lme-49&catid=16&Itemid=114.

Berry, Mary Elizabeth. *Japan in Print: Information and Nation in the Early Modern Period*. Berkeley: University of California Press, 2006.

Bettridge, Shannon, C. Scott Baker, Jay Barlow, Phillip J. Clapham, Michael Ford, David Gouveia, David K. Mattila, et al. "Status Review of the Humpback Whale (*Megaptera novaeangliae*) under the Endangered Species Act." Edited by the Department of Commerce: NOAA NMFS Southwest Fisheries Science Center, 2015.

Bitō Masahide. "Thought and Religion, 1550–1700." In *The Cambridge History of Japan*, edited by John Whitney Hall, 373–424. Cambridge: Cambridge University Press, 1991.

Bodart-Bailey, Beatrice. *The Dog Shogun: The Personality and Policies of Tokugawa Tsunayoshi*. Honolulu: University of Hawai'i Press, 2006.

Bolitho, Harold. "Travelers' Tales: Three Eighteenth-Century Travel Journals." *Harvard Journal of Asiatic Studies* 50, no. 2 (1990): 485–504.

Bolster, W. Jeffrey. *The Mortal Sea: Fishing the Atlantic in the Age of Sail*. Cambridge, MA: Belknap Press of Harvard University Press, 2012.

———. "Opportunities in Marine Environmental History." *Environmental History* 11, no. 3 (2006): 567–97.

Burnett, D. Graham. *Trying Leviathan: The Nineteenth-Century New York Court Case That Put the Whale on Trial and Challenged the Order of Nature*. Princeton: Princeton University Press, 2007.

Culik, Boris M. "*Berardius bairdii*, Baird's Beaked Whale." Convention on Migratory Species (CMS/UNEP) Secretariat, www.cms.int/reports/small_cetaceans/data/b_bairdii/b_bairdii.htm.

Cullen, Louis M. *A History of Japan 1582–1941: Internal and External Worlds*. Cambridge: Cambridge University Press, 2003.

———. "Statistics of Tokugawa Coastal Trade and Bakumatsu and Early Meiji Foreign Trade." *Japan Review* 21 (2009): 183–223.

Cushman, Gregory T. *Guano and the Opening of the Pacific World: A Global Ecological History*. New York: Cambridge University Press, 2013.

Daimaru Hideshi. "Dōbutsu no ohaka." 2006. www.asahi-net.or.jp/~rn2h-dimr/ohaka2/index.html.

Davis, Lance E., Robert E. Gallman, and Karin Gleiter. *In Pursuit of Leviathan: Technology, Institutions, Productivity, and Profits in American Whaling, 1816–1906*. Chicago: University of Chicago Press, 1997.

de Bary, William Theodore, Donald Keene, George Tanabe, and Paul Varley. *Sources of Japanese Tradition*. Vol. 1. 2nd ed. New York: Columbia University Press, 2001.

de Bary, William Theodore, William M. Bodiford, Jurgis Elisonas, Philip Yampolsky, Yoshiko Kurata Dykstra, Carol Gluck, Arthur E. Teidemann, and Andrew E. Barshay. *Sources of Japanese Tradition*. Vol. 2. 2nd ed. New York: Columbia University Press, 2005.

de Ganon, Pieter S. "The Animal Economy." PhD diss., Princeton University, 2011.

Diamond, Jared. *Collapse: How Societies Choose to Fail or Succeed*. New York: Viking, 2005.

Dohi Kazuo. "Saikai oyobi Ikishima ni okeru kujiragumi to Dohi kujiragumi ni kankei suru nendaibetsu no nagare." *Sora-ou 300nen kinenki Web-han* (2010). http://mtv17.ninpou.jp/iki2/sora/dohi.htm.

Dolin, Eric Jay. *Leviathan: The History of Whaling in America*. New York: W. W. Norton, 2007.

Dorsey, Kurkpatrick. *Whales and Nations: Environmental Diplomacy on the High Seas.* Seattle: University of Washington Press, 2013.

Ehime Prefectural Lifelong Learning Center. "Uwakai to seikatsu bunka (Heisei 4 nendo)." 2009. http://www.i-manabi.jp/system/regionals/regionals/ecode:1/2 /contents.

Ellis, Richard. *Men and Whales.* New York: Knopf, 1991.

Flershem, Robert G., and Yoshiko N. Flershem. "Migratory Fishermen on the Japan Sea Coast in the Tokugawa Period." *Japan Forum* 3, no. 1 (1991): 71–90.

Foucault, Michel. *The Order of Things: An Archaeology of the Human Sciences.* New York: Vintage, 1973.

Fujimoto Takashi. "Geiyū no ryūtsū to chihō shiba no keisei" (The circulation of whale oil and the formation of the local market]. *Bulletin of the Institute of Research in Kyushu Cultural History,* no. 12 (1968): 125–54.

Fukumoto Kazuo. *Nihon hogei shiwa: Kujiragumi manyufakuchua no shiteki kōsatsu o chūshin ni.* Kyōyō sensho, vol. 83. Tokyo: Hōsei Daigaku Shuppankyoku, 1993.

Fukuoka, Maki. *The Premise of Fidelity: Science, Visuality, and Representing the Real in Nineteenth-Century Japan.* Stanford: Stanford University Press, 2012.

Fukuoka daigaku sōgō kenkyūsho. *Kinsei saikai hogeigyō shiryō: Yamagata-ken bunsho.* Vol. 8. Fukuoka-shi: Fukuoka Insatsu, 1994.

Fukuoka-shi hakubutsukan. "Fukuoka-shi hakubutsukan tokubetsu kikakuten: Nihon to kujira." Fukuoka: Shunhōsha Shashin Insatsu, 2011.

Geijer, Christina K. A., Giuseppe Notarbartolo di Sciara, and Simone Panigada. "Mysticete Migration Revisited: Are Mediterranean Fin Whales an Anomaly?" *Mammal Review* 46, no. 4 (2016): 284–96.

Hain, J. H. W., J. D. Hampp, S. A. McKenney, J. A. Albert, and R. D. Kenney. "Swim Speed, Behavior, and Movement of North Atlantic Right Whales (*Eubalaena glacialis*) in Coastal Waters of Northeastern Florida, USA." *PLoS ONE* 8, no. 1 (2013): e54340. https://doi.org/10.1371/journal.pone.0054340.

Hamanaka Eikichi. *Taiji chōshi.* Wakayama-ken Taiji-chō: Taijichō, 1979.

Hanley, Susan B. "A High Standard of Living in Nineteenth-Century Japan: Fact or Fantasy?" *Journal of Economic History* 43, no. 1 (1983): 183–92.

Harada Nobuo. *Edo no ryōrishi: Ryōribon to ryōri bunka.* Chūkō shinsho. Tokyo: Chūō Kōronsha, 1989.

———. *Edo no shokuseikatsu.* Tokyo: Iwanami Shoten, 2003.

———. *Rekishi no naka no kome to niku: Shokumotsu to tennō, sabetsu.* Tokyo: Heibonsha, 1993.

Hardacre, Helen. *Marketing the Menacing Fetus in Japan.* Berkeley: University of California Press, 1997.

Hashiura Yasuo. "Whaling at Taijiura, a Series of Scrolls." In *A History of Whaling at Taijiura, Kumano,* edited by the Committee for the Compilation of a History of Whaling at Taijiura. Tokyo: Heibonsha, 1969.

Hawley, Frank. *Whales and Whaling in Japan.* Miscellanea Japonica. Kyoto: Kawakita Printing, 1958.

Hayami, Akira. *The Historical Demography of Pre-Modern Japan*. Tokyo: University of Tokyo Press, 2001.

Higuchi, Toshihiro. "Japan as an Organic Empire: Commercial Fertilizers, Nitrogen Supply, and Japan's Core-Peripheral Relationship." In *Environment and Society in the Japanese Islands: From Prehistory to the Present*, edited by Bruce L. Batten and Phillip C. Brown, 139–57. Corvallis: Oregon State University Press, 2015.

Hirado-shi kyōiku iinkai. *Saikai geigeiki*. Hirado: Hirado-shi kyōiku iinkai, 1980.

Hiraguchi, Tetsuo. "Catching Dolphins at the Mawaki Site, Central Japan, and Its Contribution to Jomon Society." In *Pacific Northeast Asia in Prehistory: Hunter-Fisher-Gatherers, Farmers, and Sociopolitical Elites*, edited by C. Melvin Aikens and Song Nai Rhee, 35–45. Pullman: Washington State University Press, 1992.

Hobsbawm, Eric, and Terence Ranger. *The Invention of Tradition*. Cambridge: Cambridge University Press, 1983.

Howell, David L. *Capitalism from Within: Economy, Society and the State in a Japanese Fishery*. Berkeley: University of California Press, 1995.

———. "Foreign Encounters and Informal Diplomacy in Early Modern Japan." *Journal of Japanese Studies* 40, no. 2 (2014): 295–327.

———. "Urbanization, Trade, and Merchants." In *Japan Emerging: Premodern History to 1850*, edited by Karl F. Friday, 356–65. Boulder: Westview Press, 2012.

Hur, Nam-Lin. *Death and Social Order in Tokugawa Japan: Buddhism, Anti-Christianity, and the Danka System*. Harvard East Asian Monographs. Cambridge, MA: Harvard University Press, 2007.

Igler, David. *The Great Ocean: Pacific Worlds from Captain Cook to the Gold Rush*. New York: Oxford University Press, 2013.

Imahashi Riko. *Edo no dōbutsuga: Kinsei bijutsu to bunka no kōkogaku*. Tokyo: Tokyo Daigaku Shuppankai, 2004.

International Court of Justice. "Whaling in the Antarctic (Australia v. Japan: New Zealand intervening)." News release, March 31, 2014.

International Fund for Animal Welfare. "The Economics of Japanese Whaling: A Collapsing Industry Burdens Taxpayers." Yarmouthport, MA: International Fund for Animal Welfare, 2013.

International Whaling Commission. "Whale Population Estimates." https://iwc .int/estimate.

Isono Naohide. "Edo jidai kujirarui zusetsu kō (Old Illustrations of Whales)." *Hiyoshi Review of Natural Science*, no. 16 (1994): 25–36.

Iwasaki Masami and Nomoto Masahiro. "Nihon ni okeru kita no kai no hogei." In *Hogei no bunka jinruigaku*, edited by Kishigami Nobuhiro, 172–86. Tokyo: Seizandō Shoten, 2012.

Jackson, Terrence. *Network of Knowledge: Western Science and the Tokugawa Information Revolution*. Honolulu: University of Hawai'i Press, 2016.

Jaffe, Richard M. "The Debate over Meat Eating in Japanese Buddhism." In *Going Forth: Visions of Buddhist Vinaya*, edited by William M. Bodiford, 255–75. Honolulu: University of Hawai'i Press, 2005.

Jannetta, Ann Bowman. "Famine Mortality in Nineteenth-Century Japan: The Evidence from a Temple Death Register." *Population Studies* 46, no. 3 (1992): 427–43.

Jiji. "Endangered Gray Whale Spotted in Aichi Bay." *Japan Times*, May 3, 2012.

Jones, Ryan Tucker. "Running into Whales: The History of the North Pacific from below the Waves." *American Historical Review* 118, no. 2 (2013): 349–77.

Kajūji Harutoyo. "Seihōki." 1579–82. National Diet Library of Japan. Tokyo.

Kalland, Arne. *Fishing Villages in Tokugawa Japan*. Nordic Institute of Asian Studies, recent monographs, no. 69. Honolulu: University of Hawai'i Press, 1995.

Kalland, Arne, and Pamela J. Asquith. "Japanese Perceptions of Nature: Ideals and Illusions." In *Japanese Images of Nature: Cultural Perceptions*, edited by Pamela J. Asquith and Arne Kalland, 1–35. London: Curzon Press, 1997.

Kalland, Arne, and Brian Moeran. *Japanese Whaling: End of an Era?* Nordic Institute of Asian Studies, monograph series no. 61. London: Curzon Press, 1992.

Kanō Kōkichi and Saigusa Hiroto. *Sangyō gijutsu hen. Nōgyō, seizōgyō, gyogyō*. Nihon kagaku koten zensho. Vol. 11. Tokyo: Asahi Shinbunsha, 1944.

Kasahara Masao. *Kinsei gyoson no shiteki kenkyū: Kishū no gyoson o sozai to shite*. Tokyo: Meicho Shuppan, 1993.

Kato, Kumi. "Prayers for the Whales: Spirituality and Ethics of a Former Whaling Community—Intangible Cultural Heritage for Sustainability." *International Journal of Cultural Property* 14 (2007): 283–313.

Kawaoka Takeharu. *Umi no tani: Gyoson no rekishi to minzoku*. Tokyo: Heibonsha, 1987.

Kimbrough, R. Keller. "Preaching the Animal Realm in Late Medieval Japan." *Asian Folklore Studies* 65, no. 2 (2006): 179–204.

Kirita Miyoshi. *Kakochō: eien ni ikiteitru na no hakken* Tokyo: Maruzen, 2003.

Kiyomizu Seishi. "Kujira no haka • gyokai no kuyōhi o tazunete—hogei • kujira shokubunka kara shuchō." *Wakayama chiri* 20 (2000): 37–46.

Koga Yasushi. "Saikai hogeigyō ni okeru chūshō kujiragumi no keiei to soshiki: Bakumatsuki Ojikajima Ōsakaya o chūshin ni" (Small whaling enterprises in the Japanese traditional whaling industry: The case of mid-nineteenth-century northern Kyushu region)." *Bulletin of the Kyushu University Museum* 10 (2012): 99–126.

———. "Saikai hogeigyō ni okeru geiniku ryūtsu: Bakumatsuki Iki konaya no hanbai kōdō o chūshin ni" (Distribution of whale meat in mid-nineteenth-century northern Kyushu region). *Bulletin of the Kyushu University Museum*, no. 9 (2011): 47–68.

Komatsu Masayuki. *Kujira sono rekishi to bunka*. Tokyo: Goma Shobō, 2005.

———. *Kujira to Nihonjin: Tabetekoso kyōson dekiru ningen to umi no kankei*. Intelligence Playbooks, vol. 16. Tokyo: Seishun Shuppansha, 2002.

———. *Kujira to sanpo: Edo Tōkyōwan kara Bōsō • Miura hantō o tazunete Hōjō no umi*. Tokyo: Goma Shobō, 2004.

———. *Rekishi to bunka tanbō: Nihonjin to kujira*. Tokyo: Goma Shobō, 2007.

———. *Yoku wakaru kujira ronsō: Hogei no mirai o hiraku*. Berusō bukkusu, vol. 22. Tokyo: Seizandō Shoten, 2005.

Kondō Isao. *Nihon engan hogei no kōbō*. Kokubunji-shi: San'yōsha, 2001.

Kretschmer, Angelika. "Mortuary Rites for Inanimate Objects: The Case of Hari Kuyō." *Japanese Journal of Religious Studies* 27, nos. 3/4, Mortuary Rites in Japan (2000): 379–404.

Kuboi Norio. *Zusetsu shokuniku • shuryō no bunkashi: Sesshō kindan kara inochi o ikasu bunka e*. Tokyo: Tsuge Shobō Shinsha, 2007.

Kuramoto Tameichirō. *Kumanonada (Owase chihō) gyoson shiryō shū*. Tsu, Mie-ken: Kyōdo Shiryō Kankōkai, 1968.

Kuriyama, Shigehisa. *The Expressiveness of the Body and the Divergence of Greek and Chinese Medicine*. New York: Zone Books, 1999.

Kushimoto chōshi hen-san iinkai. *Kozachō shiryō—Hogei hen kaiga shiryō*. Kozachō shiryō. Kushimoto-chō: Nishioka Sōgō Insatsu, 2008.

LaFleur, William R. *Liquid Life: Abortion and Buddhism in Japan*. Princeton: Princeton University Press, 1992.

Lenček, Lena, and Gideon Bosker. *The Beach: The History of Paradise on Earth*. New York: Viking, 1998.

Long, Hoyt. "Grateful Animal or Spiritual Being? Buddhist Gratitude Tales and Changing Conceptions of Deer in Early Japan." In *JAPANimals: History and Culture in Japan's Animal Life*, edited by Gregory M. Pflugfelder and Brett L. Walker, 21–58. Ann Arbor: Center for Japanese Studies, University of Michigan, 2005.

Lovejoy, Arthur O. *The Great Chain of Being: A Study of the History of an Idea*. Cambridge, MA: Harvard University Press, 1936.

Maeda Keijiro and Teraoka Yoshiro. *Hogei*. Tokyo: Nihon Hogei Kyokai, 1952.

Marcon, Federico. "Inventorying Nature: Tokugawa Yoshimune and the Sponsorship of *Honzōgaku* in Eighteenth-Century Japan." In *Japan at Nature's Edge: The Environmental Context of a Global Power*, edited by Ian Jared Miller, Julia Adeney Thomas, and Brett L. Walker, 189–206. Honolulu: University of Hawai'i Press, 2013.

———. *The Knowledge of Nature and the Nature of Knowledge in Early Modern Japan*. Chicago: University of Chicago Press, 2015.

———. "The Names of Nature: The Development of Natural History in Japan, 1600–1900." PhD diss., Columbia University, 2007.

———. "Satō Nobuhiro and the Political Economy of Natural History in Nineteenth-Century Japan." *Japanese Studies* 34, no. 3 (2014): 265–87.

Markus, Andrew. "The Carnival of Edo: Misemono Spectacles from Contemporary Accounts." *Harvard Journal of Asiatic Studies* 45, no. 2 (1985): 499–541.

Marra, Michele. *Representations of Power: The Literary Politics of Medieval Japan.* Honolulu: University of Hawai'i Press, 1993.

Matsubara Hiromichi. *Nihon nōgakushi nenpyō.* Tokyo: Gakkai Shuppan, 1984.

Matsuda, Matt K. *Pacific Worlds: A History of Seas, Peoples and Cultures.* New York: Cambridge University Press, 2012.

Matsuzaki Kenzō. *Gendai kuyō ronkō: Hito, mono, dō-shokubutsu no irei.* Tokyo: Keiyūsha, 2004.

McWilliams, James E. *American Pests: The Losing War on Insects from Colonial Times to DDT.* New York: Columbia University Press, 2008.

Mie-ken Owase shiyakusho. *Owase-shi shi.* Tsu-shi: Tōa Insatsu, 1969.

Miyamoto Tsuneichi. *Umi no tani.* Tokyo: Miraisha, 1975.

Miyawaki Kazuto and Hosokawa Takao. *Kujirazuka kara mietekuru Nihonjin no kokoro: Bungo Suidōkaiiki no kujira no kioku o tadotte.* Tokyo: Norin Tōkei Shuppansha, 2008.

Mori Hiroko and Miyazaki Katsunori. "Bunka 5, Ōtsuki Seijun 'Geishikō' seiritsu no seijiteki haikei." *Seinan gakuin daigaku kokusai bunka ronshū* 25, no. 2 (3/2011): 53–82.

———. "Tenpō sannen 'Isanatori ekotoba' hankō no haikei" (The publication of 'ISANATORIEKOTOBA' (whaling picture) in the Edo period). *Bulletin of the Kyushu University Museum* 8 (2010): 1–16.

Morikawa, Jun. *Whaling in Japan: Power, Politics and Diplomacy.* New York: Columbia University Press, 2009.

Morita Katsuaki. *Kujira to hogei no bunkashi.* Nagoya-shi: Nagoya Daigaku Shuppankai, 1994.

Morris, Gerald E., and Llewellyn Howland III. *Yachting in America: A Bibliography Embracing the History, Practice, and Equipment of American Yachting and Pleasure Boating from Earliest Beginnings to Circa 1988.* Mystic, CT: Mystic Seaport Museum, 1997.

Muroto-shi shi henshu iinkai. *Muroto-shi shi.* Muroto: Muroto-shi, 1989.

Muscolino, Micah. "The Yellow Croaker War: Fishery Disputes between China and Japan, 1925–1935." *Environmental History* 13, no. 2 (2008): 306–24.

Nagata Seiji. *Kachōga.* Hokusai Bijutsukan, vol. 1. Tokyo: Shūeisha, 1990.

Nagayama Hisao. *Tabemono Edo shi.* Tokyo: Shin Jinbutsu Ōraisha, 1976.

Nakajima Hisae. *Mono ni naru dōbutsu no karada: Hone, chi, suji, zōki no riyōshi.* Tokyo: Hihyōsha, 2005.

Nakamura Ikuo. *Nihonjin no shūkyō to dōbutsukan: sesshū to nikujiki.* Tokyo: Yoshikawa Kōbunkan, 2010.

———. *Saishi to kugi: Nihonjin no shizenkan • dōbutsukan.* Kyoto: Hōzōkan, 2001.

Nakane, Chie. "Tokugawa Society." Translated by Susan Murata, translation edited by Conrad Totman. In *Tokugawa Japan: The Social and Economic*

Antecedents of Modern Japan, edited by Chie Nakane and Shinzaburō Ōishi, 213–31. Tokyo: University of Tokyo Press, 1990.

Nakazawa Katsuaki, ed. *Rekishi no naka no dōbutsutachi*. Vol. 2, *Hito to dōbutsu no Nihon shi*. Tokyo: Yoshikawa Kōbunkan, 2008.

Nakazono Shigeo. *Kujira tori no keifu: Gaisetsu Nihon hogeishi*. Nagasaki-shi: Nagasaki Shinbunsha, 2001.

Nakazono Shigeo and Yasunaga Hiroshi. *Kujiratori emonogatari*. Fukuoka-shi: Gen Shobō, 2009.

Nappi, Carla. *The Monkey and the Inkpot: Natural History and its Transformations in Early Modern China*. Cambridge, MA: Harvard University Press, 2009.

National Marine Fisheries Service. "Endangered and Threatened Species: Proposed Endangered Status for North Pacific Right Whale." *Federal Register* 71 (2006): 77694–704.

Needham, Joseph. *Science and Civilisation in China*. Vol. 3, *Mathematics and the Sciences of the Heavens and the Earth*. Cambridge: Cambridge University Press, 1959.

———. *Science and Civilisation in China*. Vol. 6, *Biology and Biological Technology: Agriculture*. Cambridge: Cambridge University Press, 2000.

Nicol, C. W. *Taiji—Winds of Change*. Tokyo: Japan Whaling Association, 1979.

Nihon kokugo daijiten. 2nd ed. Tokyo: Shōgakkan, 2000–2002.

Nippon Suisan Kaisha. *A History of Hundred Years of Nippon Suisan Kaisha, Ltd.* Tokyo: Nippon Suisan Kaisha, 2012. www.nissui.co.jp/english/corporate/100 yearsbook/pdf/100yearsbook.pdf.

Nishiura Shinsuke. "Genkainada de kiita kujira honekiri uta: Sagaken Yobuko, Iki no kujira shiseki to 'Yobuko kujiragumi' no kujira bunka fukyū katsudō." In *Kujirazuka kara mietekuru Nihonjin no kokoro II: Kujira no kioku o tadotte saikai-iki e*, edited by Hosokawa Takao, 1–54. Tokyo: Nōrin Tōkei Shuppansha, 2012.

Nishiwaki, Masahiro. "Failure of Past Regulations and the Future of Whaling." In *The Whaling Issue in U.S.-Japan Relations*, edited by John R Schmidhauser and George O. Totten III, 44–53. Boulder: Westview Press, 1978.

NOAA Fisheries. "Globe Trotting Gray Whales Slowly Reveal their Secrets." *Feature Stories*. Published electronically October 17, 2012. www.fisheries.noaa .gov/stories/2012/10/10_17_12gray_whale_mmpa_science.html.

NOAA Fisheries Office of Protected Resources. "Melon-headed Whale (*Peponocephala electra*)." 2012. www.nmfs.noaa.gov/pr/species/mammals/cetaceans /melonheadedwhale.htm.

Noad, Michael J., and Douglas H. Cato. "Swimming Speeds of Singing and Non-Singing Humpback Whales during Migration." *Marine Mammal Science* 23, no. 3 (2007): 481–95.

Normile, Dennis. "Japan's Scientific Whaling: An Expensive Proposition." *Science News* (2013). www.sciencemag.org/news/2013/02/japans-scientific -whaling-expensive-proposition.

Ogawa Teizō. "Nihon kaibōgaku shi." In *Meiji-zen Nihon igaku shi*, edited by Nihon Gakushiin Nihon kagakushi kankōkai, 49–249. Tokyo: Nihon Gakujutsu Shinkōkai, 1955.

Ohta, Masa. *Japanese Folklore in English (Eigo de yomu Nihon no minwa)*. Translated by Suzue Takagi. Vol. 3. Tokyo: Asahi Shuppansha, 1982.

Omura, Hideo. "History of Gray Whales in Japan." In *The Gray Whale: Eschrichtius robustus*, edited by Mary Lou Jones, Steven L. Swartz, and Stephen Leatherwood, 57–77. New York: Academic Press, 1984.

Ooms, Herman. *Tokugawa Village Practice: Class, Status, Power, Law*. Berkeley: University of California Press, 1996.

Ōsumi Seiji. *Kujira to Nihonjin*. Tokyo: Iwanami Shoten, 2003.

Ota, Hiroki. "Historical Development of Pesticides in Japan." *Survey Reports on the Systemization of Technologies* 18 (March 2013): 1–108.

Ōtsuka Shūichi. "Iyo no kujirazuka kara Saikaiiki no kujirazuka e, jiko jitsugen ni idomu: Kami Shibai 'Kaneko Misuzu to kujira hōe no ohanashi' no sōsaku, jistuen to sono hankyō." In *Kujirazuka kara mietekuru Nihonjin no kokoro II: Kujira no kioku o tadotte saikaiiki e*, edited by Hosokawa Takao, 135–74. Tokyo: Nōrin Tōkei Shuppansha, 2012.

Parsons, E. C. M., A. Bauer, M. P. Simmonds, A. J. Wright, and. D McCafferty. *An Introduction to Marine Mammal Biology and Conservation*. Burlington, MA: Jones & Bartlett Learning, 2013.

Perez, Louis G. "Revision of the Unequal Treaties and Abolition of Extraterritoriality." In *New Directions in the Study of Meiji Japan*, edited by Helen Hardacre, with Adam L. Kern, 320–34. Leiden: Brill, 1997.

Perryman, Wayne L., Meghan A. Donahue, Jeffrey L. Laake, and Thomas E. Martin. "Diel Variation in Migration Rates of Eastern Pacific Gray Whales Measured with Thermal Imaging Sensors." *Marine Mammal Science* 15, no. 2 (1999): 426–45.

Pomeranz, Kenneth, ed. *The Great Divergence: China, Europe, and the Making of the Modern World Economy*. Princeton: Princeton University Press, 2001.

———, ed. *The Pacific World*. Vol. 11, *The Pacific in the Age of Early Industrialization*. Burlington, VT: Ashgate, 2009.

Pratt, Edward E. *Japan's Protoindustrial Elite: The Economic Foundations of the Gōnō*. Cambridge, MA: Harvard University Press, 1999.

Qiu, B. "Kuroshio and Oyashio Currents." In *Encyclopedia of Ocean Science*, 1413–25. New York: Academic Press, 2001.

Ravina, Mark. "Tokugawa, Romanov, and Khmer: The Politics of Trade and Diplomacy in Eighteenth-Century East Asia." *Journal of World History* 26, no. 2 (2015): 269–94.

Rehmeyer, Julie. "A Whale's Tale." *Science News* 170, no. 18 (2006): 278.

Reilly, S. B., J. L. Bannister, P. B. Best, M. Brown, R. L. Brownell Jr., D. S. Butterworth, P. J. Clapham, et al. "*Eschrichtius robustus* (western subpopulation)."

The IUCN Red List of Threatened Species 2008 (2008): e.T8099A12885692. doi:10.2305/IUCN.UK.2008.RLTS.T8099A12885692.en.

———. *"Eubalaena japonica."* *The IUCN Red List of Threatened Species 2008* (2008): e.T41711A10540463. doi:10.2305/IUCN.UK.2008.RLTS. T41711A10540463.en.

———. *"Megaptera novaeangliae."* *The IUCN Red List of Threatened Species 2008* (2008): e.T13006A3405371. doi:0.2305/IUCN.UK.2008.RLTS. T13006A3405371.en.

Richards, John F. *The Unending Frontier: An Environmental History of the Early Modern World.* Berkeley: University of California Press, 2003.

Ritvo, Harriet. *The Platypus and the Mermaid, and Other Figments of the Classifying Imagination.* Cambridge, MA: Harvard University Press, 1997.

Rosenbaum, Howard C., Cristina Pomilla, Martin Mendez, Matthew S. Leslie, Peter B. Best, Ken P. Findlay, Gianna Minton, et al. "Population Structure of Humpback Whales from Their Breeding Grounds in the South Atlantic and Indian Oceans." *PLoS ONE* 4, no. 10 (2009): e7318.

Rozwadowski, Helen. "Oceans: Fusing the History of Science and Technology with Environmental History." In *A Companion to American Environmental History,* edited by Douglas Cazaux Sackman, 442–61. Malden, MA: Blackwell, 2010.

Saga kenritsu hakubutsukan. *Genkai no kujira tori: Saikai hogei no rekishi to minzoku.* Saga: Saga Kenritsu Hakubutsukan, 1980.

Saito, Osamu. "The Frequency of Famines as Demographic Correctives in the Japanese Past." In *Famine Demography: Perspectives from the Past and Present,* edited by Tim Dyson and Cormac Ó Gráda, 218–39. New York: Oxford University Press, 2002.

Sakuma, Junko. "Whale Meat Doesn't Sell: The ICR Reports Miserable Result of Auction." *IKAN-Net News,* May 22, 2012.

Satō Nobuhiro. "Baiyō hiroku." 1840. In *Nihon nōsho zenshū,* edited by Yamada Tatsuo et al., 153–406. Tokyo: Nōsangyoson Bunka Kyōkai, 1977.

Satō, Tsuneo. "Tokugawa Villages and Agriculture." Translated by Mikiso Hane, translation edited by Conrad Totman. In *Tokugawa Japan: The Social and Economic Antecedents of Modern Japan,* edited by Chie Nakane and Shinzaburō Ōishi, 37–80. Tokyo: University of Tokyo Press, 1990.

Scarff, J. E. "Historic Distribution and Abundance of the Right Whale (*Eubalaena glacialis*) in the North Pacific, Bering Sea, Sea of Okhotsk and Sea of Japan from the Maury Whale Charts. (IWC SC/42/PS-3)." *Annual Report. International Whaling Commission* 41 (1991): 467.

Screech, Timon. *The Lens Within the Heart: The Western Scientific Gaze and Popular Imagery in Later Edo Japan.* New York: Cambridge University Press, 1996.

Segawa Kiyoko. *Hisagime: Josei to shōgyō.* Tokyo: Miraisha, 1975.

Shapinsky, Peter D. "From Sea Bandits to Sea Lords: Nonstate Violence and Pirate Identities in Fifteenth- and Sixteenth-Century Japan." In *Elusive*

Pirates, Pervasive Smugglers: Violence and Clandestine Trade in the Greater China Seas, edited by Robert J. Antony, 27–42. Hong Kong: Hong Kong University Press, 2010.

———. "Predators, Protectors, and Purveyors: Pirates and Commerce in Late Medieval Japan." *Monumenta Nipponica* 64, no. 2 (2009): 273–313.

Shoemaker, Nancy. "Whale Meat in American History." *Environmental History* 10, no. 2 (2005): 269–94.

Smith, Thomas. *The Agrarian Origins of Modern Japan*. Stanford: Stanford University Press, 1959.

Starkey, David J., Poul Holm, and Michaela Barnard. *Oceans Past: Management Insights from the History of Marine Animal Populations*. Sterling, VA: Earthscan, 2008.

Statistics Bureau of Japan. "Chapter 5: Agriculture, Forestry, and Fisheries." In *Statistical Handbook of Japan 2016*. Tokyo: Statistics Bureau, Ministry of Internal Affairs and Communications, 2016. www.stat.go.jp/english/data/handbook/c0117.htm#c05.

———. "Chapter 7: Agriculture, Forestry, and Fisheries." In *Historical Statistics of Japan 2012*. Tokyo: Statistics Bureau, Ministry of Internal Affairs and Communications, 2012. www.stat.go.jp/data/chouki/07.htm.

Strange, Edward F. *Hiroshige's Woodblock Prints—A Guide*. 1983, New York: Dover, 1983. www.hiroshige.org.uk/hiroshige/strange/strange.htm.

Sueta Tomoki. *Hansai hogeigyō no tenkai: Saikai hogei to masutomi gumi*. Tokyo: Ochanomizu Shobō, 2004.

———. "Kinsei Nihon ni okeru hogei gyojō no chiikiteki shūchū no keisei katei: Saikai hogeigyō chiiki no tokushusei no bunseki."*Okayama daigaku keizai gakkai zasshi* 40, no. 4 (2009): 49–72.

Sullivan, Robert M., John D. Stack, and W. J. Houck. "Observations of Gray Whales (*Eschrichtius robustus*) along Northern California." *Journal of Mammalogy* 64, no. 4 (1983): 689–92.

Summit of Japanese Traditional Whaling Communities and Nihon Kujirarui Kenkyūjo. *Report and Proceedings*. Nagato: Institute of Cetacean Research, 2002.

Suzuki Bokushi. *Snow Country Tales: Life in the Other Japan*. Translated by Jeffrey Hunter and Rose Lesser. New York: Weatherhill, 1986.

Taiji Akira. *Taiji Kakuemon to kujirakata*. Wakayama: Nishioka Sōgō Insatsu, 2001.

Taiji Gorōsaku. "Kumano Taijiura hogei no hanashi." 1937. In *Kujira, iruka no minzoku*, edited by Tanigawa Ken'ichi, 29–86. Tokyo: San'ichi Shobō, 1997.

Takahashi Jun'ichi. *Kujira no Nihon bunkashi: Hogei bunka no kōseki o tadoru*. Nihon bunka no kokoro • sono uchi to soto. Kyoto: Tankōsha, 1992.

Takatori Masao. *Shintō no seiritsu*. Tokyo: Heibonsha, 1979.

Takigawa Teizō. *Kumano Taiji no denshō: Takigawa Teizō ikō*. Tokyo: Kōsakusha, 1982.

Tamamuro Fumio. "Local Society and the Temple-Parishoner Relationship within the Bakufu's Governance Structure." *Japanese Journal of Religious Studies* 28, nos. 3/4 (2001): 261–92.

Tanikawa Tsutomu. "A Monument of Scarified Insects in Chosei Village, Chiba Prefecture." *Japanese Journal of Pestology* 24, no. 1 (2009): 23–24.

Tanno, Dai, and Toshihide Hamazaki. "Is American Opposition to Whaling Anti-Japanese?" *Asian Affairs* 27, no. 2 (2000): 81–92.

Thomas, Julia Adeney. *Reconfiguring Modernity: Concepts of Nature in Japanese Political Ideology*. Berkeley: University of California Press, 2001.

Tokumi Mitsuzō. *Chōshū hogei kō*. Yamaguchi-ken Shimonoseki-shi: Kanmon Mingeikai, 1957.

Torisu Kyōichi. *Saikai hogei no shiteki kenkyū*. Fukuoka-shi: Kyūshū Daigaku Shuppankai, 1999.

————. *Saikai hogeigyōshi no kenkyū*. Fukuoka-shi: Kyūshū Daigaku Shuppankai, 1993.

Tōru, Yamamoto. "Kumano no kujira meguri." *Kumanoshi* 56 (2009): 6–15.

Totman, Conrad D. *Early Modern Japan*. Berkeley: University of California Press, 1995.

————. *A History of Japan*. Malden, MA: Blackwell, 2005.

————. *The Lumber Industry in Early Modern Japan*. Honolulu: University of Hawai'i Press, 1995.

Tsukamoto Manabu. *Shōrui o meguru seiji: Genroku no fōkuroa*. Tokyo: Heibonsha, 1993.

Tsutsui, William M. "The Pelagic Empire: Reconsidering Japanese Expansion." In *Japan at Nature's Edge: The Environmental Context of a Global Power*, edited by Ian Jared Miller, Julia Adeney Thomas, and Brett L. Walker, 21–38. Honolulu: University of Hawai'i Press, 2013.

Ueno Masuzō. *Nihon dōbutsugakushi*. Tokyo: Yasaka Shobō, 1987.

————. "The Western Influence on Natural History in Japan." *Monumenta Nipponica* 19, nos. 3/4 (1964): 315–39.

Unschuld, Paul U. *Medicine in China: A History of Ideas*. Berkeley: University of California Press, 1985.

Vande Walle, W. F., and Kazuhiko Kasaya. *Dodonaeus in Japan: Translation and the Scientific Mind in the Tokugawa Period*. Leuven: Leuven University Press, 2001.

Vaporis, Constantine N. *Breaking Barriers: Travel and the State in Early Modern Japan*. Cambridge, MA: Harvard University Press, 1994.

————. "To Edo and Back: Alternate Attendance and Japanese Culture in the Early Modern Period." *Journal of Japanese Studies* 23, no. 1 (1997): 25–67.

————. *Tour of Duty: Samurai, Military Service in Edo, and the Culture of Early Modern Japan*. Honolulu: University of Hawai'i Press, 2008.

Vlastos, Stephen. *Mirror of Modernity: Invented Traditions of Modern Japan*. Berkeley: University of California Press, 1998.

Wada Tsutomu. "Kinsei hogeigyo no keiei ni tsuite—Ise-wan • Kumano-nada engan o chūshin ni." *Fubito* 57, no. 1 (2005): 32–49.

Wakayama kenshi hensan iinkai. *Wakayama kenshi. Kin-gendai.* Wakayama-shi: Wakayama-ken, 1989.

———. *Wakayama kenshi. Kinsei.* Vol. 4. Wakayama-shi: Wakayama-ken, 1990.

———. *Wakayama kenshi. Kinsei shiryō.* Wakayama-shi: Wakayama-ken, 1976.

Wakayama shiritsu hakubutsukan. *Edo jidai no dōshokubutsu zukan: Kishū no honzōgaku o chūshin ni.* Wakayama: Wakayama-shi Kyōiku Iinkai, 1994.

Walker, Brett L. "Commercial Growth and Environmental Change in Early Modern Japan: Hachinohe's Wild Boar Famine of 1749." *Journal of Asian Studies* 60, no. 2 (2001): 329–51.

———. *A Concise History of Japan.* Cambridge: Cambridge University Press, 2015.

———. *The Conquest of Ainu Lands: Ecology and Culture in Japanese Expansion, 1590–1800.* Berkeley: University of California Press, 2001.

———. *Toxic Archipelago: A History of Industrial Disease in Japan.* Seattle: University of Washington Press, 2014.

Walsh, Quentin R., and P. J. Capelotti. *Whaling Expedition of the Ulysses, 1937–38.* Gainesville: University Press of Florida, 2010.

Walthall, Anne. "Peace Dividend: Agrarian Developments in Tokugawa Japan." In *Japan Emerging: Premodern History to 1850*, edited by Karl F. Friday, 391–401. Boulder: Westview Press, 2012.

Watanabe, Hiroyuki. *Japan's Whaling: The Politics of Culture in Historical Perspective.* Translated by Hugh Clarke. Melbourne: Trans Pacific Press, 2009.

Wigen, Kären. *The Making of a Japanese Periphery, 1750–1920.* Berkeley: University of California Press, 1995.

Wilson, Ben, and Angus Wilson. *The Complete Whale-Watching Handbook: A Guide to Whales, Dolphins, and Porpoises of the World.* St. Paul, MN: Voyageur Press, 2006.

Yamada Tatsuo et al. *Nihon nōsho zenshū.* 72 vols. Tokyo: Nōsan-gyoson Bunka Kyōkai, 1977–2001.

Yamashita Shōto. *Hogei I.* Tokyo: Hōsei Daigaku Shuppankyoku, 2004.

Yasuda Ken. *Edo kōki shokoku sanbutsuchō shūsei.* 16 vols. Tokyo: Kagaku Shoin, 1996–2005.

Yonemoto, Marcia. *Mapping Early Modern Japan: Space, Place, and Culture in the Tokugawa Period.* Berkeley: University of California Press, 2003.

———. "Maps and Metaphors of the 'Small Eastern Sea' in Tokugawa Japan (1603–1868)." *Geographical Review* 89, no. 2, Oceans Connect (1999): 169–87.

Yoshihara Tomokichi. *Kujira no haka.* 1977. Reprinted in *Kujira, iruka no minzoku*, edited by Tanigawa Ken'ichi, 409–78. Tokyo: San'ichi Shobō, 1997.

Zallen, Jeremy. "American Lucifers: Makers and Masters of the Means of Light, 1750–1900." PhD diss., Harvard, 2014.

Zuikōji. "Yakuyoke kaiun anzan fukutai Zuikōji." Osaka: Tōyama Bunko, 1986.

INDEX

abalone diving, 60

agriculture: Tokugawa economy and, 42, 72–73, 77, 80, 82–83; whale-based products in, 101–5

akabō kujira (Cuvier's beaked whale), 34, 35–36, 37

American Occupation of Japan, 192

American whaling: fleet size for, 8, 203n45; Japanese imperial expansion and, 184–85; Japanese whaling groups and, 71–75; origins of offshore whaling and, 34–35; Pacific whale populations and, 56, 71, 73, 184–85; sperm whales and, 34, 71. *See also* factory ship whaling

Amino Yoshihiko, 12, 199n26

anatomical drawings of whales: "Diagram of six whales" scroll and, 114–19, 115*fig.*; in "Geishikō," 125–28, 127*fig.*, 130; in *Isanatori ekotoba*, 125–26, 127*fig.*, 130; human and whale parallels and, 112–13, 116–17, 151; inspiration for, 117–19; Japanese medicine and, 116, 117; natural history knowledge and, 120; of nonwhales, 112–13, 117; Western medicine and, 112–13, 116–17, 118, 213n14

Antarctic whaling, 4, 7, 9, 20, 76, 191, 192, 199n24

archery ceremony (*oyumi no shinji*), 177

archipelagic system in Japan, ix–x; closed-system view and, 15–20, 194; foreign encroachment and, 184–85, 186, 192; Pacific environment and, 15, 17–20, 31, 44–48, 77–78; sustainability of whaling in, 192–96; Tokugawa whaling culture and, 146–48

Arctic whale migration, 3, 10, 27, 31, 51

Asuka Shrine, Taiji, Wakayama Prefecture, 177

Baird's beaked whale (*Berardius bairdii*), 34, 35–37

Bakin. *See* Takizawa Bakin

Balaenoptera acutorostrata. See minke whale

Balaenoptera borealis. See sei whales

Balaenoptera physalus. See fin whales

baleen, 7, 24, 35: uses for, 84

baleen whales, 25–34. *See also* fin whales; gray whales; humpback whales; right whales

Basque whalers, 35, 36, 209n17

beaked whales: Bōsō whalers and, 36–38, 53, 76, 199n25; historic importance of, 34, 35–36

Beiga, 113, 114–16, 115*fig.*, 119, 126–27

Beluga whale (*Delphinapteras leucas*), 39

Bencao gangmu. See Honzō kōmoku

blubber: coastal whaling and, 53–54, 86*fig.*; insulating properties of, 21; as meat, 84, 92; offshore whaling and, 34–35; whale migration and, 27, 30. *See also* whale oil

Bokushi. *See* Suzuki Bokushi

Bolster, Jeffrey, xii

bomb lance, 74–75

Bōsō Peninsula: beaked whales and, 36–38, 53, 76, 199n25; historical whaling practices and, 36–37, 53, 76; sustainability of whaling and, 36–38, 76, 199n25

bow-mounted harpoon guns, 74–75

Bryde's whale (*Balaenoptera brydei*), 201n6

Buddhism: karmic hierarchy in, 149–53; Laws of Compassion and, 150, 162, 165–67

Buddhist sutras, 151–52, 217n5

Bungo Strait, 30, 76, 155, 171–73

calving grounds, 27, 30, 31–32. *See also* fetal whales; migration routes

catcher boats, 8, 74, 198n12

Cetacea, as general category, 38–39

Oda Nobunaga, 42
Odontoceti. *See* dolphins; toothed whales
offshore whaling: American origins of,
34–35; Japanese shift to, 10, 64, 75, 187;
sustainability and, 36; targeted species
and, 34–38; techniques in, 7–8; whale
products in, 84. *See also* factory ship
whaling; prowhaling arguments
Ogasawara (Bonin) Islands, 29, 32
Ogawajima, Saga Prefecture, 49, 54, 164,
174–75, 179
Oike Shiroōemon, 62
Ojiro Shrine, Mie Prefecture, 169
Oka Jūrō, 75
oki no tonosama ("lords of the open sea"), 167
Okumiya Nizaemon, 102, 104–5
Ōkura Nagatsune, 26*fig.*, 104–5.
Omura, Hideo, 31–32
Omura's whale (*Balaenoptera omurai*), 201n6
ōnaya (whaling group members), 86–87;
investor relations and, 90–91, 92, 98. *See
also* whaling groups
Ontleedkundige Tafelen (Kulmus), 117
opportunistic harvest of whales, 6, 50, 76,
171–72, 173
organized whaling, 34–38; coastal vs. offshore species and, 34–38; commercial
character of, 191–92; culture of Tokugawa era and, 21–22; decline in local
whale populations and, 8–9, 10; discon-
tinuities with contemporary whaling
and, 6, 57, 184–89; Pacific World in Japanese history and, 12–20; resource management and, 14–15, 109, 193–95 (*see also*
resource strategies); sustainability of,
9–12, 36, 59, 192–94; techniques used in,
6–8, 51–53; Tokugawa era origins of, 6,
49–50, 57. *See also* whaling groups
Osaka: coastal trade and, 43–44; scroll
on whales from, 130–31; whale bone
bridge in, 149, 150*fig.*, 153; whale products
and, 83.
Osaka Museum of History, 134
Ōtsuki Gentaku, 125–28, 131, 145
Ōtsuki Heisen: "Geishikō" (manuscript),
51*fig.*, 125–28, 127*fig.*, 129, 130, 131, 145,
204n11, 206n47
Owase whaling area, 58, 59, 65
Oyamada Tomokiyo, 52*fig.*, 54*fig.*, 128–29
Oyashio Current, 29. *See also* Kuroshio
Current
oyumi no shinji (archery ceremony), 177

Pacific coast whaling areas, 35, 36–37, 54. *See
also* Kumano coast whaling area; Kuroshio Current; Tosa Bay whaling area
Pacific Ocean environment: cultural integration of, 19–20; global politics and, 184;
modernization as disruption and, 187–89;
political side of, 184–85, 186; territorial
boundaries and, 19, 186–87; Tokugawa
economy and, 21–22, 77–78; Tokugawa
foreign trade restrictions and, 14–15, 56.
See also archipelagic system in Japan;
marine environment; migration routes
pelagic whaling. *See* factory ship whaling;
offshore whaling
pets, 156–57
Physeter macrocephalus. See sperm whales
plant monuments, 160
political concerns: domainal surveys and,
128; Laws of Compassion and, 165–67;
natural history scholarship and, 128;
Pacific history and, 184–86, 187, 189–90,
194; treaties and, 189–90; whaling groups
and, 57. *See also* resource strategies
prayers, 170–71
prehistoric whaling, 6, 13, 49–50, 83. *See
also* Jōmon period; opportunistic harvest of whales
processing of whales: diagrams of, 132;
local workers and, 65–66; managers
of, 86–88, 90; ship-based whaling and,
8, 18–19, 35, 74, 186–87; shore-based
practices and, 18, 20–21, 49, 53–54, 55,
56, 86*fig.*; Western whalers and, 34–35.
See also whale meat; whale oil; whale
products
prowhaling arguments, 197n7, 208n4;
historical evidence and, 5–12; Japanese
culture and, 47–48, 76, 91–92, 179–82,
192, 208n4; subsistence and, 105–9;
whale product sales and, 105–9

religious ritual: food taboos and, 94–95,
108, 118; Japanese connection with natural world and, 177–82; manipulation of
natural world and, 178–82. *See also* Buddhism; memorials; Shinto tradition;
whale death
resource strategies: coastal whaling and,
14–15, 21–22, 56, 128, 129, 131, 185; commerce in whale products and, 80–85, 105–
9, 129–30, 191; domainal surveys and, 120,
123, 124, 130–31; global competition and,

texts on whaling (*continued*) and, 139–43; literary works and, 135–39. *See also* illustrated whale scrolls; natural history scholarship

Toboke, 79–80, 81, 94, 135–38

Tokugawa Ieyasu, 42, 61

Tokugawa period (1603–1868): agriculture in economy of, 42, 72–73, 77, 80, 82–83; changes in whaling practices since, 5, 38; coastal waters as resource base in, 21–22; cultural importance of whaling in, 21–22, 33, 41–48; foreign trade restrictions and, 14–15, 56; history of Pacific fisheries and, 13–20; memorial towers and, 159–61; naval forces in, 61–62; origins of whaling tradition and, 6; species of whales in, 26*fig.*, 37, 38–41; sustainability of whaling in, 9–12, 36, 59, 192–95; Tokugawa peace and, 16, 56; travel in, 42–44, 121; views of animals in, 156–57, 165–66; whale classification in, 38–39; whales in consciousness of, 146–48; whaling villages in, 41–43. *See also* cultural place of whaling in Japan; organized whaling; whaling groups

Tokugawa Tsunayoshi, 150, 162, 165–67

Tokugawa Yoshimune, 107, 120, 123, 185

Tokyo, 7, 6, 29. *See also* Edo

Tomokiyo, 129

toothed whales, 34–38. *See also* beaked whales; dolphins; sperm whales

torii (whalebone gateway), 180, 220n72

Tosa Bay whaling area: maps showing, xx–xxii; net whaling and, 54, 65, 68; whale products from, 102; whaling groups and, 30, 46, 54, 61–62, 63, 68, 99

Totman, Conrad, 16, 56

Toyotomi Hideyoshi, 42

Tōyō Whaling Company, 179–80

"traditional" or "old-style" (*koshiki hogeigyō*) whaling, 50, 76, 80, 83, 188–90, 191, 193. *See also* opportunistic harvest of whales; organized whaling; whaling groups

Traditional Whaling Summit (2002), 4

transportation. *See* travel

travel: coastal trade and, 42–44; restrictions on foreign trade and, 14–15, 56; road system and, 44, 45–47, 203n49; scholarly information gathering and, 121, 125; tribute and, 140, 146; whale meat and, 80, 97, 99, 191–92

treaties, 189–90

tsuchi kujira (Baird's beaked whale), 34, 35–37

Tsujikawa family, 85–86. *See also* Masutomi whaling group

Tsushima Current, 25, 27–29, 30

urbanization, 82

Usuki, Oita Prefecture, 171–73

Wada Chūbei Yorimoto, 60, 61, 67

Wada Yoriharu, 63, 67

Wakan sansai zue (Illustrated Sino-Japanese encyclopedia), 40–41, 122

Wakayama Prefecture. *See* Taiji; Wakayama Prefecture

Walker, Brett, 17

Walsh, Quentin, 8

Watanabe Hiroyuki, 192

wealth from whaling: memorials and, 160, 161, 162; texts on whaling and, 129–31, 140, 180; traditional whaling groups and, 191–92; whaling group managers and, 85–87, 128, 129; workers and, 87–88. *See also* Masutomi whaling group

Western viewpoints: anatomical drawings and, 112–13, 116–17, 118, 213n14; Dutch studies and, 116–18, 125–28, 141, 145; natural history and, 144, 145

Western whaling: decline of Japanese whaling groups and, 71–75; influence of whale oil in, 84; offshore operations and, 34–35, 36; population collapse and, 36; practices in, 7, 8; sperm whales and, 34–35, 36. *See also* factory ship whaling

whale anatomy. *See* anatomical drawings

whaleboats, 50, 52–53. *See also* catcher boats; factory ship whaling

"Whale-bodhisattva one-hundred-fathom monument" ("Kujira bōsatsu hyaku hiro kōryū"), 79–80, 81, 94, 135–38

whale bones: agricultural uses for, 56, 101, 108; bridge made with, 149, 150*fig.*; gateway of, 180, 220n72; sculpture of, 133

whale death: Buddhism and, 149–53, 174, 175–76; coastal whaling practices and, 51–53; death registers (*kakochō*) and, 153–57; description of (Ogawajima story), 174–76; festival practices and, 176–77; impacts of, in nonwhaling areas, 171–73; *kuyō* towers and, 158–61; marine impacts on coastal life and, 167–71; responses to, in nonwhaling areas, 76, 171–73. *See also* memorials

WEYERHAEUSER ENVIRONMENTAL BOOKS

Cultivating Nature: The Conservation of a Valencian Working Landscape, by Sarah R. Hamilton

Bringing Whales Ashore: Oceans and the Environment of Early Modern Japan, by Jakobina K. Arch

The Organic Profit: Rodale and the Making of Marketplace Environmentalism, by Andrew N. Case

Seismic City: An Environmental History of San Francisco's 1906 Earthquake, by Joanna L. Dyl

Smell Detectives: An Olfactory History of Nineteenth-Century Urban America, by Melanie A. Kiechle

Defending Giants: The Redwood Wars and the Transformation of American Environmental Politics, by Darren Frederick Speece

The City Is More Than Human: An Animal History of Seattle, by Frederick L. Brown

Wilderburbs: Communities on Nature's Edge, by Lincoln Bramwell

How to Read the American West: A Field Guide, by William Wyckoff

Behind the Curve: Science and the Politics of Global Warming, by Joshua P. Howe

Whales and Nations: Environmental Diplomacy on the High Seas, by Kurkpatrick Dorsey

Loving Nature, Fearing the State: Environmentalism and Antigovernment Politics before Reagan, by Brian Allen Drake

Pests in the City: Flies, Bedbugs, Cockroaches, and Rats, by Dawn Day Biehler

Tangled Roots: The Appalachian Trail and American Environmental Politics, by Sarah Mittlefehldt

Vacationland: Tourism and Environment in the Colorado High Country, by William Philpott

Car Country: An Environmental History, by Christopher W. Wells

Nature Next Door: Cities and Trees in the American Northeast, by Ellen Stroud

Pumpkin: The Curious History of an American Icon, by Cindy Ott

The Promise of Wilderness: American Environmental Politics since 1964, by James Morton Turner

The Republic of Nature: An Environmental History of the United States, by Mark Fiege

A Storied Wilderness: Rewilding the Apostle Islands, by James W. Feldman

Iceland Imagined: Nature, Culture, and Storytelling in the North Atlantic, by Karen Oslund

Quagmire: Nation-Building and Nature in the Mekong Delta, by David Biggs